Taking Action:

Implementing Effective Mathematics Teaching Practices

in K–Grade 5

Series Editor
Margaret S. Smith
University of Pittsburgh

DeAnn Huinker
University of Wisconsin-Milwaukee

Victoria Bill
Institute for Learning, University of Pittsburgh

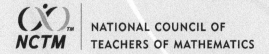

NATIONAL COUNCIL OF
TEACHERS OF MATHEMATICS

more**4U**
www.nctm.org/more4u
Access code: TAT15187

Copyright © 2017 by
The National Council of Teachers of Mathematics, Inc.
1906 Association Drive, Reston, VA 20191-1502
(703) 620-9840; (800) 235-7566; www.nctm.org
All rights reserved
Eleventh Printing 2022

Library of Congress Cataloging-in-Publication Data

Names: Huinker, DeAnn. | Bill, Victoria.
Title: Implementing effective mathematics teaching practices in
  Kindergarten-grade 5 / DeAnn Huinker, University of Wisconsin-Milwaukee,
  Victoria Bill, Institute for Learning, University of Pittsburgh.
Description: Reston, VA : National Council of Teachers of Mathematics,
[2017]
  | Series: Taking action | Includes bibliographical references.
Identifiers: LCCN 2016057992 (print) | LCCN 2017008089 (ebook) | ISBN
  9780873539692 (pbk.) | ISBN 9781680540000 (ebook)
Subjects: LCSH: Mathematics--Study and teaching (Elementary)--United
States.
Classification: LCC QA135.6 .H846 2017 (print) | LCC QA135.6 (ebook) | DDC
  372.70973--dc23
LC record available at https://lccn.loc.gov/2016057992

The National Council of Teachers of Mathematics advocates for high-quality
mathematics teaching and learning for each and every student.

Printed in the United States of America

Contents

PREFACE

In April 2014, the National Council of Teachers of Mathematics (NCTM) published *Principles to Actions: Ensuring Mathematical Success for All*. The purpose of that book is to provide support to teachers, schools, and districts in creating learning environments that support the mathematics learning of each and every student.

Principles to Actions articulates a set of six guiding principles for school mathematics—Teaching and Learning, Access and Equity, Curriculum, Tools and Technology, Assessment, and Professionalism. These principles describe a "system of essential elements of excellent mathematics programs" (NCTM 2014, p. 59). The overarching message of *Principles to Actions* is that "effective teaching is the nonnegotiable core that ensures that all students learn mathematics at high levels and that such teaching requires a range of actions at the state or provincial, district, school, and classroom levels" (p. 4). The eight "effective teaching practices" delineated in the "Teaching and Learning Principle" (see chapter 1 of this book) are intended to guide and focus the teaching of mathematics across grade levels and content areas. Decades of empirical research in mathematics classrooms support these teaching practices.

Following the publication of *Principles to Actions*, NCTM president Diane Briars appointed a working group to develop the *Principles to Actions Professional Learning Toolkit* (http://www .nctm.org/ptatoolkit/) to support teacher learning of the eight effective mathematics teaching practices. The professional development resources in the Toolkit consist of grade-band modules that engage teachers in analyzing artifacts of teaching (e.g., mathematical tasks, narrative and video cases, student work samples). The Toolkit modules use a "practice-based" approach to professional development, in which materials taken from real classrooms give teachers opportunities to explore, critique, and examine new practices (Ball and Cohen 1999; Smith 2001).

The Toolkit represents a collaborative effort between the National Council of Teachers of Mathematics and the Institute for Learning (IFL) at the University of Pittsburgh. The Institute for Learning (IFL) is an outreach of the University of Pittsburgh's Learning Research and Development Center (LRDC) and has worked to improve teaching and learning in large urban school districts for more than twenty years. Through this partnership, the IFL made available to the working group a library of classroom videos featuring teachers engaged in ambitious teaching. These videos, a key component of many of the modules in the Toolkit, offer positive narratives of ambitious teaching in urban classrooms.

The Taking Action series includes three grade-band books: grades K–5, grades 6–8, and grades 9–12. These books draw on the Toolkit modules but go far beyond the modules in several important ways. Each book presents a coherent set of professional learning experiences, with the specific goal of fostering teachers' development of the effective mathematics teaching practices. The authors intentionally sequenced the chapters to scaffold teachers' exploration of the eight teaching practices using practice-based materials, including additional tasks, instructional episodes, and student work to extend the range of mathematical content and instructional practices featured in each book, thus providing a richer set of experiences to bring the practices to life. Although each Toolkit module affords an opportunity to investigate an effective teaching practice, the books provide materials for extended learning experiences around an individual teaching practice and across the set of eight effective practices as a whole. The books also give connections to resources in research and equity. In fact, a central element of the book is the attention to issues of equity, access, and identity, with each chapter identifying how the focal effective teaching practice supports equitable mathematics teaching and learning. Each chapter features key ideas and literature surrounding ambitious and equitable mathematics instruction to support the focal practice and provides pathways for teachers' further investigation.

We hope this book will become a valuable resource to classroom teachers and those who support them in strengthening mathematics teaching and learning.

Margaret Smith, Series Editor
Melissa Boston
DeAnn Huinker

ACKNOWLEDGMENTS

The activities in this book are drawn in part from **Principles to Actions Professional Learning Toolkit: Teaching and Learning** created by the team that includes Margaret Smith (chair) and Victoria Bill (co-chair), Melissa Boston, Frederick Dillon, Amy Hillen, DeAnn Huinker, Stephen Miller, Mary Lynn Raith, and Michael Steele. This project is a partnership between the National Council of Teachers of Mathematics and the Institute for Learning at the University of Pittsburgh. The Toolkit can be accessed at **http://www.nctm.org/PtAToolkit/**.

The video clips used in the Toolkit and in this book were taken from the video archive of the Institute for Learning at the University of Pittsburgh. The teachers featured in the videos allowed us to film their teaching in an effort to open a dialogue about teaching and learning with others who are working to improve their instruction. We thank them for their bravery in sharing their practice with us so that others can learn from their efforts.

CHAPTER 1

Setting the Stage

Imagine walking into a first-grade classroom where students are sitting on a rug and their teacher, Ms. Bouchard, is reading _The Very Hungry Caterpillar_ by Eric Carle. After discussing the story, she comments, "I wonder how many pieces of fruit were eaten through by that caterpillar? He sure was hungry." This question prompts the task shown in figure 1.1 and launches her students into a mathematical investigation.

On Monday, the hungry caterpillar ate through one apple, but he was still hungry. On Tuesday he ate through two pears, but he was still hungry. On Wednesday he ate through three plums. On Thursday he ate through four strawberries. On Friday he ate through five oranges. How many pieces of fruit did the hungry caterpillar eat during the week?

Fig. 1.1. The Caterpillar task

Some students use cubes, while other students start drawing on paper. Regardless of how the students solve the problem, the teacher expects all students to "put their thinking on paper." As the students work, Ms. Bouchard makes her way around the classroom asking questions, "So, tell me about your picture" or "How does the picture show your thinking?" or "How does the picture show the story?" The teacher also makes note of their approaches so she can decide which students she wants to present their work, and in which order, later during the whole-class discussion. The work of two students, Aidan and Maya, are shown in figure 1.2.

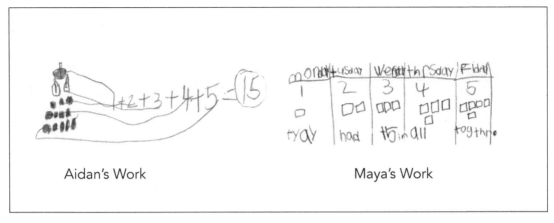

Aidan's Work   Maya's Work

Fig. 1.2. Samples of student work for the Caterpillar task

Before holding a class discussion, the teacher asks students to describe their picture to a partner. This gives all students a chance to share their own thinking, and begins orienting them to the thinking of other students, certainly not an easy task for first-grade students. Next the class gathers on the rug to present and compare their work. Throughout the lively discussion, Ms. Bouchard focuses her students on the mathematics learning goals for the lesson—to see and model the mathematical elements in a contextual problem, to understand addition as putting together sets of objects, and to understand that counting can be used to answer "how many" questions. To close the lesson, Ms. Bouchard asks each student to look at their picture and to revise it so that it better shows their thinking using ideas they got by looking at and talking about the work of their classmates.

A Vision for Students as Mathematics Learners and Doers

The lesson portrayed in the opening scenario exemplifies the vision of school mathematics that the National Council of Teachers of Mathematics (NCTM) has been advocating in a series of policy documents over the last twenty-five years (NCTM 1989, 2000, 2006). In this vision, as in the scenario, students are active learners, constructing their knowledge of mathematics through exploration, discussion, and reflection. The tasks in which students engage are both challenging and interesting and cannot be answered quickly by applying a known rule or procedure. Students must reason about and make sense of a situation and persevere when a pathway is not immediately evident. Students use a range of tools to support their thinking and collaborate with their peers to test and refine their ideas. A whole-class discussion provides a forum for students to share ideas and clarify understandings, develop convincing arguments, and learn to see things from other students' perspectives.

In the Caterpillar scenario, students were encouraged to use their imagination to envision the caterpillar eating his way through the apple, the pears, the plums, the strawberries, and the oranges. Through this context, they were presented with mathematical work to find the total number of pieces of fruit. Even though combining five quantities was a challenge for these young learners, all students could enter the problem by using their choice of materials. The context interested the students and they persevered in making sense of the situation and keeping track of all those quantities. Putting their thinking on paper, while not new to the students, was difficult for them. Presenting their work to a partner had multiple purposes. It allowed some students to get help from a peer in revising their drawing while allowing all students the opportunity to communicate their own mathematical thinking and to consider the reasoning of other students. During the whole-class discussion, students were pressed to not only analyze the work of individual students but to compare approaches and discuss how they were similar and different. In this way, the teacher introduced students to new ways to represent and organize their thinking on paper, such as with realistic pictures, math drawings, or equations (e.g., $1 + 2 + 3 + 4 + 5 = 15$). While most students counted by ones, other students shared how they had grouped the numbers such as making fives, $(1 + 4) + (2 + 3) + 5$, or how they discovered that adding $1 + 2 + 3 + 4$ made 10. During the closing minutes of the lesson students were allowed time to revise their drawings, reinforcing that mathematical work occurs within a community of practice in which we develop shared understanding and learn from each other.

The vision for student learning advocated by NCTM, and represented in our opening scenario, has gained growing support over the past decade as states and provinces have put into place world-class standards (e.g., National Governors Association Center for Best Practices and Council of Chief State School Officers 2010). These standards focus on developing conceptual understanding of important mathematical ideas, flexible use of representations, strategies, and procedures, and the ability to engage in a set of mathematical practices that include reasoning, problem solving, and communicating mathematically.

A Vision for Teachers as Facilitators of Student Learning

Meeting the demands of world-class standards for student learning requires teachers to engage in what has been referred to as "ambitious teaching." Ambitious teaching stands in sharp contrast to what many teachers experienced themselves as learners of mathematics. On one hand, many of us remember memorizing facts and procedures with little emphasis on understanding, problem solving, and application. Ambitious teaching, on the other hand, views students as capable of making sense of mathematical ideas and being able to use their understanding to solve authentic problems (Lampert, Boerst, and Graziani 2011) and values students' thinking, including emergent understanding and errors, and attends to student thinking in an equitable and responsive manner (Anthony et al. 2015).

In ambitious teaching, the teacher engages students in challenging tasks and collaborative inquiry, and then observes and listens as students work so that she or he can provide an appropriate level of support to diverse learners. The goal is to ensure that each and every student succeeds in doing meaningful, high-quality work, not simply executing procedures with speed and accuracy. In our opening scenario with Ms. Bouchard, we see a teacher who is engaging her students in mathematics reasoning and problem solving. She presents an authentic task for her students to explore that emerges naturally from reading the children's literature book. She provides resources to support their work, such cubes, paper, and crayons, as well as partners with whom to exchange ideas, and monitors their actions providing support as needed. During the whole-class discussion, the teacher orchestrates discourse that builds on students' ways of thinking about the task while making connections to important mathematical ideas. It is this central focus on student sense making, thinking, and reasoning that exemplifies ambitious teaching. As Anthony and colleagues (Anthony et al. 2015, p. 46) underscore:

> Ambitious mathematics teaching involves skilled ways of eliciting and responding to each and every student in the class so that they learn worthwhile mathematics and come to view themselves as competent mathematicians.

This book is intended to support teachers in meeting the challenge and complexities of ambitious teaching by describing and illustrating a set of teaching practices that facilitate the type of "responsive and discipline-connected instruction" (Lampert et al. 2010, p. 130) that is at the heart of ambitious teaching.

Support for Ambitious Teaching

Principles to Actions: Ensuring Mathematical Success for All (NCTM 2014) provides guidance on what it will take to make ambitious teaching, and rigorous content standards, a reality in classrooms, schools, and districts in order to support mathematical success for each and every student. At the heart of this book is a set of eight teaching practices that provide a framework for strengthening the teaching and learning of mathematics (see fig. 1.3). These teaching practices describe intentional and purposeful actions taken by teachers to support the engagement and learning of every student. These teaching practices, based on knowledge of mathematics teaching and learning accumulated over more than two decades, represents "a core set of high-leverage practices and essential teaching skills necessary to promote deep learning of mathematics" (NCTM 2014, p. 9). Each of these teaching practices is examined in more depth through illustrations and discussions in the subsequent chapters of this book.

Establish mathematics goals to focus learning. Effective teaching of mathematics establishes clear goals for the mathematics that students are learning, situates goals within learning progressions, and uses the goals to guide instructional decisions.
Implement tasks that promote reasoning and problem solving. Effective teaching of mathematics engages students in solving and discussing tasks that promote mathematical reasoning and problem solving and allow multiple entry points and varied solution strategies.
Use and connect mathematical representations. Effective teaching of mathematics engages students in making connections among mathematical representations to deepen understanding of mathematics concepts and procedures and as tools for problem solving.
Facilitate meaningful mathematical discourse. Effective teaching of mathematics facilitates discourse among students to build shared understanding of mathematical ideas by analyzing and comparing student approaches and arguments.
Pose purposeful questions. Effective teaching of mathematics uses purposeful questions to assess and advance students' reasoning and sense making about important mathematical ideas and relationships.
Build procedural fluency from conceptual understanding. Effective teaching of mathematics builds fluency with procedures on a foundation of conceptual understanding so that students, over time, become skillful in using procedures flexibly as they solve contextual and mathematical problems.
Support productive struggle in learning mathematics. Effective teaching of mathematics consistently provides students, individually and collectively, with opportunities and supports to engage in productive struggle as they grapple with mathematical ideas and relationships.
Elicit and use evidence of student thinking. Effective teaching of mathematics uses evidence of student thinking to assess progress toward mathematical understanding and to adjust instruction continually in ways that support and extend learning.

Fig. 1.3. Eight effective teaching practices for mathematics

Ambitious mathematics teaching must be equitable. Driscoll and his colleagues (Driscoll, Nikula, and DePiper 2016, pp. ix-x) acknowledge that defining equity can be elusive, but argue that equity is really about fairness in terms of providing access to "each learner with alternative ways to achieve, no matter the obstacles they face" and believing in each student's potential "to do challenging mathematical reasoning and problem solving." Hence teachers need to pay attention to the instructional opportunities that are provided to students, particularly to historically underserved or marginalized youth (i.e., students who are Black, Latina/Latino, American Indian, low income) (Gutierrez 2013, p. 7). Every student has the right to participate substantially in all phases of a mathematics lesson and be challenged and supported in developing deep understanding and proficiency in mathematics (Jackson and Cobb 2010).

Toward this end, throughout this book we relate the eight effective teaching practices to specific equity-based practices (see fig. 1.4) shown to strengthen mathematical learning and cultivate positive student mathematical identities (Aguirre, Mayfield-Ingram, and Martin 2013). Equitable mathematics classrooms provide every student with access to meaningful mathematics by leveraging students' strengths (mathematical competencies), drawing on students as resources of knowledge, and challenging spaces of marginality. These classroom communities of collaboration and coherent discourse position each and every student to make sense of mathematics and develop positive mathematics identities.

Go deep with mathematics. Develop students' conceptual understanding, procedural fluency, and problem solving and reasoning.
Leverage multiple mathematical competencies. Use students' different mathematical strengths as a resource for learning.
Affirm mathematics learners' identities. Promote student participation and value different ways of contributing.
Challenge spaces of marginality. Embrace student competencies, diminish status, value multiple mathematical contributions.
Draw on multiple resources of knowledge (math, language, culture, family). Tap students' knowledge and experiences as resources for mathematics learning.

Fig. 1.4. Five equity-based practices to support mathematics learning

Central to ambitious teaching, and at the core of the five equity-based practices, is helping each and every student develop an identity as a capable member of a mathematical community of practice. Aguirre and her colleagues (Aguirre et al. 2013, p. 14) define mathematical identities as

> the dispositions and deeply held beliefs that students develop about their ability to participate and perform effectively in mathematical contexts and to use mathematics in powerful ways across the contexts of their lives.

Students enter elementary school eager to engage in collaborative, mathematical problem solving. Yet as students progress through these early years of their education, beliefs about their mathematical abilities sometimes shift. It is sad when such young learners begin to see themselves as "not good at math" and question their own sense-making abilities, as well as wonder whether they have a place in mathematical communities. When students begin to approach mathematics with fear, anxiety, and lack of confidence, it is too often the result of unambitious instructional practices based on the belief that not everyone can do serious mathematics (Delpit 2012). Allen and Schnell (2016, p. 398) argue, "teachers have a unique opportunity to steer their students' mathematical development in a more positive direction." The effective teaching practices discussed and illustrated in this book are intended to help in this regard.

Contents of this Book

This book is written for teachers and teacher educators who are committed to ambitious teaching that provides their students with increased opportunities to experience mathematics as meaningful, challenging, and worthwhile. It is likely, however, that any education professional working with teachers would benefit from the illustrations and discussions of the effective teaching practices for mathematics.

This book can be used in several ways. Teachers can read through the book on their own, stopping to engage in the activities suggested and trying out the ideas in their own classrooms. Alternatively, and perhaps more powerfully, teachers can work their way through the book with colleagues in professional learning communities, grade-level meetings, or staff development sessions. Working together to discuss and examine teaching practices brings considerable added value to our professional learning. Teacher educators or professional developers might use this book in college or university education courses for prospective teachers or in professional development workshops during the summer or school year. The book would be a good choice for a face-to-face or online book study for any group of mathematics teachers interested in improving their instructional practices.

In this book we provide a rationale for and discussion of each of the eight effective mathematics teaching practices, and when appropriate, connect them to the equity-based practices for mathematics classrooms. We provide examples and activities intended to help elementary teachers develop their understanding of each teaching practice, how it can be enacted in the classroom, and how it can promote equity in student learning. Towards this end, we invite the reader to actively engage in two types of activities that are presented throughout the book: Analyzing Teaching and Learning (ATL) and Taking Action in Your Classroom. The Analyzing Teaching and Learning activities invite the reader to engage with specific artifacts of classroom practice (e.g., mathematics tasks, narrative cases of classroom instruction, teacher-student dialogues, video clips, and student work samples). Taking Action in Your Classroom provides specific suggestions for a teacher to begin exploring specific teaching practices in her or his own classroom. The ATLs are drawn, in part, from activities found in the Principles to Actions Professional Learning Toolkit (http://www.nctm.org/PtAToolkit/). Additional activities, beyond what can be found in the Toolkit, have been added in order to provide a more extensive investigation of each of the eight effective mathematics teaching practices.

The video clips, featured in several Analyzing Teaching and Learning activities, show teachers endeavoring to engage in ambitious instruction in their urban classrooms and show students preserving in solving mathematical tasks that require reasoning and problem solving. The videos, made available by the Institute for Learning at the University of Pittsburgh, provide images of effective mathematics teaching. As such, they are examples to be analyzed rather than models to be copied. You can access and download the videos and their transcripts by visiting NCTM's More4U website (nctm.org/more4u). The access code can be found on the title page of this book.

As you read this book and engage with both types of activities, we encourage you to keep a journal or notebook in which you record your responses to questions that are posed, as well as make note of issues and new ideas that emerge. These written records can serve as the basis for your own personal reflections, informal conversations with other teachers, or for planned discussions with colleagues.

Each of the next eight chapters focuses explicitly on one of the eight effective teaching practices for mathematics. We have arranged the chapters in an order that makes it possible to highlight the ways in which the teaching practices are interrelated. (Note that this order differs from the one shown in figure 1.2 and in *Principles to Actions* [NCTM 2014]).

Chapter 2: Establish Mathematics Goals to Focus Learning

Chapter 3: Implement Tasks that Promote Reasoning and Problem Solving

Chapter 4: Build Procedural Fluency from Conceptual Understanding

Chapter 5: Pose Purposeful Questions

Chapter 6: Use and Connect Mathematical Representations

Chapter 7: Facilitate Meaningful Mathematical Discourse

Chapter 8: Elicit and Use Evidence of Student Thinking

Chapter 9: Support Productive Struggle in Learning Mathematics

Each of these chapters will follow a similar structure. We begin a chapter with a short discussion of the focal teaching practice. Then we ask the reader to engage in a series of Analyzing Teaching and Learning (ATL) activities that highlight key features of the teaching practice for teachers and students through artifacts of classroom practice. Each chapter also includes a summary of research findings related to the focal teaching practice, and describes how the teaching practice promotes equity in mathematics classrooms. We end each chapter with suggestions for Taking Action in Your Classroom. This includes a summary of the key messages regarding the focal teaching practice and an activity in which the reader is encouraged to apply aspects of the teaching practice in her or his own classroom instruction.

In the final chapter of the book (Chapter 10: Pulling It All Together), we consider how the set of eight effective mathematics teaching practices are related and how they work in concert to support student learning of mathematics. In chapter 10 we also consider the importance of thoughtful and thorough planning in advance of a lesson and evidence-based reflection following a lesson as critical components of the teaching cycle and necessary for successful use of the effective teaching practices.

An Exploration of Teaching and Learning

We close this chapter with the first Analyzing Teaching and Learning activity, which takes you into the classroom of Mr. Harris, where his third-grade students are exploring representations for multiplication. The case presents a situation from his classroom in which his students are first exploring and solving the Band Concert task and then engaging in a whole-class discussion to analyze and compare the various strategies they used.

When new teaching practices are introduced in chapters 2 through 9, we occasionally refer the new teaching practice to some aspect of the Case of Mr. Harris and the Band Concert task. In so doing, we are using the case as a touchstone throughout the book to relate the teaching practices. Hence the case provides a unifying thread that brings coherence to the book and makes salient the synergy of the effective mathematics teaching practices (i.e., the combined effect of the effective teaching practices is greater than the impact of any individual teaching practice).

As you read the case of Mr. Robert Harris, consider the follow questions and record your observations in your journal or notebook so that you can revisit them when we refer to Mr. Harris and the Band Concert task in subsequent chapters:

- What does Mr. Harris do during the lesson to support his students' engagement in and learning of mathematics?

- What aspects of Mr. Harris's teaching are similar to or different from your own teaching of mathematics?

- Which aspects of his teaching might you want to incorporate into your own teaching of mathematics?

- In what ways does the case illustrate the eight effective teaching practices in support of ambitious teaching of mathematics?

Exploring Representations for Multiplication
The Case of Robert Harris and the Band Concert Task

1   Robert Harris wanted his third-grade students to understand the structure of
2   multiplication and decided to develop a task that would allow students to explore
3   multiplication as equal groups through a familiar context—the upcoming spring band
4   concert. He thought that the Band Concert task (see next page) would prompt students
5   to make or draw arrays and provide an opportunity to build conceptual understanding
6   toward fluency in multiplying one-digit whole numbers by multiples of 10 using
7   strategies based on place value and properties of operations—all key aspects of the
8   standards for third-grade students. He felt that the task aligned well with his math goals
9   for the lesson and supported progress along math learning progressions, had multiple
10   entry points, would provide opportunities for mathematical discourse, and would
11   challenge his students. As students worked on the task he would be looking for evidence
12   that his students could identify the number of equal groups and the size of each group
13   within visual or physical representations, such as collections or arrays, and connect these
14   representations to multiplication equations.

[Handwritten margin notes: "Make arrays", "Build conceptual understanding towards fluency", "Place value & Properties of operation"]

	The Band Concert Task
15	
16	The third-grade class is responsible for setting up the chairs for the spring band
17	concert. In preparation, the class needs to determine the total number of chairs
18	that will be needed and ask the school's engineer to retrieve that many chairs
19	from the central storage area. The class needs to set up 7 rows of chairs with 20
20	chairs in each row, leaving space for a center aisle. How many chairs does the
21	school's engineer need to retrieve from the central storage area?

22   Mr. Harris began the lesson by asking students to consider how they might represent
23 the problem. "Before you begin working on the task, think about a representation you
24 might want to use and why, and then turn and share your ideas with a partner." The class
25 held a short conversation sharing their suggestions, such as using cubes or drawing a
26 picture. Then the students began working individually on the task.

Begin Task 27   As Mr. Harris made his way around the classroom, he noticed many students drawing
28 pictures. Some students struggled to organize the information, particularly those who
29 tried to represent each individual chair. He prompted these students to pause and review
30 their work by asking, "So, tell me about your picture. How does it show the set up of the
31 chairs for the band concert?" Other students used symbolic approaches, such as repeated *Structured*
32 addition or partial products, and a few students chose to use cubes or grid paper. He *questions*
33 made note of the various approaches so he could decide which students he wanted to *for*
34 present their work, and in which order, later during the whole-class discussion. *Elaboration*

maintain 35   In planning for the lesson, Mr. Harris prepared key questions that he could use to *and*
High 36 press students to consider critical features of their representations related to the structure
Levels 37 of multiplication. As the students worked, he often asked "How does your drawing show *Clarification*
38 the seven rows? How does your drawing show that there are 20 chairs in each row?"
39 "Why are you adding all those twenties?" "How many twenties are you adding and why?"
40   He also noticed a few students changed representations as they worked. Dominique
41 started to draw tally marks, but switched to using a table. When Mr. Harris asked her
42 why, she explained she got tired of making all those marks. Similarly, Jamal started to
43 build an array with cubes, but then switched to drawing an array. Their initial attempts
44 were valuable, if not essential, in helping each of these students make sense of the
45 situation.
46   Before holding a whole-class discussion, Mr. Harris asked the students to find a
47 classmate who had used a different representation and directed them to take turns
48 explaining and comparing their work as well as their solutions. He encouraged them to
49 also consider how their representations were similar and different. For example, Jasmine
50 who had drawn a diagram compared her work with Kenneth who had used equations

51   (see fig. 1.5). Jasmine noted that they had gotten the same answer and Kenneth said they
52   both had the number 20 written down seven times. Molly, in particular, was a student
53   who benefited from this sharing process because she was able to acknowledge how
54   confused she had gotten in drawing all those squares (see fig. 1.5) and had lost track of
55   her counting. Her partner helped her mark off the chairs in each row in groups of ten
56   and recount them. The teacher repeated this process once more as students found another
57   classmate and held another sharing and comparing session.

58   During the whole-class discussion, Mr. Harris asked the presenting students to
59   explain what they had done and why and to answer questions posed by their peers. He
60   asked Jasmine to present first since her diagram accurately modeled the situation, and
61   it would likely be accessible to all students. Kenneth went next as his approach was
62   similar to Jasmine's but without the diagram. Both clearly showed the number 20 written
63   seven times. Then Teresa presented. Her approach allowed the class to discuss how skip
64   counting by twenties was related to the task and to multiplication, a connection not
65   apparent for many students. Below is an excerpt from this discussion.

66   **Mr. H:**   So, Teresa skipped counted by twenties. How does this relate to the Band
67   Concert situation?

68   **Connor:**   She counted seven times like she wrote on her paper.
69   **Mr. H:**   I'm not sure I understand. Can someone add on to what Connor was saying?
70   **Grace:**   Well each time she counted it was like adding 20 more chairs, just like what
71   Kenneth did.
72   **Mr. H:**   Do others agree with what Grace is saying? Can anyone explain it in their own
73   words?
74   **Mason:**   Yeah, the numbers on top are like the 7 rows and the numbers on the bottom
75   are the total number of chairs for that many rows.
76   **Mr. H:**   This is interesting. So what does the number 100 mean under the 5?
77   **Mason:**   It means that altogether five rows have 100 total chairs, because there are 20
78   chairs in each row.
79   **Mr. H:**   Then what does the 140 mean?
80   **Mason:**   It means that seven rows would have a total of 140 chairs.
81   **Mr. H:**   [*Mr. Harris paused to write this equation on the board:* $7 \times 20 = 140$.] Some of
82   you wrote this equation on your papers. How does this equation relate to each
83   of the strategies that we have discussed so far? Turn and talk to a partner about
84   this equation.
85   [*After a few minutes, the whole-class discussion continued and Grace shared what*
86   *she talked about with her partner.*]

87 **Grace:** Well, we talked about how the 7 means seven rows like Jasmine showed in her
88 picture and how Teresa showed. And the 20 is the number of chairs that go
89 in each row like Jasmine showed, and like how Kenneth wrote down. Teresa
90 didn't write down all those twenties but we know she counted by twenty.

91 Toward the end of the lesson, Mr. Harris had Tyrell and Ananda present their
92 representations (see fig. 1.5) because they considered the aisle and worked with tens
93 rather than with twenties. After giving the students a chance to turn and talk with a
94 partner, he asked them to respond in writing whether it was okay to represent and solve
95 the task using either of these approaches and to justify their answers. He knew this
96 informal experience with the distributive property would be important in subsequent
97 lessons, and the student writing would provide him with some insight into whether or
98 not his students understood that quantities could be decomposed as a strategy in solving
99 multiplication problems.

The case was written by DeAnn Huinker (University of Wisconsin-Milwaukee), drawing on her professional
experiences with teachers and students in the Milwaukee area.

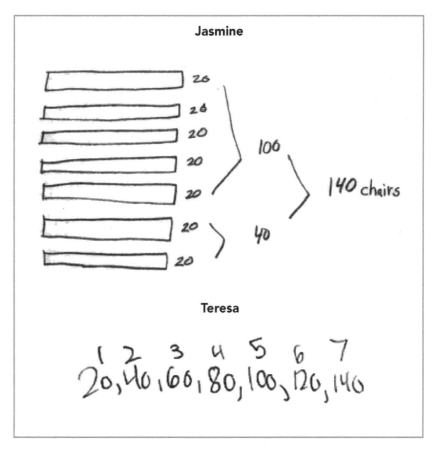

Fig. 1.5. Student work for the Band Concert task
(*continued on next page*)

Kenneth

20 + 20 + 20 + 20 + 20 + 20 + 20

40 + 40 = 80
80 + 20 = 100
100 + 20 = 120
120 + 20 = 140

140 chairs

Molly

160

Fig. 1.5. Student work for the Band Concert task
(*continued on next page*)

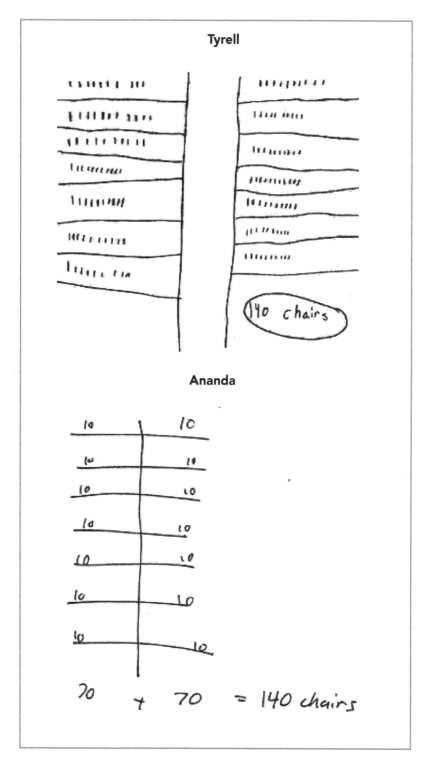

Fig. 1.5. Student work for the Band Concert task

Moving Forward

The case of Robert Harris presents many noteworthy aspects of mathematics instruction and examples of his use of the effective mathematics teaching practices. However, we are not going to provide an analysis of this case here. Rather, as you work your way through chapters 2 through 9 you will revisit the case of Robert Harris and consider the extent to which he engaged in the effective mathematics teaching practices and the impact it appeared to have on student learning and engagement. As you progress through the chapters, you may want to return to the observations you made during your initial reading of the case and consider the extent to which you are now seeing aspects of the case through a new lens.

As you read the chapters that follow, we encourage you to continue to reflect on your own instruction and how the effective teaching practices can help you in improving your teaching of mathematics. The Taking Action in Your Classroom activity at the end of each chapter is intended to support you in this process. Cultivating a habit of systematic and deliberate reflection holds the key to improving one's teaching as well as sustaining lifelong professional learning.

CHAPTER 2

Establish Mathematics Goals to Focus Learning

Learning goals inform the important decisions teachers make in planning and preparing for instruction, implementing lesson activities, and guiding student learning. In this chapter, you will explore the effective mathematics teaching practice, *establish mathematics goals to focus learning*. According to *Principles to Actions: Ensuring Mathematical Success for All* (NCTM 2014, p. 12):

> Effective teaching of mathematics establishes clear goals for the mathematics that students are learning, situates goals within learning progressions, and uses the goals to guide instructional decisions.

Establishing clear and specific mathematics goals for student learning in a lesson sets the stage and provides the direction for teachers' instructional decisions. Goals inform selecting the task on which students will work, formulating purposeful questions to determine what students already know related to the goal and help move them toward it, and structuring class discussions so that the work of students can be used as a basis for achieving lesson goals. In essence, the goals serve as both the destination and the road map for a lesson. As such, goals need to identify what students will come to understand about mathematics during the lesson rather than focusing on what students will do. Teachers must also be aware of how the goals for today's lesson or a sequence of lessons are situated within the mathematical landscape, because students' learning today contributes to the gradual development and deepening of students' mathematical knowledge over time.

The chapter includes four Analyzing Teaching and Learning (ATL) activities.

- ATL 2.1: Compare and contrast three goal statements for a multiplication lesson and examine how each goal relates to expected student learning.

- ATL 2.2: View a video clip from a kindergarten classroom and notice how the learning goals are connected to specific teaching actions that occur throughout the lesson.
- ATL 2.3: View a video clip from a fifth-grade classroom on defining polygons and observe how the learning goals inform instructional decisions.
- ATL 2.4: Revisit the kindergarten classroom and consider how the learning goals inform each of the other effective mathematics teaching practices.

For each ATL, we encourage you to make note of your responses, and if possible, share and discuss your ideas with colleagues. Once you have shared or written down your thoughts, continue reading the analysis of the ATL in which we relate the activity to the chapter's focal teaching practice. After the ATL activities, the chapter includes research findings on formulating and using goals and examines how the focal teaching practice promotes equity for students. We end the chapter by offering suggestions for analyzing your own lesson goals and applying the information on goals in your own classroom.

Establishing Goals for Mathematics Instruction

Effective teaching begins by establishing lesson goals that clarify the mathematics that students are learning during a lesson or sequence of lessons. With goals in mind teachers can select a task, anticipate possible student responses, and write questions that will guide students so they advance their understanding of the mathematics goal. Goals are the core of the work and everything else is based on them.

Engage in ATL 2.1: Comparing Goal Statements for a Multiplication Lesson

We return to the Band Concert task from the Case of Robert Harris presented in chapter 1, and consider how mathematics learning goals help focus a lesson. Before beginning the Analyzing Teaching and Learning activity, take a moment and glance back at the Band Concert task in ATL 1.1 (page 11) and consider the mathematical opportunities afforded by this task. Then work through ATL 2.1. Here we ask you to examine three different goal statements for a multiplication lesson using the Band Concert task and consider the potential of each goal statement for guiding the actions of the teacher in focusing student learning throughout the lesson.

The three goal statements, shown below, are being considered for a lesson in which students will explore multiplication using the Band Concert task. Examine the goal statements, and then consider the following questions:

- How are the goal statements the same and how are they different?
- What mathematics is the focus of each goal statement?
- What potential does each goal hold to guide teacher actions in focusing student learning on understanding the operation of multiplication?

Goal 1: Students will solve a variety of multiplication word problems and write the related multiplication equations.

Goal 2: Students will write equations for multiplication word problems and label the meaning of each factor in their equations as it relates to the context of the word problem.

Goal 3: Students will understand the structure of multiplication as comprising equal groups within visual or physical representations (e.g., collections or arrays), understand the numbers in multiplication equations (i.e., number of equal groups, size of each group, total amount), and connect representations to multiplication equations.

Analysis of ATL 2.1: Learning Goals versus Performance Goals

The three goal statements in ATL 2.1 are similar in a number of ways. All three goals are focused on multiplication. Each goal involves students working with multiplication contexts and multiplication equations. The goal statements are mathematical in nature and highlight actions appropriate for elementary students. Although some similarities exist between the goal statements, a number of important differences are also evident in their expectations of students.

Statements 1 and 2 focus on what students should be able to do—they should solve word problems and write equations, and in statement 2, also label the factors. We refer to these types of statements as performance goals. Performance goals are statements that describe what we want students to say, write, show, or demonstrate as a result of the lesson. They indicate what students should be able to do and do not necessarily require that students understand the mathematical ideas underlying their actions or performance.

Statement 3 focuses on what students should understand about multiplication. We refer to this type of statement as a learning goal. Learning goals describe what students should understand about a mathematics topic as an outcome of instruction. These goal statements portray a deeper grasp of mathematical concepts, insight into reasons why procedures work, and relationships or connections among mathematical ideas. While statement 2 hints at understanding because students relate the factors in their equations to the problem situation, it would not be clear what students understood about the underlying structure of multiplication irrespective of context. Statement 3, which happens to be Mr. Harris's lesson goal, clarifies the key understandings that students are developing—multiplication comprises working with equal groups, multiplication appears in a variety of contexts and representations, and multiplicative equations include factors and products with similar meaning across contexts. The underlying mathematical idea worth engaging students in learning is one that generalizes beyond the given problem of the day such as the meaning of the factors.

Mr. Harris's implementation of the band concert lesson was clearly guided by goal 3. Several opportunities existed for students to talk about the meaning of the factors in the Band Concert task. The teacher focused students' attention on the meaning of the factors and how they related to their representations as they worked independently and in pairs, as well as during the whole-class discussion. These exchanges reinforced the structure of multiplication that will not change regardless of the context or the visual representations. Students who achieve goal 3 are much more likely to be able to apply and transfer their learning to a wider range of problems as compared to students who only achieve goals 1 or 2.

While both performance and learning goals can be written for a lesson, it is hard, however, to imagine designing and implementing a lesson with only a performance goal as a guide. A learning goal is critical. The learning goal sets the stage for lesson planning and implementation of the lesson (Hiebert et al. 2007). Without a clear learning goal, that is, a clear sense of the specific mathematical understandings being targeted in a lesson, teachers would not know what to listen or look for in student responses nor what questions to ask to press students further when a response has not fully met all aspects of the learning goal. For example, goal 3 guides the teacher in pressing students to compare and contrast how equal groups are shown in different representations. The learning goal acts as a gauge against which the teacher can continually align and monitor student responses. Over time, as learning goals are used to plan and guide instruction, students are continually pressed to find and discuss mathematical connections and relationships and to explain the meaning of the mathematical topic. As a result students come to view this way of work as the norm for doing mathematics.

A strong mathematics learning goal should also be situated within a learning progression (Daro, Mosher, and Corcoran 2011) and connect to bigger mathematical ideas (Charles 2005). This ensures the teacher has a clear sense of how the current learning builds on prior knowledge and where the mathematics is going. With this insight, the teacher can help students connect what they already know to the current work, as well as glance ahead to where the learning is going. Classroom learning based on performance goals, such goals 1 and 2 in ATL 2.1, often presents a narrow view of mathematics. Whereas classroom instruction based on learning goals, such as goal 3, lead students to become more aware of the broader mathematical landscape and the coherence of mathematics.

Using Learning Goals to Inform Teacher Actions

Another aspect of the teaching practice on goals concerns how they are used to guide instructional decisions when enacted in a lesson. In this next Analyzing Teaching and Learning activity, we go into the classroom of Amanda Smith and watch a video clip in which her kindergarten students are trying to determine the total number of donuts when combining two sets of donuts. First familiarize yourself with the Donut task (see fig. 2.1) and then reflect on the mathematical ideas that could be explored with students through this task.

The Donut Task

1. Dion chooses 3 chocolate donuts and 4 vanilla donuts. Draw a picture and write an equation to show Dion's donuts.

2. Tamika has 4 vanilla donuts and 3 chocolate donuts. Draw a picture and write an equation to show Tamika's donuts.

3. Tamika claims that she has more donuts than Dion. Who has more donuts, Dion or Tamika? Draw a picture and write an equation to show how you know who has more donuts.

Adapted from Institute for Learning (2012a). Lesson guides and student workbooks available at ifl.pitt.edu

Handwritten annotations:

$$C C C$$
$$V V V V$$
$$3 + 4 = \boxed{7}$$

$$V V V V$$
$$C C C$$
$$4 + 3 = \boxed{7}$$

They have the same amount of Donuts

$$4 + 3 = 3 + 4$$
$$V V V V \quad V V V V$$
$$C C C \quad C C C$$

Fig. 2.1. Kindergarten task for exploring addition concepts and properties

Engage in ATL 2.2: Observing How Goals Guide Teacher-Student Interactions

Now we turn to ATL 2.2. The video clip features the first in a series of lessons used by Ms. Smith to develop students' understanding of the commutative property of addition. Her kindergarten students are well aware of the classroom expectations that they will represent situational problems on their work mats and will be ready to publicly explain how they solved the problems to their peers. In this lesson, Ms. Smith has two mathematics learning goals for students:

1. Students will understand and justify that the total amount of two or more sets can be combined in more than one way (i.e., counting all, counting on, or use of known facts) because the same set of items are counted.

2. Students will understand that regardless of the order of the addends in a problem situation, the total amount remains the same because no additional items are added or removed.

The lesson begins with a discussion of several students' representations of the donuts and their strategies for determining the total of 3 + 4 and 4 + 3. The teacher honors multiple ways of representing and solving the task in order to give many students an opportunity to share their problem-solving methods and to expose others to alternative strategies. Students are challenged to determine and to compare the two expressions. In the video clip, we join the whole-class discussion at the point in which Ms. Smith focuses on students' informal understanding and insights related to the intended learning goals. A transcript is included in Appendix A to support your viewing of the video and its analysis.

[handwritten note in left margin: Counting on 4, 5, 6, 7]

Analyzing Teaching and Learning 2.2 more4U

Observing How Goals Guide Teacher-Student Interactions

Watch the video clip of Ms. Smith and her students discussing the donut task.

- What were some ways the teacher kept students focused on the mathematics learning goal of the lesson during the discussion?

- Make a list of specific instances in which Ms. Smith made an instructional decision that was directly related to her learning goals.

- Think further about the specific teacher actions: what did students say or do as a result of the intentional moves by the teacher?

You can access this video online by visiting NCTM's More4U website (nctm.org/more4u). The access code can be found on the title page of this book.

[handwritten note in left margin: It just got switched around — had the class reiterate that]

[handwritten note at bottom: how would we write that]

Analysis of ATL 2.2: The Use of Goals to Inform Lesson Implementation

In the video clip you just watched, as well as throughout the lesson, the learning goals guided Ms. Smith in preparing the lesson and in its implementation. In her planning, she made several decisions that made it possible for her to attain her goals for the lesson. She considered and designed a lesson that built on students' prior knowledge. It was just one of a series of related lessons that engaged students in solving word problems. Therefore, students entered this lesson with prior knowledge of how to represent a situational problem and determine the total amount of two or more sets.

Ms. Smith decided the sequence of the discussion shown in the video clip on the basis of the learning goals. The goals also what she anticipated she would hear and see from her students. She moved from a discussion of problem-solving strategies for the first two prompts to a discussion of the commutative property of addition using the third prompt: Tamika claims that she has more donuts than Dion. Who has more donuts, Dion or Tamika? By designing the task prompts to specifically target the learning goals, Ms. Smith increased the likelihood that students would have to address those mathematical ideas in the lesson.

To prompt discussion of the commutative property of addition, Ms. Smith intentionally moved the set of 4 counters on the overhead projector to the left of the set of 3 counters transforming 3 + 4 into 4 + 3. She stated, "If I can think about my problem as 4 vanilla and 3 chocolate…can I think like that?" (lines 16–18 in the video transcript). This teacher move made it possible to probe students and engage them in an informal but lively discussion of the commutative property of addition. In response, Clair excitedly realizes and yells out that, "it still makes 7" (line 19). The teacher did not immediately acknowledge whether Clair was right or wrong, but rather put a perplexed expression on her face as she asked the class, "Clair says that still makes 7. Do you agree with her?" (line 20). This next teacher move brought more students into the class discourse by slowing down the thinking of some students and providing other students with more time to consider the mathematical dilemma.

Ms. Smith knew what she wanted to hear from students to assess whether they were making progress toward the learning goals. As she monitored the learning, she noted that students were beginning to demonstrate an understanding of the commutative property when they recognized that the amounts are combined in a different order and that both expressions resulted in the total of 7. The teacher decided to ask Clair to show and explain her observation to the class. Specifically, Clair was able to construct and argue why the two amounts were the same. As Clair pointed to the counters projected on the overhead screen, she explained, "If 4 vanilla were over here and 3 chocolate were over here and we switched them, it would still make 7, but it just got switched around" (line 23–25). The teacher move of having students explain rather than herself at this point in the lesson gives the authority of the mathematical ideas to the students.

As the discussion continued, the teacher purposefully selected students to publicly demonstrate the ways they used the manipulatives, created math drawings, explain how they arrived at a solution, as well as share mathematical observations and curiosities. These are ongoing expectations in this kindergarten classroom. In the early grade levels, it is helpful if the teacher or students name new strategies. This makes it easier to examine and discuss specific ones. It also values the use of different strategies as approaches to solving problems. Ms. Smith made public counting on from one addend and named it for the students. She said, "How many?" and launched into counting on from 3, signaling to students to join her. Together they counted, "4, 5, 6, 7. So can we count on and get 7?" (lines 43–44). Ms. Smith knew that many students in the class had not yet committed 3 + 4 to memory; therefore, the teacher moved to engage the whole class in counting on and naming the strategy, signaling that counting on is an acceptable means of finding the total amount of donuts.

The intentional teacher actions ensured a sustained focus and discussion among her students of the important mathematical ideas articulated in her learning goals for the lesson. This was particularly impressive given that these were five-year-olds having an extended conversation of problem-solving strategies and informal understanding of the commutative property of addition. Ms. Smith knows that learning goals will extend across a set of related lessons because these ideas are complex and will take time for all students to grasp. She will continue to monitor student learning to determine those students who are making sense of and using the mathematical ideas and strategies examined in this lesson during their independent problem-solving time and she will use the evidence of student thinking to revisit her learning goals for this lesson in order to plan next steps for her students' learning.

Using Learning Goals as a Roadmap for Instruction

In planning and then teaching a lesson, teachers must make numerous decisions. To make these determinations, we go back to the notion of learning goals as both the destination and road map for a lesson. It is the mathematics learning goals that inform teachers' planning for instruction, including the selection of tasks, the plan for implementing the task, and the preparation of key questions to check on students' prior understanding related to the goal and to help move students toward the goal. During instruction, the learning goals continue to affect teachers' decisions. The learning goals inform what we look and listen for as students engage with the task, and help us decide which student ideas to take up and pursue further and which ideas to merely acknowledge and note, as well as which ideas to surface for examination and discussion with other students in the class.

Engage in ATL 2.3: Examining How Goals Inform Instructional Decisions

In our next Analyzing Teaching and Learning activity, you will watch a short video clip from Kristin Walker's fifth-grade classroom. This is the first of a series of geometry lessons in which students are investigating the defining characteristics of geometric figures. In this particular lesson, students are identifying which two-dimensional figures are polygons and which are not polygons, thus working to determine the attributes that define a polygon. Her mathematics learning goals for students are as follows:

- Students will understand the defining attributes of polygons—closed figures made of straight line segments that come together at points called vertices; closed figures divide the plane into two distinct regions, one "inside" and the other "outside" the polygon.

- Students will understand that polygons cannot have curved lines, straight-line segments that cross each other, line segments that extend out from the figure, nor have openings.

Take a moment and familiarize yourself with the Polygon task (see fig. 2.2). Which figures are polygons and which are not polygons? Which features of specific figures do you think will be perplexing for students?

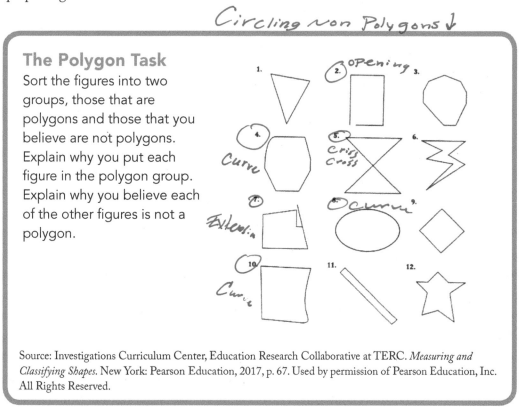

The Polygon Task

Sort the figures into two groups, those that are polygons and those that you believe are not polygons. Explain why you put each figure in the polygon group. Explain why you believe each of the other figures is not a polygon.

Fig. 2.2. The Polygon Task

To launch the lesson, Ms. Walker shows students three figures that fall into the category of polygons and three figures that are not polygons. Students make some initial observations about each group of figures, such as, "I think polygons have straight sides." However, all contributions are treated as just that, observations and ideas, and no formal definition of polygons is given to students. In ATL 2.3, we join the class as the students review the directions for the task. They are to sort the figures into two categories, polygons and non-polygons, and to explain their reasons for how they sorted each figure. The students work in pairs or small groups on the task. Each group is given one copy of a handout that contains the twelve figures shown in figure 2.2. In the video clip, we see students discussing the figures with a partner or in small groups and writing about their reasons for why the figure is or is not a polygon. Several visiting teachers and the principal are circulating and asking questions as students examine and discuss the geometric figures. A transcript is included in Appendix B to support your viewing of the video clip and its analysis.

Analyzing Teaching and Learning 2.3 more
Examining How Goals Inform Instructional Decisions

Watch the video clip from Kristen Walker's classroom as her students work on the Polygon task (see fig. 2.2) and consider how the mathematics learning goals served as a road map for the lesson.

- How did the learning goals inform selection of the task and how it was implemented?

- How did the learning goals inform what the teacher and visiting teachers were noticing and listening for in student thinking, both in what students said and what they wrote on their papers?

- How did the learning goals inform the questions the teachers asked students?

You can access this video online by visiting NCTM's More4U website (nctm.org/more4u). The access code can be found on the title page of this book.

Analysis of ATL 2.3: How Goals Inform Tasks, Noticing, and Questioning

The Polygon task was well aligned with the teacher's mathematics learning goals for her students. Based on the three polygon examples and three non-polygon examples presented at the beginning of the lesson, students had to carefully analyze, compare, and contrast the features of each of the twelve figures. The students could and did draw on each other's ideas as resources as they discussed and debated how to classify each figure. The manner in which the task was launched and implemented also gave students the ownership of the definitions that they would eventually formulate for a polygon. Consider the difference in student learning if Ms. Walker had launched her lesson by presenting students with a formal definition of a polygon at the start of the lesson and then gave students the same set of twelve figures to sort based on that formal definition. While both approaches might have gotten students to "perform" by accurately sorting the twelve figures, we would argue that the learning residue of the task would have been much different. Ms. Walker established clear learning goals for the lesson, not performance goals. Her goals were about learning, not about just performing. She wanted students to understand what determines whether a shape is or is not a polygon and she wanted students to generate a definition that had meaning for them and for which they had ownership. Thus the mathematics learning goals informed both the task she selected and the manner in which she implemented the task with her students.

The mathematics learning goals informed what the teacher and visiting teachers were listening for and noticing in student thinking and reasoning. For example, the teachers were listening for student observations about figures being closed, about the use of straight-line segments, and about how those line segments meet up with other line segments at the vertices (figs. 1, 3, 4, 6, 9, 11, and 12). They were also listening for student observations about curved lines (figs. 8 and 10), line segments that extend out from the figure (fig. 7), line segments that cross (fig. 5), and figures that have a gap or are open (fig. 2).

We heard students in the video asking each other questions and pressing each other for reasons why they called a figure a polygon or why they believed the figure was not a polygon. We heard students making claims and supporting their claims by relating attributes of specific figures to one of the figures displayed on the board as examples and non-examples of polygons. The first group with two girls was naming attributes of the polygon group on display in the front of the room. Student 2 stated, "Some of those are all straight lines, but they're not polygons" (line 5 in the video transcript) thus recognizing that a figure can have straight lines yet not be a polygon. Student 3 noticed that "they're connected" (line 11), that is, she saw that the line segments met at a vertex.

In the second group shown in the video, the two boys were questioning whether figure 11 is a polygon. Student 5 commented, "Because, it doesn't make sense, the little picture, how it's shown. See, it's just like a little straight line, with another parallel line to it" (lines 17–18). The rectangle is slanted which confused the student. He did not hold himself to making a comparison to the attributes of the polygons on display. If he had, he would have realized that some figures in the group identified as polygons also have parallel lines.

In the third group shown in the video, two girls were comparing figure 5 with a figure that was not a polygon. Student 7 commented, "It's not exactly the same kind, 'cause it's slanted," and then stated, "So I think this would be a polygon" (lines 20–22). It appeared, however, that her partner did not agree, so she conceded saying, "Put a question mark beside it." The teacher had been listening in on the conversation and asked, "What part of it makes you question it" (line 24)? This question supports the mathematics learning goals because the teacher was pressing students to talk about a specific attribute of figure 5 that had caused them to question its classification.

The fourth group was discussing the figures with straight lines with the principal. They noticed that several figures had straight lines, so they were trying to figure out what needed to be true about the straight lines in order for the figure to be a polygon. They commented that figure 2 was not closed (lines 37–38), that the lines crossed in figure 5 (line 39), and for figure 7, it was not "completely closed" (line 45) and a line was "going out" (line 47). The principal directed them to figure 12 and asked, "Does it fit with your definition so far?" (line 51). His questions supported the teacher's learning goal for the students to understand the defining attributes of polygons, which entail more than just a figure that has straight sides. He asked the girls to look at figure 12 and test out the definition they were forming. Figure 12, which looks somewhat like a star, challenged the girls. While they could tell it had straight lines (line 52), they were not convinced that it was a polygon. The principal pressed them a bit further to explain what aspect of that shape was causing them to question its classification.

Reflecting on this short video clip of the fifth-grade classroom, you can begin to see how establishing clear mathematics learning goals can serve as a road map for planning and then teaching a lesson. The Polygon task and the manner in which it was implemented supported student learning toward the intended mathematics goal of understanding what determines whether a shape is a polygon. The students were given time to grapple with the mathematics of the task as they worked in small groups and thought deeply about the attributes of figures, such as realizing that two figures can both have straight lines, but both might not be polygons. The learning goals also guided what the teachers looked and listened for as students talked or wrote, as well as influenced the questions teachers asked to probe students' thinking related to the intended mathematics learning goals.

Starting to Build a Teaching Framework

The eight effective mathematics teaching practices provide a research-informed framework for strengthening the teaching and learning of mathematics. This core set of teaching practices reflects knowledge that has accumulated over the last two decades about the components of ambitious teaching that support students toward high levels of mathematical success. The focal practice in this chapter, *establish mathematics goals to focus learning*, is a critical first step in that it guides instructional decisions related to each of the other teaching practices (shown in fig. 2.3) in both the planning and implementation of lessons.

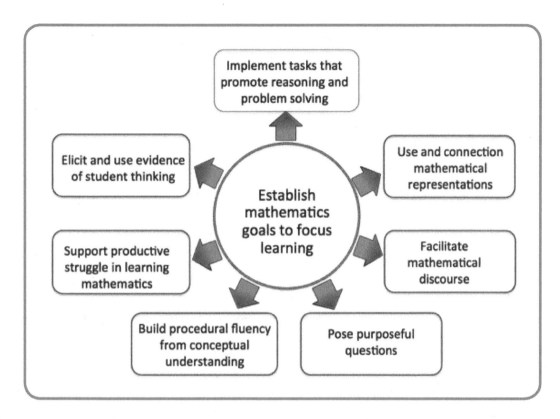

Fig. 2.3. The importance of starting with clear mathematics learning goals

Engage in ATL 2.4: Relating Goals to the Other Teaching Practices

In ATL 2.4, we ask you to revisit Ms. Smith's lesson on the Donuts task and briefly consider how the mathematics learning goals informed her decisions related to other teacher practices. In particular, we ask you to focus on the relationship of goals to the selection and design of tasks that promote reasoning and problem solving, the posing of purposeful questions, the use of mathematical representations, and the facilitation of meaningful mathematical discourse. While each of these teaching practices will be examined in much more detail in subsequent chapters, here we ask you to reflect upon these relationships as a start to strengthening your own teaching framework with the core set of teaching practices identified by NCTM (2014).

Analysis of ATL 2.4: The Importance of Starting with Learning Goals

The teacher's use of the Donut task provided students with interesting mathematical ideas to examine and discuss long before they themselves might have discovered and raised these ideas independently. Had the teacher merely asked students to solve the two word problems (see fig. 2.1) and not built in the third prompt, the lesson might have simply been a "show and tell" of one counting strategy after the other (Ball 1993; Stein et al. 2008; Schoenfeld 1998). The addition of the third prompt ensures that students will wrestle with the teacher's goal, the underlying ideas related to the commutative property. Implementing tasks that promote reasoning and problem solving such as this one increases the likelihood that students will have opportunities to make progress toward the mathematical goals of the lesson.

According to Weiss and Pasley (2014), "Teachers' questions are crucial in helping students make connections and learn important mathematics and science concepts" (p. 26). By posing questions, Ms. Smith was able to gather information and check on student understanding of the mathematical ideas (Boaler and Brodie 2004). Without probing for student's mathematical reasoning, the teacher cannot be sure what students are and are not understanding in relation to the mathematics learning goals. Facilitating meaningful mathematical discourse also depends on the teacher having clear mathematics goals for the lesson. With the goals in mind, the teacher can observe and listen more intentionally to students as they work individually and in small groups on tasks, and use this insight to structure whole-class discussions that can advance all students further toward the learning goals of the lesson (Smith and Stein 2011).

Effective teaching of mathematics engages students in making connections among mathematical representations to deepen understanding of mathematics concepts and procedures and to use representations as tools for problem solving (NCTM 2014). By asking students to represent contextual situations visually, then symbolically, while soliciting an explanation from students, the students learn the meaning of the symbols. The teacher also gets a window into student learning of the goal. Ms. Smith invited students to publicly display the physical and visual representations, to write equations, and to share their reasoning so that students saw themselves as capable of representing the situational problems in a variety of ways. Challenges that ask students to compare different representations lead students to move between representations. This allows students to see the mathematical ideas through other lenses, which advances their understanding toward the intended mathematics learning goals.

What the Research Says: Establishing and Using Learning Goals

Establishing learning goals that clearly and explicitly describe the mathematics students are learning is an essential component of effective teaching because goal setting influences teacher decisions and student learning in several important ways (Hattie 2009; Lipsey and Wilson 1993). According to Hiebert and colleagues (2007), "Formulating clear, explicit learning goals sets the stage for everything else" (p. 51). Not only do the goals determine the selection and design of tasks and the assessment of student learning but they are also influential in all aspects of the planning and enacting of lessons. In addition, goals influence student views on the nature of mathematics and what it means to be successful in the mathematics classroom.

Moss, Brookhart, and Long (2011) highlight the importance of distinguishing between the goals that inform teacher actions and decisions and the lesson goals as communicated to students. They define learning goals as being "derived from content standards, written in teacher language, and used to guide teaching during a lesson or across a series of lessons" (p. 66). Throughout this chapter we have focused on the establishment of learning goals designed to inform teacher actions and decisions in both the planning and implementation of lessons. However, it is also important to communicate the mathematical intent of a lesson to students (Marzano 1997; Wiliam and Leahy 2015).

Students must understand the mathematical learning expectations for their work. In such classrooms, students tend to perform at higher levels than in classrooms where the learning expectations are unclear (Hattie 2009; Haystead and Marzano 2009). How the learning goals are communicated to students is debatable. While it might not be necessary to post the goals on the classroom wall or project then on the whiteboard screen, "the mathematical purpose of a lesson should not be a mystery to students" (NCTM 2014, p. 13). Moss and colleagues (2011) label the learning goals as communicated to students as "shared learning targets." They explained that a "shared learning target frames the lesson from the students' point of view. A shared learning target helps students grasp the lesson's purpose—why it is crucial to learn this chunk of information, on this day, and in this way" (p. 66). Yet merely posting a learning target is insufficient. Michaels and colleagues (2010) suggest the use of "marking" and "recapping" throughout a lesson so that students know the significant contributions that are noteworthy in the lesson. Marking involves bringing "everyone's attention to a key point" (p. 27) and explaining why that mathematical point is important in relation to the learning goal for the lesson. Recapping involves "making public in a concise, coherent form" (p. 28) a summary that supports shared understanding of the mathematics. Thus, teachers need to discuss with students, as appropriate throughout a lesson, the mathematical aim of their current work to help students understand how the activities support the intended learning (Wiggins and McTighe 2005). As NCTM (2014, p. 13) noted, both teachers and students need to be aware of the following:

- What mathematics is being learned?
- Why is it important?
- How does it relate to what has already been learned?
- Where are these mathematical ideas going?

The focus of this teaching practice is on the importance of establishing learning goals, not performance goals. Learning goals describe the mathematical understandings students are developing as a result of instruction, whereas performance goals describe what students are expected to demonstrate or do during a lesson. The goals students perceive as salient in the classroom influence their motivation for learning (Ames and Archer 1988). Learning goals support development of a productive disposition toward mathematics (Gresalfi and Cobb 2006; Gresalfi 2009); overemphasis on performance goals has negative effects on student motivation (Ryan et al. 1998). The lesson goals as communicated to students also influence their attributions of learning (Elliot and Dweck 1988; Grant and Dweck 2003). Students who perceive an emphasis on learning goals in the classroom use more effective strategies, prefer challenging tasks, persist in face of difficulties, have a more positive attitude toward the class, and have a stronger belief that success follows from one's effort. In other words, students are more likely to exhibit characteristics of a growth mindset and believe that their abilities in mathematics can be developed through learning. In contrast, students who perceive performance goals as salient in the classroom often seek the easiest and quickest way to achieve the goals, give up in the face of challenge, and tend to attribute failure to lack of ability. These students are more likely to exhibit characteristics of a fixed mindset and believe that mathematical ability is simply a fixed trait that cannot be improved through learning. Dweck (2008) and her colleagues have noted that students tend to have more of a fixed view of learning mathematics than of other disciplines. Unfortunately, this may partly be related to the preponderance of performance goals communicated to students in mathematics classrooms without linking those performances to the underlying mathematical understandings.

Clear mathematics learning goals also suggest the kind of evidence teachers need to determine student achievement (Jansen, Bartell, and Berk 2009). The mathematics goals serve as a lens through which the teacher can monitor student learning and prepare to ask students questions designed to assess what they know related to the goals (Stein et al. 2008). As Hiebert and colleagues (2007) noted, "Without explicit learning goals, it is difficult to know what counts as evidence of student learning, how students learning can be linked to particular instructional activities, and how to revise instruction to facilitate student learning more effectively" (p. 51). In addition, learning goals provide guidance for the feedback teachers give to students focused on filling the gap between what a learner understands and what should be understood (Sadler 1989). When feedback is descriptive and addresses the mathematical goal of the task, rather than being evaluative, students are more likely to gain the guidance that helps them advance their learning (Hattie and Temperley 2007; Nelson and Schunn 2009).

Promoting Equity by Establishing Mathematics Goals to Focus Learning

An equitable mathematics program provides all students with opportunities to learn mathematics with understanding, actively building new knowledge by engaging in problem solving and connecting to prior knowledge. In addition, students are learning mathematics in ways that develop conceptual understanding of mathematical ideas, operations, and relationships while at the same time developing fluency with procedures. What is the balance between using learning goals that are focused on mathematical ideas and those focused on meaningful use of strategies? Are some students given access to learning goals more regularly than others?

Ms. Smith established a learning goal for her young learners focused on meaningful use of strategies. She presented the task in a manner that was open, thus allowing for multiple entry points and giving her students a choice to select and use varied strategies to approach and solve the task. Some students represented the situation with counters and counted all to arrive at the total amount. Some students counted on from a given amount, and others had already committed the fact to memory. Ms. Smith was well aware of the learning trajectory related to problem-solving strategies and supported the range of learners in how she enacted the task. Regardless of the strategy used by students, all students had entry into solving the problem. Equitable education is not about all students getting the same at the same time, but all students getting what they need. Expecting that all learners will use the same problem-solving approach hinders student access because you have to start where each child is in the learning process in order to authentically meet the students' academic needs and help the students grow (Alber 2010). Although we want students to use methods that make sense to them, it is important to note that it is still the responsibility of the teacher to identify the students' current level of understanding and strategy and then use effective teaching practices to advance student learning (Weiss and Pasley 2004). It is not acceptable to merely acknowledge a students' current level of understanding. Thus, situating lesson goals within mathematics learning progressions is critical for teachers to meet students where they are at and support them in advancing their understanding of important mathematics ideas and use of meaningful strategies.

It is not easy for students to make connections and to articulate the reasoning behind their problem-solving strategies. Most students, especially English language learners, learners with special needs, and learners who struggle with math, benefit from the use of visual and physical representations. These representations give the students a specific point of reference that assist their explanations and make it possible for them to engage more fully in classroom discussions (Fuson and Murata 2007). For some students the situational context is needed to help them make meaning of the mathematics by connecting it to their own everyday or familiar experiences. Students do not enter the classroom knowing how to use representations, but we know that strengthening students' ability to move between and among the representations strengthens conceptual understanding as students form rich relationships among mathematical ideas (Lesh, Post, and Behr 1987). Students who are asked to publicly demonstrate the ways they used manipulatives, to recreate their math drawings for others, or to share their reasoning become students who see themselves as mathematical authorities in the classroom capable of representing and solving mathematical problems (Bishop 1985; Nathan and Knuth 2003; Webel 2010).

Taking Action in Your Classroom

Throughout this chapter, you have analyzed lesson goals and considered how goals inform teacher actions in the classroom and help teachers monitor student progress. Here we summarize some of the key messages for you to keep in mind as you take action in your own classroom.

- Learning goals should describe what students are to understand about a mathematics topic—concepts, reasons for why procedures work, relationships, and connections—as a result of engaging in a lesson.

- Goals inform the selection and design of tasks so that they provide opportunities for students to gain access to important mathematical ideas.

- Planning and facilitating lessons, as well as eliciting evidence of student thinking, are guided by the identified mathematics learning goals.

- The enactment of learning goals, rather than performance goals, sends messages to students about the nature of mathematics and influences how they view their own agency as capable and contributing members of the mathematics classroom community.

We now invite you to take action in your own professional setting. Explore how you can make your goals for student learning more explicit in regard to the expected mathematical understanding, and consider how these more explicit goals better inform your actions related to the other effective mathematics teaching practices in selecting tasks, posing intentional questions, and eliciting and using evidence of student learning.

Taking Action in Your Classroom
Examining My Math Learning Goals for a Lesson

Select a lesson that you recently taught and re-examine the goals for that lesson.

- Would you classify the goals as learning goals or performance goals?
- In what ways did you communicate the purpose of the lesson to your students?

Now imagine you will be teaching the lesson again.

- What is it that you want students to understand about the mathematics of the lesson? Rewrite the goals so they are clearly learning goals that make explicit the mathematical ideas, concepts, and relationships you want students to understand.
- How might these more explicit goal statements better guide your decision-making as you prepare for the lesson and teach the lesson?
- Using the revised and more explicit learning goals, develop two questions for assessing your students' progress toward the goals during the lesson, and design an exit prompt or task (e.g., an exit ticket) related to the goals to gain information for planning subsequent lessons.

CHAPTER 3

Implement Tasks that Promote Reasoning and Problem Solving

The opportunities afforded by mathematics tasks determine how students come to comprehend what it means to learn and understand mathematics. Students who have opportunities to engage in solving and discussing high-level tasks have different opportunities to learn than those who are only asked to solve low-level tasks. In this chapter, you will examine the effective teaching practice, *implement tasks that promote reasoning and problem solving*. According to *Principles to Actions: Ensuring Mathematical Success for All* (NCTM 2014, p. 17):

> Effective teaching of mathematics engages students in solving and discussing tasks that promote mathematical reasoning and problem solving and allow multiple entry points and varied solution strategies.

Tasks that promote reasoning and problem solving provide opportunities for students to engage in mathematical sense making. These types of high-level tasks do not have a prescribed pathway for students to follow in solving the task, but rather encourage students to enter into the task in multiple ways (e.g., using different types of representations) and to work toward solutions using varied approaches and strategies that make sense to them. In solving such tasks, students wrestle with how to approach them as they work toward understanding underlying mathematical ideas and relationships. One reason to discuss solutions to these types of tasks is to have students analyze and compare the varied solution pathways, leading to new and deeper mathematical insights.

The chapter includes four Analyzing Teaching and Learning (ATL) activities.

- ATL 3.1: Compare two multiplication tasks and identify how the tasks do or do not promote reasoning and problem solving among students.

- ATL 3.2: Analyze a collection of mathematics tasks and decide on the level and type of thinking required of students to engage with each task.

- ATL 3.3: Compare instruction in two classrooms and determine factors that contribute to the maintenance or decline of high-level thinking opportunities afforded by a task.

- ATL 3.4: Analyze a sequence of related tasks and consider how the tasks build upon each other to advance student learning.

As you engage in each ATL, we encourage you to make note of your responses, and if possible, share and discuss your thoughts and ideas with colleagues. Once you share or write down your thoughts, continue reading the analysis of the ATL in which we relate the activity to the chapter's focal teaching practice. After the Analyzing Teaching and Learning activities, the chapter includes research findings on the use of high-level tasks, and then examines how the focal teaching practice promotes equity among students. We end the chapter by offering suggestions for applying the ideas to tasks in your own classroom.

Comparing and Contrasting Mathematical Tasks

Tasks vary in the mathematical opportunities they afford students. Some tasks engage students in thinking and reasoning and some tasks do not. "Over time, the cumulative effect of the use of mathematics tasks is students' implicit development of ideas about the nature of mathematics—about whether mathematics is something that they personally can make sense of and how long and how hard they should have to work to solve any mathematical task" (NCTM 2014, p. 20).

Engage in ATL 3.1: Comparison of Two Multiplication Tasks

In ATL 3.1, we ask you to compare two multiplication tasks. Both tasks ask students to work with multiples of ten but in very different ways. As you engage in the activity, consider the level of thinking and reasoning required in each task. Then reflect on how the task permits or does not permit students to enter into the mathematical work in multiple ways and how the task affords or limits students opportunities to demonstrate their reasoning and understanding.

Analyzing Teaching and Learning 3.1
Comparison of Two Multiplication Tasks

Solve the Multiples of Ten task and the Band Concert task (shown below). Make note of the mathematical knowledge you drew upon and the strategies you used to solve each task.

1. What features of each task lead you to use particular strategies to solve it?

2. In what ways are the two tasks similar and different in regard to the targeted mathematical ideas?

3. Which task is more likely to promote reasoning and problem solving among students? Why?

Multiples of Ten Task	The Band Concert Task
Solve the following multiplication problems: $7 \times 10 =$ _____ $7 \times 20 =$ _____ $5 \times 50 =$_____ $40 \times 7 =$ _____ $10 \times 9 =$ _____ $5 \times 20 =$ _____ $3 \times 20 =$ _____ $30 \times 4 =$ _____	The third-grade class is responsible for setting up the chairs for the spring band concert. In preparation, the class needs to determine the total number of chairs that will be needed and ask the school's engineer to retrieve that many chairs from the central storage area. The class needs to set up 7 rows of chairs with 20 chairs per row, leaving space for a center aisle. How many chairs does the school's engineer need to retrieve from the central storage area?

Analysis of ATL 3.1: The Cognitive Demands of Tasks

Both of these tasks could be found in a third-grade unit on multiplication. At a basic level, each task involves solving a multiplication equation. However, a deeper analysis of the tasks shows that they are, in fact, quite different in terms of the level and kind of thinking in which students might engage to solve each task.

In the Band Concert task, the students must expend effort to find a strategy for solving the task and justify why their approach makes sense because no solution strategy is stated or implied by the task. This task can be solved in multiple ways, as seen by the range of student strategies and explanations in the Case of Robert Harris, presented in chapter 1 (see page 10). Some of Mr. Harris's students build 7 rows with 20 chairs in each row each either physically (using manipulatives to represent each chair) or by drawing all of the chairs. Other students use repeated additions of 20 chairs or skip counting to find the total number of chairs. Some students also decompose the 20 and show 7 groups of 10 chairs on each side of an aisle. It is clear in the case that students had access to the mathematics of the Band Concert task. That is, when presented with the task, all students are able to do *something* at their current level of understanding that helped them make progress towards the mathematical goals of the lesson. Although the Band Concert task could be solved using a multiplication equation, this task is best used before students learn multiplication procedures, as was the case in Mr. Harris's classroom. Mr. Harris was developing students' conceptual understanding of multiplication on which he could later build toward procedural fluency. (This will be discussed in more depth in chapter 4.)

By contrast, the Multiples of Ten task implies different expectations for students. The goal of the task is to find the correct product for each multiplication equation. The way in which the task is set up, and the directions given, implies that students know a procedure for solving such equations. However, if students do not know a procedure and have limited understanding of the meaning of multiplication equations, it is likely that they have limited or no entry into the task. While such tasks serve a function in the curriculum in that they provide an opportunity for students to practice learned procedures, they do not require students to engage in thinking, reasoning, and problem solving. Further, the use of such tasks without first laying a foundation of conceptual understanding—what it means to multiply two numbers, relationship of addition and multiplication, informal understanding of properties of the operations, and decomposing numbers—can reinforce students applying rules with limited or no understanding of why they work or when they should be applied.

The Task Analysis Guide, shown in figure 3.1, provides criteria for determining the level of thinking or cognitive demand required in order to solve a task (Smith and Stein 1998). This taxonomy, developed by Stein, Grover, and Henningsen (1996), places tasks into four categories: (1) memorization, (2) procedures without connections, (3) procedures with connections, and (4) doing mathematics. Tasks that place higher-level cognitive demands on students engage them in mathematical investigations or in using procedures in ways that are meaningfully connected with conceptual understanding. Tasks that place lower-level cognitive demands on students ask them to use procedures, formulas, or algorithms detached from related concepts or consist primarily of memorization or the recall of previously memorized facts.

The Band Concert task is considered to be a task with a high level of cognitive demands while the Multiples of Ten task is considered to be a task with a low level of cognitive demands. High demand tasks, such as the Band Concert task, have the potential to engage students in reasoning and problem solving. Specifically, the Band Concert task is categorized as *doing mathematics* (the last category in fig. 3.1) because the task does not prescribe what students need to do or how they should do it, and considerable effort must be expended to determine a course of action. Most important students must wrestle with the meaning of multiplication as an array having 7 rows with 20 chairs in each row, and wrestle with an informal understanding of the distributive property as the chairs are split into 7 rows of 10 chairs each separated by the center aisle.

Low demand tasks, such as the Multiples of Ten task, focus on recalling facts and rules and the use of known procedures. Specifically, the Multiples of Ten task would be categorized as *procedures without connections* because it expects use of a previously learned procedure and has no connection to the concepts or meaning that underline the procedure. The task is focused on students producing correct answers and not on developing mathematical understanding.

While students need opportunities to engage in all types of tasks, research shows that experience with high-level tasks is critical if we want students to develop the capacity to engage in thinking, reasoning, and problem solving (Stein and Lane 1996). Students who are only asked to solve low-level tasks develop very different beliefs about mathematics than those who regularly engage with high-level tasks. It is through the use of high-level tasks that students come to view mathematics as a sense-making endeavor.

Task Analysis Guide

Lower-level demands: Memorization

- Involve either reproducing previously learned facts, rules, formulas, or definitions or committing facts, rules, formulas or definitions to memory.

- Cannot be solved using procedures because a procedure does not exist or because the time frame in which the task is being completed is too short to use a procedure.

- Are not ambiguous. Such tasks involve the exact reproduction of previously seen material, and what is to be reproduced is clearly and directly stated.

- Have no connection to the concepts or meaning that underlie the facts, rules, formulas, or definitions being learned or reproduced.

Lower-level demands: Procedures Without Connections

- Are algorithmic. Use of the procedure either is specifically called for or is evident from prior instruction, experience, or placement of the task.

- Require limited cognitive demand for successful completion. Little ambiguity exists about what needs to be done and how to do it.

- Have no connection to the concepts or meaning that underlie the procedure being used.

- Are focused on producing correct answers instead of on developing mathematical understanding.

Continued on next page

Fig. 3.1. A guide for examining the cognitive demand of mathematical tasks (From Smith and Stein 1998, p. 348)

- Require no explanations or explanations that focus solely on describing the procedure that was used.

Higher-level demands: Procedures With Connections

- Focus students' attention on the use of procedures for the purpose of developing deeper levels of understanding of mathematical concepts and ideas.
- Suggest explicitly or implicitly pathways to follow that are broad general procedures that have close connections to underlying conceptual ideas as opposed to narrow algorithms that are opaque with respect to underlying concepts.
- Usually are represented in multiple ways, such as visual diagrams, manipulatives, symbols, and problem situations. Making connections among multiple representations helps develop meaning.
- Require some degree of cognitive effort. Although general procedures may be followed, they cannot be followed mindlessly. Students need to engage with conceptual ideas that underlie the procedures to complete the task successfully and that develop understanding.

Higher-level demands: Doing Mathematics

- Require complex and nonalgorithmic thinking—a predictable, well-rehearsed approach or pathway is not explicitly suggested by the task, task instructions, or a worked-out example.
- Require students to explore and understand the nature of mathematical concepts, processes, or relationships.
- Demand self-monitoring or self-regulation of one's own cognitive processes.
- Require students to access relevant knowledge and experiences and make appropriate use of them in working through the task.
- Require students to analyze the task and actively examine task constraints that may limit possible solution strategies and solutions.
- Require considerable cognitive effort and may involve some level of anxiety for the student because of the unpredictable nature of the solution process required.

These characteristics are derived from the work of Doyle on academic tasks (1988) and Resnick on high-level-thinking skills (1987), the *Professional Standards for Teaching Mathematics* (NCTM 1991), and the examination and categorization of hundreds of tasks used in QUASAR classrooms (Stein, Grover, and Henningsen 1996; Stein, Lane, and Silver 1996).

Fig. 3.1. A guide for examining the cognitive demand of mathematical tasks

Examining the Mathematical Thinking Potential of Tasks

All students, even those in pre-kindergarten, can engage with high-level tasks that promote mathematical reasoning and problem solving. While it is important for students throughout the elementary grades to have regular opportunities to solve and discuss solutions to high-level tasks, Stein and Smith (1998, p. 269) remind us:

> Tasks that ask students to perform a memorized procedure in a routine manner lead to one type of opportunity for student thinking; tasks that require students to think conceptually and that stimulate students to make connections lead to a different set of opportunities for student thinking.

Thus, the point is not that one type of task is inherently better than another type of task but that different tasks afford different opportunities for student thinking. As teachers, we need to be able to assess the potential of the tasks that we select and use with our students and to ensure that the tasks align with our mathematics learning goals for students.

Engage in ATL 3.2: Sorting Tasks by Cognitive Demand

In ATL 3.2, you will use the Task Analysis Guide introduced in the previous section (see fig. 3.1) to analyze a collection of elementary grade tasks. The tasks demand different levels of cognitive effort on the part of students. As you study the tasks, envision how elementary students would engage with the mathematics of the task and work toward a solution. Will students be engaged in mathematical reasoning and problem solving at higher levels of cognitive demand? Will students be engaged with mathematical ideas at lower levels of cognitive demand?

▷ How are elementary students engaging in the math of the task & how do they work toward a solution

▷ Are students engaged in mathematical reasoning? ⟶ and Problem Solving at higher Levels of cognitive Demand

▷ higher or Lower cognitive Demand

Analyzing Teaching and Learning 3.2
Sorting Tasks by Cognitive Demand

Solve each of the 10 tasks shown below and consider whether the task engages you in reasoning and problem solving (high-level demands) or whether the task asks you to recall a known piece of information or apply a specific procedure (lower-level demands).

1. Do an initial sort of the tasks into two categories, tasks with lower-level demands and tasks with higher-level demands.

2. Using the Task Analysis Guide (shown in fig. 3.1), sort each category further into one of the four levels of cognitive demand that best describes the type of thinking required to solve each task.

   - Memorization (lower-level demands)

   - Procedures without connections (lower-level demands)

   - Procedures with connections (higher-level demands)

   - Doing mathematics (higher-level demands)

3. Finally, identify the specific criteria (i.e., the specific bulleted statements) from the Task Analysis Guide to support your categorization of the task.

Task A	**Task B**
Find common denominators and solve each addition equation.	Describe a real-life situation for the following equation and then solve it.

Task A

$$\frac{2}{5} + \frac{5}{10} =$$

$$\frac{2}{6} + \frac{3}{4} =$$

$$\frac{5}{6} + \frac{5}{3} =$$

Task B

$$488 \div 13 =$$

Explain how your answer makes sense in your story situation.

Task C

1. Make a diagram showing how you can find the answer to 43 − 29. Explain how you know your answer is correct.

2. Your friend solved 43 − 29 by starting with the equation 43 − 30. Explain what your friend will have to do next in order to find the correct answer to 43 − 29.

Task D

Compare the two fractions in each row. Circle the fraction that is greatest.

$$\frac{3}{8} \quad \text{or} \quad \frac{2}{3}$$

$$\frac{10}{12} \quad \text{or} \quad \frac{5}{4}$$

$$\frac{3}{6} \quad \text{or} \quad \frac{2}{3}$$

$$\frac{3}{10} \quad \text{or} \quad \frac{3}{5}$$

Task E

Ramon is solving the problem 6 + 9. He claims, "When you add two numbers, it doesn't matter what order you add them in. Either way, the answer will be the same. I'll show you, 6 + 9 = 15 and 9 + 6 = 15."

1. Is Ramon right or wrong? Use diagrams and examples for 6 + 9 and 9 + 6 to justify your answer.

2. Is Ramon's claim true for the problem 4 + 3? Show a diagram or explain how Ramon's claim is true for this problem.

3. Write two other addition problems for which the claim is true.

Task F

Solve these addition problems.

4 + 3 = _____

3 + 5 = _____

6 + 5 = _____

4 + 5 = _____

5 + 3 = _____

4 + 6 = _____

5 + 7 = _____

Task G

1. Shade in about ⁵⁄₈ of this rectangle.

2. Name three other fractions that are close in size to ⁵⁄₈. Explain your reasoning for each fraction.

Task H

1. The area of each whole rectangle is 1. Shade an area of each rectangle equal to the fraction underneath it.

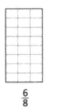

$$\frac{6}{8} \qquad \frac{2}{3}$$

2. Which fraction is larger? How do you know?

3. Name another fraction that describes the shaded portion of each rectangle.

Task I

Provide a defintion for each of the following geometric figures.

Rectangle:

Trapezoid:

Parallelogram:

Angle:

Line segment:

Task J

1. Solve each word problem:

Jamie and Alex baked 48 cookies for the bake sale and packaged them in groups of 8 cookies per bag. How many bags did they pack?

If 48 cookies are divided equally among 8 students, how many cookies will each student receive?

2. Jamie claims that the two word problems are the same but Alex claims the problems are different. Alex is correct. Show and explain how the two problems differ from each other.

Analysis of ATL 3.2: The Potential of Tasks

Students might encounter each of these tasks at some point in their learning across grades 1–5. The tasks address important mathematical topics that students study across these grades. The tasks, however, differ in terms of cognitive demand, that is, the level of thinking required to solve a specific task.

Tasks B and J are *doing mathematics* tasks. These tasks do not suggest nor imply a specific pathway. In each task, the student must decide how to approach it. For task B, the student must create a context or story problem that aligns with the given equation, 448 ÷ 13. This requires the students to draw from their own experiences and demonstrate understanding of the operation of division. The second prompt asks students to "explain how your answer makes sense in your story situation" and may require students to revise their story problem as they consider the task constraint of a remainder in that equation. Task J engages students in comparing two types of division situations, partitive and measurement, thus requiring students to explore the nature of the concept of division. Both tasks can be solved in more than one way and require considerable cognitive effort on the part of the students. The tasks also require nonalgorithmic thinking, that is, a specific solution pathway is not explicitly suggested by the task and students must draw upon their own understanding and experiences as they engage in making sense of the mathematics.

Tasks C, E, G, and H are *procedures with connections* tasks. Each of these tasks focus students on developing deeper levels of understanding mathematical concepts that are related to the use of procedures. The tasks suggest a general pathway for students to explore that is closely grounded in the underlying conceptual ideas. For task C, students begin by drawing a diagram that shows their own reasoning. This use of multiple representations helps students access the task and supports deepening understanding of subtraction strategies for 43 – 29. Students are then challenged to make sense of the strategy used by a friend. The "start with" prompt explicitly directs students to a solution path, but then students must bring meaning to using 43 – 30 and figure out how to proceed in solving the problem. For example, a student might reason, 43 – 29 = (43 – 30) + 1, realizing that subtracting one extra for ease of operation, means that the one extra must be added back on to arrive at the difference when solving 43 – 29. While the task guides students to use a compensation strategy, it also invites students into engaging with the conceptual ideas that underlie the strategy and which they must draw upon to successfully solve the task. Similarly, task E uses a worked-out example by asking students to critique Ramon's claim, thus directing students to examine and make sense of the commutative property, and then apply the strategy when asked to "write two other addition problems for which the claim is true." Task G asks students to name several fractions that are close in size to $\frac{5}{8}$ and share their reasoning, thus developing deeper levels of understanding of mathematical concepts and ideas. Task H asks students to represent fractions by shading two same-size rectangles that are each partitioned into 24 equal parts (i.e., 8 rows and 3 columns). The task is challenging for students as they must reconcile how to represent thirds and eighths on the given grids. The task prompts students to use a visual representation to make connections among thirds, eighths, and the meaning of finding a common denominator. It is the connection to meaning—linking strategies or procedures to conceptual ideas—that makes these procedures-with-connections tasks.

Both tasks A and D are *procedures without connections* tasks. A procedure which students have likely been taught is suggested by each task and little ambiguity exists about what needs to be done and how to do it. Task A tells students to find common denominators to add the fractions. Task D expects students to compare the fractions and select the one that is greater. Each task is a straightforward application of a procedure with the aim to produce correct answers. Students are not asked to make a drawing, demonstrate understanding, or provide an explanation. If students have forgotten or confuse the steps of a specified procedure, they have no options of making sense of the task on their own.

We are all familiar with *memorization* tasks which usually also have a feature of requesting rapid recall of facts, formulas, definitions, or rules. Tasks F and I are memorization tasks. Task F asks students to recall basic addition facts and Task I asks students to reproduce definitions of geometric figures. The tasks are not ambiguous. Students are successful if they can reproduce the requested information and unsuccessful if they cannot. These tasks have no explicit connection to underlying concepts or meaning.

Does the potential of the task matter? High-demand tasks that involve doing mathematics and linking procedures with connections are the only types of tasks that have the *potential* to engage students in reasoning and problem solving. As Boston and Wilhelm (2015 p. 24) note:

> In general, the potential of the task sets the ceiling for implementation—
> that is, a task almost never increases in cognitive demand during
> implementation. This finding, robust in its consistency across several studies,
> suggests that high-level instructional tasks are a necessary condition for
> ambitious mathematics instruction.

It is important to note, however, that the use of high-level tasks does not guarantee that its potential will be realized during instruction. The interactions of teachers and students during the implementation of such tasks determine whether or not students actually engage in higher levels of mathematical thinking and reasoning. Therefore, it is important to pay attention to what occurs during instruction to ensure that the demands of the task do indeed remain at a high level.

Considering How Task Implementation Impacts Learning Opportunities

The use of high-level tasks in classrooms makes it possible for students to engage in problem solving and mathematical reasoning. However, such thinking and reasoning does not always occur due to the manner in which teachers implement those high-level tasks (Stein, Grover, and Henningsen 1996; Stigler and Hiebert 2004). Even though well-intentioned, sometimes the demands of high-level tasks are reduced by teachers, almost subconsciously, in their attempts to help students move beyond confusions and struggles in order to reach correct solutions.

Here we aim to raise your consciousness to those factors that contribute to lowering, as well as to those that maintain, the cognitive demand of high-level tasks, so that you can be more intentional in supporting your students productively in higher levels of thinking. Henningsen and Stein (1997) studied the implementation of high-level tasks in urban classrooms. They identified a set of recurring factors that contributed to ways in which teachers were able to maintain the potential for thinking and reasoning afforded by high-level tasks, as well as teacher-student interactions that lead to a lowering of the cognitive effort afforded by the tasks. These factors of teacher-student dynamics are summarized in figure 3.2. Many of these factors are ones all of us recognize as having occurred in our classrooms at some point in time. Take a moment and read through the two sets of factors. Which factors are recognizable in your own teaching? Which factors caused you to pause and wonder?

Factors Associated with Decline of High-Level Tasks	Factors Associated with Maintenance of High-Level Tasks
1. Problematic aspects of the task become routinized (e.g., students press teacher to reduce task complexity by specifying explicit procedures or steps to perform; teacher "takes over" difficult pieces of the task and performs them for the students or tells them how to do it).	1. Scaffolding (i.e., task is simplified so student can solve it; complexity is maintained, but greater resources are made available). Could occur during whole class discussion, presentations, or during group or pair work.
2. Teacher shifts emphasis from meaning, concepts, or understanding to correctness or completeness of the answer.	2. Students are provided with the means of monitoring their own progress (e.g., rubrics are discussed and used to judge performance; means for testing conjectures are made explicit and used).
3. Not enought time is provided for students to wrestle with the demanding aspects of the task or too much time is provided and students flounder or drift off task.	3. The teacher or capable students model high-level performance.
	Continued on next page

Fig. 3.2. Factors of decline and maintenance in implementing high-level tasks (Adapted from Stein et al. 2009, p. 16.)

Factors Associated with Decline of High-Level Tasks	Factors Associated with Maintenance of High-Level Tasks
4. Classroom management problems prevent sustained engagement. 5. Task is inappropriate for the group of students (e.g., lack of interest, lack of motivation, lack of prior knowledge needed to perform, task expectations not clear enough to put students in the right cognitive space). 6. Students not held accountable for high-level products or processes (e.g., although asked to explain their thinking, unclear or incorrect student explanations are accepted; students were given the impression that their work would not "count" (i.e., be used to determine grades).	4. Sustained press for justifications, explanations, meaning through teacher questioning, comments, feedback. 5. Tasks are selected that build on students' prior knowledge. 6. Teacher draws frequent conceptual connections. 7. Sufficient time to explore (not too little, not too much).

Fig. 3.2. Factors of decline and maintenance in implementing high-level tasks

Engage in ATL 3.3: Comparing Instruction in Two Classrooms

One means of increasing the likelihood that a task remains at a high level of cognitive demand is by engaging in careful lesson planning. After selecting a high-level task, teachers can plan ways to support students who cannot get started, who may make a mistake, or who get stuck or lost in their thinking, as well as those students who need a push or some encouragement. Generally, the scaffolds to support high-levels of reasoning are in the form of teacher questions that press students for elaborations, explanations, and justifications. Without anticipating student approaches and potential struggles, teachers must decide in the moment how to respond to students, and with all the competing needs within a class full of students, these decisions might, unintentionally, lower the cognitive demand required of students.

In ATL 3.3, you will analyze the implementation of the Band Concert task in two different third-grade classrooms. In this way, you can study specific examples of ways in which the demands of the task are maintained or lowered and what factors account for these outcomes. We refer you back to the Case of Robert Harris introduced in chapter 1 (page 11), as well as introduce a new case, that of Mr. Stevenson.

Comparing Instruction in Two Classrooms

Reread the Case of Robert Harris and the Band Concert task (introduced in ATL 1.1) with a new lens, examining whether he maintained or lowered the cognitive demand of student engagement with the Band Concert task; then read the Case of Mr. Stevenson, shown below, with the same lens.

1. How are the two classes the same and how they are different?

2. What factors associated with the maintenance and decline of implementing high-level tasks (see fig. 3.2) might help account for the differences?

3. In what ways do the differences impact student learning?

The Case of Mr. Stevenson and the Band Concert Task

1   Mr. Stevenson teaches third grade. He wants his students to understand multiplication
2   and decided to use the Band Concert task (shown below) because it will allow his
3   students to explore multiplication in a contextual setting. He likes how the task prompts
4   students to make or draw arrays, something his students need more experience with
5   as a representation for multiplication. The task also provides an opportunity to move
6   his students toward fluency in multiplying with multiples of 10, an expectation of the
7   standards for third grade students.

8   The third-grade class is responsible for setting up the chairs for the
9   spring band concert. In preparation, the class needs to determine the
10 total number of chairs that will be needed and ask the school's engineer
11 to retrieve that many chairs from the central storage area. The class needs
12 to set up 7 rows of chairs with 20 chairs in each row, leaving space for a
13 center aisle. How many chairs does the school's engineer need to retrieve
14 from the central storage area?

15 Mr. Stevenson began by asking a student to retell the story to the whole class and
16 clarify what the question was asking, that is, to find the total number of chairs. Next he
17 stated, "I expect each of you to represent the problem and to write an equation. To show
18 the problem you can use cubes or you can draw a picture on paper. If you look up here I'll

He is explaining it, but it's taking away from the learning → Kind of Changing the goals from Learning to Performance.

Not letting students come up with their own representations

19 show you some possible ways you could do it. One way is to use grid paper. First, I mark
20 off 7 rows, then I count 20 squares to be in each row for the chairs, and then marked that
21 off." (*Mr. Stevenson draws a 7 by 20 array on a grid on the smart board.*) "Because it says
22 there is a center aisle, you could also make two 7 × 10 arrays, one on each side of that
23 center aisle." (*The teacher draws two 7 by 10 arrays on the grid paper on the smart board.*)
24 "You can use cubes or draw the picture in other ways. You decide."

25 As the students were about to start working, Mr. Stevenson emphasized that if they
26 chose to make a math picture, he did not want them drawing all the individual chairs,
27 but that they could use numbers to label parts of their drawings. He then reminded them
28 that they were in the "multiplication unit" and to keep this in mind as they worked on
29 the task. → Basically Telling them What to do.

30 The students worked individually for about five minutes. As the teacher made his
31 way around the classroom, he noticed most students were making arrays on grid paper
32 and a few students were drawing pictures or using connecting cubes. He was pleased
33 that students did not seem to struggle to represent the problem situation. He also had
34 prepared some key questions while planning for the lesson that he asked individual
35 students as they worked. These included: What multiplication problem can you write to
36 tell about the 7 rows with 20 chairs in each row? What is the product of 7 × 20? How
37 can you get the answer to 7 × 20 quickly?

38 Mr. Stevenson noted that students were coming up with different answers, 140 or 160
39 or 180 chairs. He observed many students skip-counting by tens or twenties, and some
40 students using repeated addition on scratch paper. It seemed that students were having
41 trouble keeping track of the number of tens or twenties as they skip-counted or added. If
42 students had the wrong answer, he first had them recheck their drawing or representation
43 to make sure they had the right number of rows, and then he had the students skip-count
44 with him to get the answer either by tens or twenties depending on their representation.

45 During the class discussion, Mr. Stevenson asked students to explain what they had
46 done and why and to answer questions posed by their peers. Jeffrey presented first.

47 **Jeffrey:**   I did it like Mr. S. showed us. I made 7 rows of 20 on the grid paper. Then
48   I counted by twenties up to 140.
49 **Teacher:**   What was your equation?
50 **Jeffrey:**   7 × 20.

51 Kendra went next. She also used grid paper, but had drawn two 7 × 10 arrays, and had
52 written the equation 7 × 20. He asked the class if they had any questions for Kendra, but
53 there were no questions, so the teacher began a dialogue with her.
54 **Teacher:**   Kendra, why did you write 7 × 20 and how does it relate to your diagram?
55 **Kendra:**   Well… I…. well the story problem says 7 rows with 20.

56	**Teacher:**	Well that's true, but your picture shows 7 rows of 10 and then another 7
57		rows of 10. It doesn't show 7 rows of 20. I wonder how all of this might
58		relate to each other?
59	**Kendra:**	*(Kendra had a puzzled look on her face as did her classmates. She just shrugged*
60		*her shoulders indicating she didn't know. Finally, DeShawn raised his hand.)*
61	**DeShawn:**	Well isn't 7 × 20 the right equation?

62   Mr. Stevenson acknowledged that 7 × 20 was the right equation for the situation, but
63 he wanted the students to also see that the 20 could be decomposed into 2 tens; thus
64 leading to the procedure he wanted them to use for multiplying multiples of ten. The
65 discussion continued.

66	**Teacher:**	Let's look at Kendra's diagram. How many rows are in this part?
67	**Students:**	7.
68	**Teacher:**	How many chairs are in each row on this side of the aisle?
69	**Students:**	10.
70	**Teacher:**	How many chairs are in that row on the other side of the aisle?
71	**Students:**	10.
72	**Teacher:**	Oh, so there are 2 tens in each row. So to multiply 7 × 20, you could think
73		of it as multiplying 7 × 2 tens. How many tens does that give you?
74	**Students:**	14.
75	**Teacher:**	Right, and then you just need to add a zero because it's 14 tens.

76   In the last few minutes of class, the teacher asked the students to check to make sure
77 they had written an equation and the answer on their papers and to turn them in as the
78 class ended.

Analysis of ATL 3.3: The Maintenance and Decline of Learning Opportunities

Although Mr. Harris and Mr. Stevenson both used the Band Concert task as the basis for instruction, the opportunities afforded each of their students were very different. Most notably, Mr. Harris supported sustained engagement of his students in reasoning and problem solving without taking over their thinking. On the other hand, Mr. Stevenson appeared to be doing most of the thinking in his classroom.

   Several factors associated with the maintenance of high-level tasks (see fig. 3.2) help account for the success of Mr. Harris's lesson. The teacher selected a task that built on students' prior knowledge (Factor 5). Students could approach this task by drawing a diagram and counting, as Molly did, by using skip counting like Teresa, or by using prior knowledge of repeated addition. Mr. Harris also provided appropriate scaffolding for his students (Factor 1) by asking probing questions and prompting students to reflect on their work rather than telling students what to do. For example, he asked, "So, tell me about your picture. How does it show the set up of the chairs for the band concert (line 30–31)? He also used students as supports for each other during the several "turn and talk" opportunities (lines 23–24, 46–57, 83–84) which forced students to slow down their thinking and engage a bit deeper with the mathematical ideas.

Mr. Harris's continual press for students to explain their thinking was another factor that maintained cognitive effort among the students (Factor 4). His questions pressed individual students to reflect on their work (lines 29–31) as well as the whole class as they built a shared understanding of the connections among skip counting, repeated addition, and multiplication (lines 66–80). His purposeful use of student presentations during the class discussion (lines 58–63, 91–93) provided models of high-level performance (Factor 3). Throughout the lesson, Mr. Harris made frequent conceptual connections (Factor 6), such as the relationship between repeated addition and multiplication (lines 66-80) and the connection of the multiplication equation to student diagrams (lines 81-90). Finally, and perhaps most importantly, he had a clear goal for student learning (as discussed in chapter 2), he selected a task that was aligned with his goals, and all of his efforts throughout the lesson were focused on helping students reach the goals he had set.

Although Mr. Stevenson began the lesson with a high-level task, the level of demand declined during implementation as he interacted with the students. His case illustrates how several factors associated with the decline of high-level tasks (see fig. 3.2) account for the shift in students' opportunities to think and reason. Mr. Stevenson removed problematic aspects of the tasks (Factor 1). Toward the beginning of the lesson, he showed students how they might use grid paper to represent the problem (lines 18–23). While he did not require students to use grid paper, his demonstration strongly influenced how students approached representing the problem situation (lines 30–31). Jeffrey even commented, "I did it like Mr. S showed us" (line 47). Students likely inferred that the "right way" to represent the situation was the one emphasized by the teacher, namely, showing arrays on grid paper. Consequently, students did not need to draw on their prior knowledge or experiences nor take ownership of the ideas as evidenced by Jeffrey's comment (line 47) and Kendra's inability to connect her equation to her drawing that she had just replicated from the teacher's diagram (lines 54–60). Toward the end of the whole-class discussion, Mr. Stevenson takes over the difficult thinking of connecting the decomposition of 20 into 2 tens to the procedure he wanted them to use for multiplying multiples of ten (lines 72–75). The other major contributing factor to the decline in cognitive effort among the students occurred as Mr. Stevenson shifted the emphasis to correctness and completeness of the answer (Factor 2) rather than probing students' ideas. He pushed for correctness as he interacted with individual students who had gotten the wrong answer and helped them skip-count to the correct answer (lines 41–44). He also noted that they were in the multiplication unit (lines 27–28), thus inferring that they should write a multiplication equation rather than an addition equation. At the end of the lesson he pushed for completeness by telling students to check their papers and make sure they included an equation and the answer (lines 76–78). Throughout the lesson, students were not held accountable for high-level thinking or written work (Factor 6). While Mr. Stevenson's goal was to help his students understand multiplication more deeply, the implementation of the lesson focused more on getting a correct answer and pushing students toward the teacher's procedure for multiplying multiples of ten. It is likely that the students have little understanding of the teacher's procedure, as they had limited opportunities to engage in their own sense making with the problem situation or to understand and evaluate the usefulness of varied strategies.

The differences between the two classes matter for student learning. Even though both teachers used the same high-level task, the students had very different opportunities to learn mathematics and to see themselves as capable or not capable of doing mathematics. In Mr. Harris's class, students learned that they could make sense of problems and persevere. Students learned that they could figure out their own solution paths as authors and owners of mathematical ideas. Struggle was a norm in Mr. Harris's classroom, as was the collaborative community he developed in which students not only worked on their own solution paths but also strove to understand the reasoning of their classmates. The goal to understand the mathematics was also a norm in this classroom. Students understood that they were to refer to the context of the problem as they discussed the meaning of the numbers in the task and they were to find relationships among different strategies, such as repeated addition and skip counting, and connect them to the meaning of multiplication.

In Mr. Stevenson's class students learned very little about the meaning of multiplication and made few connections between prior knowledge of skip counting or repeated addition and the new concept of study, multiplication. We do not know if Mr. Stevenson's students can persevere in solving situational problems because they were not given the opportunity to do so in this lesson. If the case depicts typical teacher-student dynamics, we wonder whether the students will come to believe that the teacher is the source of mathematical knowledge and grow dependent upon him for ways to solve problems. Students quickly realize that if they wait, the teacher will usually tell them what to do or guide them step-by-step to a solution. Additionally, as shown through this case, students come to view the purpose of lessons as getting to the answer rather than striving to understand the underlying mathematics. Becoming aware of the factors that contribute to the maintenance or decline of high-level tasks might help Mr. Stevenson more purposefully plan his lessons to keep the cognitive effort at a high-level throughout the implementation of his lessons.

Sequencing Tasks to Build Mathematical Understanding

The use of high-level tasks, such as the Band Concert task, have the potential to impact students' learning of mathematics and their dispositions for approaching and engaging with mathematics, but this rarely happens from the implementation of just one high-level task. The learning of important mathematical ideas occurs over time, across many lessons, through the use of related tasks that build upon, develop, and extend student learning. As Hiebert and his colleagues noted (Hiebert et al. 1997, p. 31):

> A teacher's role in selecting tasks goes well beyond choosing good individual tasks, one after another. Teachers need to select sequences of tasks so that, over time, students' experiences add up to something important. Teachers need to consider the residue left behind by sets of tasks, not just individual tasks.

Engage in ATL 3.4: Exploring a Sequence of Tasks

In ATL 3.4, we ask you to analyze a sequence of five subtraction tasks from a first-grade unit on exploring the relationship between addition and subtraction. As you study the set of tasks, consider what learning "residue" (Hiebert et al. 1997) might be left behind with respect to students' understanding of the underlying structure of subtraction and the relationship between addition and subtraction.

Analyzing Teaching and Learning 3.4
Exploring a Sequence of Related Tasks

Study the five tasks shown below. These tasks are from a first-grade unit on addition and subtraction. The sequence of the tasks reflects the order in which they appeared in the unit of study but not necessarily consecutive lessons.

1. How would you classify the cognitive demands of each task (i.e., doing mathematics, procedures with connections, procedures without connections, memorization)? Refer to the characteristics of tasks listed in the Task Analysis Guide (see fig. 3.1).

2. In what ways does each individual task contribute to students' understanding of the relationship between addition and subtraction?

3. What might be the added value of each subsequent task for student learning as a class progresses through the sequence, as well as the learning value of the overall set of tasks?

Task 1

The Playground

1. For each story problem, make a picture or diagram, write an equation, and find the answer.

   - There were 13 first-grade students on the playground. Then 9 first-grade students go back to the classroom. How many first-grade students are still on the playground? $13 - 9 = \boxed{}$

   - There were 16 second-grade students on the playground. Then (some) of the second-grade students go back to the classroom. There are now 10 second-grade students on the playground. How many second-grade students went back to the classroom? $16 - \boxed{} = 10$

2. How are the two story problems similar and how are they different?

Task 2

Pet Store

A pet store owner keeps track of the number of pets that she has at the start of the day and the number of pets she has at the end of the day.

Animal	Starting Amount	Sold Amount	Ending Amount
Dogs	11		6
Cats	18		8
Hamster	13		7

Use the information in the table to determine which type of pet was sold the most on this day. Use pictures, numbers, and/or words to help you figure out and explain how you know which type of pet was sold the most.

Task 3

The Party

1. For each story problem, make a picture or a diagram, write an equation, and find the answer.

   • Thomas is decorating cupcakes for the party. He has 5 cupcakes decorated so far. He needs a total of 12 cupcakes for the party. How many more cupcakes does he need to decorate?

   • The package contained 12 balloons that need to be blown up for the party. Robert blew up some of the balloons. There are still 5 balloons that need to be blown up. How many balloons did Robert blow up?

2. How are the two story problems similar and how are they different?

Task 4

Reading a Book

Allee has read 9 pages of her book. The book has 15 pages in it. How many more pages does she need to read to finish the book?

Jenna claims she can add on in jumps. She explains, "9 and jump 1 more gets me to 10. Then jump 5 more gets me to 15…And 1 and 5 is 6. She has 6 pages to read."

Daniel says he can subtract back in chunks. He explains, "I start at 15 then I subtract 5 to get back to 10. Then I subtract 1 more to get to 9. So a 5 chunk and a 1 chunk is 6. The answer is 6."

Why do Jenna and Daniel each get the same answer when they used different strategies? Does this always work? Draw a picture to help you explain.

Analysis of ATL 3.4: Building Understanding Over Time

The set of tasks is intended to support student progress toward meeting the expectations of state standards for first grade. Students are expected to use addition and subtraction within 20 to solve story problems that include problem situations of joining, separating, putting together, taking apart, and comparing, with unknowns in all positions. Students should be able to demonstrate how to find the solutions by using objects to act out the situation or by making drawings. They are also expected to write equations that match the story problems showing the unknown in all positions, those being, result unknown, change unknown, and start unknown positions. Students are also expected to solve addition and subtraction equations with the unknown in any position.

Each of the five tasks engages students in high-levels of mathematical reasoning. Tasks 1, 2, 3, and 5 are classified as *doing mathematics* tasks because no specific pathway is suggested by the tasks and each requires students to explore and understand the concept of subtraction. Task 4 is a *procedures with connections* task because it focuses students explicitly on two strategies for solving the story problem. Both strategies use ten, but Jenna adds on in jumps while Daniel subtracts back in chunks. The task prompts students to think about the underlying mathematical ideas and to draw a picture helping them make connections among representations in order to develop meaning for the relationship between subtraction and addition.

Task 1 begins with a familiar type of subtraction story problem, "a separate situation with the result unknown." Students are to draw a diagram and write an equation, which will likely be $13 - 9 = [4]$. Next, students represent and solve a harder type of subtraction story problem, "a separate-change-unknown situation." In this problem, students start with the whole amount of second graders but are confronted with an unknown number of second-grade children who go back into the school; then students are given the number of second-graders who remain on the playground. Research indicates that some students will say they cannot solve problem two because they do not know how many students went into school because it says "some" (Carpenter and Moser 1984). It is likely that students will also struggle with writing the equation and marking the unknown amount. The final question in the task directly asks students to compare and contrast the two story situations. While it is likely that some students will identify superficial differences, such as the grade level of students and the number of students, the intent is to focus students on the underlying mathematical structure. That is, in both situations the whole amount is known and one part is unknown. The difference is that the position of the unknown part varies.

Task 2 provides continued experience with separate-change-unknown problem situations. The value added for student learning with this task is two-fold. First, students get more experience with these harder problem types. Second, the task is not straightforward, as students must discern how to make sense of the data table and how to determine which type of animal was sold the most at the pet store.

Task 3 is similar in format to Task 1, but includes a new type of story problem for students to represent and solve, "join-change-unknown." It is likely that students will write the equation as $5 + [7] = 12$ for the cupcake story. The second story problem is a separate change-unknown situation with the matching equation of $12 - [7] = 5$. The value added of this task is a direct comparison and discussion of the relationship of addition and subtraction in the story situations and in the equations. Even though both situations sound very different, the underlying structure is the same. The whole amount is known and one part is unknown.

The first three tasks asked students to focus on understanding the problem situation and to find a solution. Task 4 asks students to analyze and make sense of two different solution strategies that utilize number relationships. Jenna finds the difference between 9 and 15 by adding on in jumps. She starts at 9 pages and then adds 1 page to get to 10, an important benchmark, and then realizes that she needs 5 more pages to reach 15 total pages. She then knows that the solution is the sum of her jumps, $1 + 5 = 6$. Daniel also uses number relationships to find the difference between 9 and 15, but he starts at 15 and then jumps back in chunks. Similar to Jenna's method, he uses 10 as an important benchmark. He subtracts 5 from 15 to get to 10 and then realizes he needs to subtract 1 more to reach 9. He also knows that the solution is the sum of the chunks he subtracted, $5 + 1 = 6$. This task forces students to examine strategies based on number relationships and the use of 10 as an important benchmark rather than using strategies based on direct modeling and counting. Furthermore, students must consider the relationship between addition and subtraction and how either approach, building up or subtracting back, can both be used to find the difference of two numbers. The value added with this task is that it prompts students to notice and then justify a generalization about the relationship between addition and subtraction.

The final task, Task 5, alternates the direction of the earlier work. Here students are asked to pose three word problems, each of which matches the structure of a different equation. The value added of this task is that it will challenge, as well as assess, students' knowledge of the contextual differences modeled by each equation. The goal is to see whether students can create and use their own contexts as a means of making sense of the different equations.

While an individual task can be an interesting exploration for students, it is the set of related tasks, worked out in sequence, that together have the potential to build and deepen students' conceptual understanding of a mathematical idea. Hence the residue—the underlying mathematical understanding—that is left behind is a result of engagement with the set of related tasks. This set of five tasks gave us a glimpse into considering how the same mathematical idea, in this case the relationship of addition and subtraction, can be examined and explored from multiple perspectives. The intent of each new view is to advance and deepen students' understanding of the underlying mathematical structure. The five tasks provide an example of how a sequence of high-level mathematics tasks can be used to incrementally build student understanding of a mathematical idea.

What Research Says: Implementing High-Level Tasks

A rich history of research, spanning several decades, has established the importance of high-level tasks for students' learning of mathematics. If we want students to develop proficiency in mathematical reasoning and problem solving, then we must create environments that support students in developing those abilities. This begins with tasks. Given that not all tasks provide the same opportunities for student thinking and learning, teachers need to attend to the cognitive demand of tasks they use with their students (Hiebert et al. 1997). Several taxonomies of thinking exist (e.g., Hess 2009; Krathwohl 2002), but most are general in nature. In this chapter, we utilized the Task Analysis Guide (see fig. 3.1) developed by Smith and Stein (1998) to study four levels of cognitive demand unique to mathematical tasks. The four levels include: (1) memorization, (2) procedures without connections, (3) procedures with connections, and (4) doing mathematics. These levels of cognitive demand provide a way of classifying mathematical tasks according to the level or type of thinking that tasks could potentially elicit from students (Silver and Stein 1996; Stein et al. 2009). Tasks determine the potential of classroom instruction for engaging students in high-level thinking and reasoning.

Student learning is related to the tasks students experience. Students who have on-going opportunities to engage in high-level mathematical tasks show greater learning gains than students who spend the majority of their time engaged in procedural tasks (Boaler and Staples 2008; Hiebert and Wearne 1993; Stein and Lane 1996). Large national studies of mathematics instruction consider the implementation of cognitively challenging tasks as a key indicator of mathematics instruction that promotes students' learning (e.g., Weiss and Pasley 2004). Studies of mathematics curriculum implementation consistently associate higher student achievement with mathematics curricula that contain a predominance of cognitively challenging tasks (e.g., Cai et al. 2011; Riordan and Noyce 2001; Schoenfeld 2002).

For example, Hiebert and Wearne (1993) studied six second-grade classrooms during instruction on place value and multi-digit addition and subtraction. Those classes that engaged students with high-level tasks and more mathematical discourse, as compared to the classes using the conventional textbook approach and mainly low-level tasks, showed higher levels of performance by the end of the school year on place value, routine computation, and novel computation. They concluded that "teaching and learning can be related through the kinds of instructional tasks provided and the nature of classroom discourse" (p. 422) because higher levels of student performance are supported "by the increased opportunities to engage in reflective thought and self-expression, two processes that can be linked to the nature of instructional tasks and classroom discourse." In other words, increasing opportunities for students to engage in high-level tasks and extended discourse on those tasks results in greater student learning. Another example, the QUASAR Project (Quantitative Understanding: Amplifying Student Achievement and Reasoning) sought to improve student learning in middle schools serving economically disadvantaged students by regularly engaging students with high-level tasks. This four-year study looked at student performance on project-developed measures of reasoning and problem solving and found that student performance was greatest in classrooms in which teachers set up and implemented tasks at high levels of cognitive demand (Stein and Lane 1996).

This brings us to our third and final point. To recap: First, teachers must be able to identify and select high-level tasks. Second, students need to have regular opportunities to engage with high-level tasks. Third, teachers need to maintain the cognitive demand of high-level tasks when implementing them with students. Unfortunately, high-level tasks are the most difficult to implement well. As students engage with high-level tasks, teachers often lower the level of thinking in their attempts to support student progress toward a solution (Stein, Grover, and Henningsen 1996; Stigler and Hiebert 2009). The factors associated with the maintenance and decline of high-level tasks, examined earlier in this chapter (see fig. 3.3), describe how students' engagement with high-level tasks that originally promoted reasoning and problem solving can decline into less rigorous mathematical activity (Henningsen and Stein 1997). For example, Mr. Stevenson (see ATL 3.3), removed the "productive struggle" often accompanying cognitively challenging tasks by taking over the thinking of his students and funneling them toward a correct answer and a specific procedure. International studies have also examined the implementation of high-level tasks. A major, unfortunate finding was that teachers in U.S. classrooms almost always, and far more than higher achieving countries, lowered the cognitive demand of high-level tasks, turning opportunities to engage students in reasoning and sense making into procedural steps to memorize and follow (Stigler and Hiebert 2004). Higher achieving countries, conversely, were more successful in maintaining the high-level demands of tasks during implementation, and thus, provided their students with more opportunities to engage in understanding the underlying mathematical ideas for procedures, make connections among concepts, and engage in mathematical reasoning and problem solving.

Promoting Equity by Implementing Tasks that Promote Reasoning and Problem Solving

One of the essential elements of excellent mathematics programs is a focus on access and equity (NCTM 2014). All students must "have access to a high-quality mathematics curriculum, effective teaching and learning, high expectations, and the support and resources needed to maximize their learning potential" (p. 59). One aspect of high-quality curricula is a focus on providing each and every student with access to high-level tasks, that is, tasks that promote reasoning and problem solving. *Opportunity gaps* (Flores 2007) are created when some groups of students, particularly students who have been traditionally marginalized in mathematics (e.g., children of minority groups, children for whom English is not their first language, children of poverty, and children who have previously struggled in mathematics), are provided different opportunities to learn mathematics than other students by disparities such as the nature of mathematical tasks and how tasks are implemented during instruction.

High-level tasks not only hold high mathematical expectations for every student, one aspect of equitable classrooms, they also "allow multiple entry points and varied solution strategies" (NCTM 2014, p. 17). Thus, tasks that promote reasoning and problem solving provide ways for each and every student to enter into the mathematics and encourage students to demonstrate their knowledge in multiple ways. Many, but not all, high-level tasks are also "low threshold, high ceiling tasks" (McClure 2011). Similar to the idea of multiple entry points, such tasks are ones that *all* students can enter and explore at some level (low threshold). These tasks also hold the potential for extending student learning beyond the immediate learning goals (high ceiling). That is, the teacher might prompt students to examine additional aspects of the task or the mathematics, or students might challenge themselves. For example, the Band Concert task (ATL 3.1) would be considered a low-threshold, high-ceiling task, as would many of the other high-level tasks included in this book.

Making high-level tasks accessible to all students (i.e., low threshold) requires launching the task so that students understand what is expected of them and providing students with appropriate resources that will support their entry into the task in ways that allow students to *draw on multiple resources of knowledge,* one of the five equity-based practices for mathematics classrooms (Aguirre, Mayfield-Ingram, and Martin 2013). For example, in launching the Band Concert task, Robert Harris (ATL 1.1, page 10) asked students to turn and talk in pairs about their ideas for representing the problem. This allowed students to draw on each other as resources in understanding and clarifying task expectations, as well as draw from their own experiences, as they considered how to represent and solve the task.

Engaging students in high-level tasks affords them the opportunity to *go deep with mathematics*, another of the equity-based practices in mathematics (Aguirre, Mayfield-Ingram, and Martin 2013). The Band Concert task, and other high-level tasks that we have discussed in this chapter, have a high ceiling, that is, the potential to engage students in challenging mathematics beyond the immediate learning goals. As we saw in the Case of Robert Harris, the task engaged students in deepening their understanding of multiplication while also exposing students to the structure underlying the distributive property of multiplication. Eventually students will form a generalization that one (or both) of the factors can be decomposed in different ways, then multiplied by the other factor (or factors), and finally those partial products can be combined to obtain an answer equivalent to the original multiplication equation.

The high-level tasks that we have been discussing can also be considered group-worthy tasks—tasks that support students in collaborating with peers on important mathematical ideas (Lotan 2005). Group-worthy tasks contain many of the characteristics already identified as important (e.g., opportunities for problem solving, multiple points of entry) while also requiring productive interactions between students, group and individual accountability, and clear criteria for evaluation of the group's product. The nonroutine nature of high-level tasks provides an ideal setting for students to collaboratively work together toward a common goal, drawing on the strengths of each group member, and using each other as resources of knowledge. However, such collaborative work, particularly at the elementary level, requires establishing socio-mathematical norms (Cobb and Hodge 2002) and expectations for students to work collaboratively in small groups. This includes valuing the mathematical competence and contributions of each group member and reinforcing the expectations that each group member must be involved in both the decision-making and in the mathematical work.

Positioning students as valuable contributors to mathematical work, even as authors and owners of mathematical ideas (Yamakawa, Forman, and Ansell 2009), supports the development of positive mathematical identities and agency as mathematical thinkers. Martin (2012) defines mathematical identity as "dispositions and deeply held beliefs that individuals develop about their ability to participate and perform effectively in mathematical contexts and to use mathematics to change the conditions of their lives" (p. 57–58). In other words, mathematical identity comprises how students see themselves in relation to mathematics and their ability to engage in mathematics. Schoenfeld (2014) defines mathematical agency as students' "capacity and willingness to engage mathematically" (p. 407). Regular opportunities for each and every student to engage in high-level tasks, which promote reasoning and problem solving, provide multiple entry points (low threshold), and encourage use and discussion of varied solution strategies (high ceiling), are an important step toward establishing and enhancing students' positive identities and sense of agency in mathematics.

Taking Action in Your Classroom

Throughout this chapter, you have compared the cognitive demand of tasks and identified characteristics of tasks with a high-level of cognitive demand. You have also examined and considered ways that teachers can maintain the cognitive demand during the implementation of high-level tasks. Here we summarize some of the key messages for you to keep in mind as you take action in your own classroom.

- Mathematical tasks vary in the level of cognitive demand required of students; high-level tasks offer opportunities for reasoning, sense making, and problem solving while low-level tasks promote recall of procedures and information.

- Tasks that promote reasoning and problem solving (i.e., high-level tasks) lead to the greatest learning gains for students when the demands of the task are maintained during implementation with students.

- Tasks, such as low-threshold, high-ceiling tasks, provide students with multiple entry points into the tasks, thus providing greater student access to mathematical reasoning and problem solving.

- Sequences of related tasks, rather than individual tasks, provide students, over time, with greater opportunities to develop and deepen mathematical understanding and strengthen mathematical proficiencies.

We now invite you to take action as you consider implications of the ideas discussed in this chapter for your own professional setting. We encourage you to begin this process by using the Task Analysis Guide to look more closely at the tasks you have used over the past few weeks in your own classroom. Then we suggest you teach a lesson based on a high-level task and pay particular attention to the factors influencing whether or not your implementation of the task maintains the cognitive demand.

Taking Action in Your Classroom
Use the Task Analysis Guide to Examine Learning Opportunities

Use the Task Analysis Guide (see fig. 3.1) to analyze the mathematics tasks you used with your students over the past few weeks.

- Approximately what percent of the tasks were at each of the four levels of cognitive demand?

- What are some implications for your mathematics program on providing your students with the opportunity to engage in high-level tasks that promote reasoning and problem solving?

Use the Factors of Maintenance and Decline to Explain Learning Outcomes

Teach a mathematics lesson based on a high-level task. Then consider the factors (see fig. 3.2) that influenced task implementation and student learning outcomes. You may want to audio or video record the lesson so that you have record of what occurred during the lesson.

- In what ways was the implementation of your lesson more similar to that of Mr. Harris or Mr. Stevenson?

- Which factors influenced your decisions that might have lead to a decline of cognitive demand during task implementation and limited student learning?

- Which factors influenced your decisions that supported a high-level of cognitive demand during task implementation and deepened student learning?

CHAPTER 4

Build Procedural Fluency from Conceptual Understanding

Conceptual understanding and procedural fluency are both important components of students' mathematical proficiency, and need to be integrated and woven together (National Research Council, 2001). In this chapter, you will examine the effective teaching practice, *build procedural fluency from conceptual understanding.* According to *Principles to Actions: Ensuring Mathematical Success for All (*NCTM 2014, p. 42)*:*

> Effective teaching of mathematics builds fluency with procedures on a foundation of conceptual understanding so that students, over time, become skillful in using procedures flexibly as they solve contextual and mathematical problems.

At the elementary level, students establish their mathematical foundation upon which rests all subsequent learning of mathematics. It is essential that this foundation be resilient, and that requires, first and foremost, deep conceptual understanding of mathematical ideas, relationships, and operations. From this base of understanding, students can move gradually to meaningful learning of basic number combinations, formulas, and computational procedures. The phrase "over time" in the teaching practice statement above cautions us that rushing students into learning procedures can be dangerous and even undermine students' own agency and confidence in using mathematics. When we prematurely ask students to learn procedures without a solid foundation of understanding, students begin to see mathematics as isolated bits of knowledge to be memorized rather than viewing it as a connected and coherent discipline. When knowledge of procedures builds from conceptual understanding, students see mathematics as making sense and are able to use mathematical procedures meaningfully and appropriately to solve contextual and mathematical problems.

The chapter includes four Analyzing Teaching and Learning (ATL) activities.

- ATL 4.1: Examine how a teacher sequences student work from the Band Concert task for a class discussion that lays a conceptual foundation for building meaningful use of procedures.

- ATL 4.2: Watch a video clip and investigate how a teacher helps her first-grade students make progress toward fluency by extending addition strategies to larger numbers.

- ATL 4.3: Study a sequence of tasks and consider how it can support fourth-grade students in building from conceptual understanding toward procedural fluency with multi-digit multiplication.

- ATL 4.4: Examine student work from the task sequence on multi-digit multiplication and discern the gradual movement of students toward fluency.

For each ATL, we encourage you to make note of your responses, and if possible, share and discuss your thoughts and ideas with colleagues. Once you have shared or written down your thoughts, continue reading the analysis of the ATL in which we relate the activity to the chapter's focal teaching practice. After the analyzing teaching activities, the chapter includes research findings on the relationship of conceptual understanding and procedural fluency and examines how the focal teaching practice promotes equity among students. We end the chapter by offering suggestions for applying the ideas on understanding and fluency in your own classroom.

Building a Foundation of Conceptual Understanding

Students with positive mathematics identities and strong mathematical agency—the capacity and willingness to engage mathematically—are often those students who have deep conceptual understanding of mathematical ideas, relationships, and operations. These students are able to use mathematical procedures meaningfully because they understand why they work and when it is appropriate to use them. This ability to use procedures meaningfully occurs gradually, over months and years, and evolves from conceptual understanding. In fact, we take the stance that conceptual understanding must come first and be the foundation upon which to build procedural fluency. At the same time as we guide students in developing conceptual understanding, we should do so with an eye toward the eventual connections to procedures.

Engage in ATL 4.1: Mathematical Affordances of a Task

In our first Analyzing Teaching and Learning activity in this chapter, we revisit the Case of Robert Harris and the Band Concert Task (page 10). You might want to first take a few minutes and reread the case before continuing. In ATL 4.1, you will examine the mathematical affordances of the Band Concert task from a lens of laying the conceptual groundwork needed for moving to procedures with multiplication. Then we ask you to examine two sequences of student work discussed with the whole class over two consecutive days. One sequence of student work was discussed on Day 1. The other sequence of student work was discussed in depth on Day 2.

Analyzing Teaching and Learning 4.1
Mathematical Affordances of a Task

Revisit the Band Concert task (shown below) and consider its mathematical prospects.

- What mathematical affordances might the Band Concert task allow for establishing the conceptual foundation needed for building meaningful use of multiplication procedures?

Then study the two sequences of student work (shown below).

- In what ways does the Day 1 sequence help students deepen their understanding of multiplication?

- How does the Day 2 sequence help students develop informal understanding of properties of the operations?

The Band Concert Task

The third-grade class is responsible for setting up the chairs for the spring band concert. In preparation, the class needs to determine the total number of chairs that will be needed and ask the school's engineer to retrieve that many chairs from the central storage area. The class needs to set up 7 rows of chairs with 20 chairs in each row, leaving space for a center aisle. How many chairs does the school's engineer need to retrieve from the central storage area?

Day 1 Student Work Sequence #1

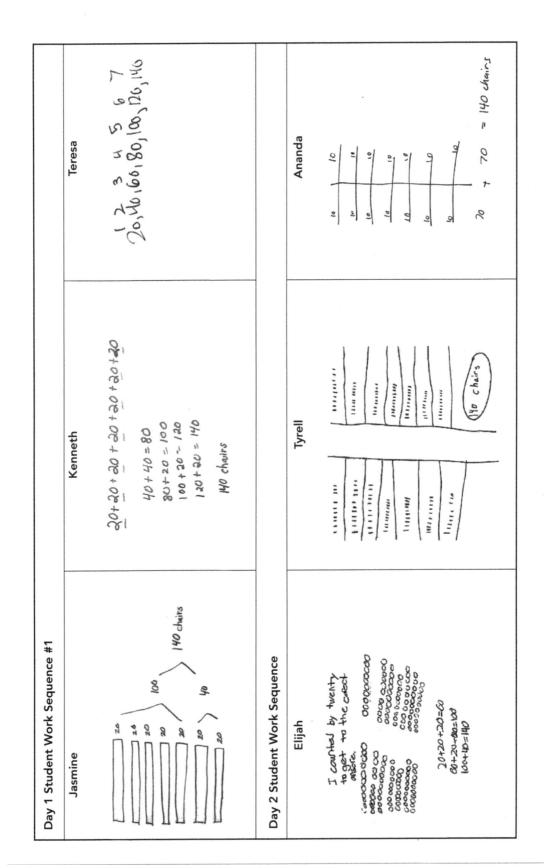

Jasmine

Kenneth

$20 + 20 + 20 + 20 + 20 + 20 + 20$

$40 + 40 = 80$
$80 + 20 = 100$
$100 + 20 = 120$
$120 + 20 = 140$

140 chairs

Teresa

1 2 3 4 5 6 7
20, 40, 60, 80, 100, 120, 140

Day 2 Student Work Sequence

Elijah

I counted by twenty to get to the correct answer.

$20 + 20 + 20 = 60$
$60 + 20 + 20 = 100$
$100 + 40 = 140$

Tyrell

140 chairs

Ananda

10   10
10   10
10   10
10   10
10   10
20   20

20 + 70 = 140 chairs

Analysis of ATL 4.1: Developing Conceptual Foundations for Procedures

Robert Harris spent two days on the Band Concert task. This extended lesson provided students with time to explore and discuss many important mathematical ideas. The main learning goal of the lesson was to strengthen students' conceptual understanding of multiplication. The design of the task also provided an opportunity to build informal understanding of properties of the operations as a foundation for moving toward meaningful use of multiplication procedures.

Mathematical Affordances of the Task

Mr. Harris selected the Band Concert task because it afforded his third-grade students with many mathematical opportunities. The task provided a context for his students to examine the structure of multiplication in everyday contexts and to make connections to the structure of multiplication equations. In addition he knew his students needed more experiences with arrays, and the band concert prompted his students to visualize an array of chairs. Specifically, students were to show how "to set up 7 rows of chairs with 20 chairs in each row." The teacher knows that understanding and working with arrays is an important step toward use of area models for multiplication with larger numbers. The Band Concert task also supports student progress toward meeting conceptual understanding expectations of state standards for third grade, specifically that students are to know the meaning of each factor in a multiplication equation as they relate to problem situations involving equal groups, arrays, and measurement quantities.

As Mr. Harris selects tasks for his students, he always tries to keep an eye on the mathematical horizon and consider how the current math work is establishing the conceptual foundation needed to eventually understand and use procedures meaningfully. The numbers in the Band Concert task were purposefully chosen to build toward a fluency expectation for third grade—students are to multiply one-digit whole numbers by multiples of 10 in the range 10–90 using strategies based on place value and properties of the operations. The Band Concert task provided a contextual situation that allowed students to develop and discuss informal strategies for multiplying multiples of 10 as a precursor to more general procedures for multiplying multi-digit numbers.

One additional affordance of the task involves the mention of "leaving space for a center aisle." While some students disregarded this nuance of the task, other students attended to it, which prompted them to decompose the 20 into 2 tens and to informally use the distributive property. Mr. Harris knows that he and his students will be doing lots of work in the near future on building arrays and area models and then decomposing and re-composing those representations as a foundation for understanding the properties of multiplication, as well as division procedures, with multi-digit numbers. This work begins to address additional state expectations at third grade—students are to understand properties of multiplication and use area models to represent the distributive property, even though they are not expected to use formal terms for properties. The Band Concert task elicited students' informal reasoning and understanding of the distributive property and provided an opportunity to strengthen this important conceptual foundation with properties of operations. With any task, Mr. Harris considers its affordances for developing conceptual understanding among his students, as well as which mathematical concepts and relationships can and should be emphasized as important foundations for moving his students toward fluency and meaningful use of procedures.

Day 1 Student Work Sequence

For the whole-class discussion, Mr. Harris purposefully selected the first sequence of student work (Jasmine, Kenneth, Teresa). He did not just ask for student volunteers, but chose work that allowed him to probe individual student's reasoning with the intent to build shared understanding of multiplication as it relates to repeated addition and the meaning of each factor in an array model. He asked Jasmine to present first because her diagram accurately modeled the situation and it was likely accessible to all students (ATL 1.1, lines 58–65). Jasmine explained how the 7 rectangles represented the rows of chairs and that each row had 20 chairs. She then combined 5 rows to get 100 chairs, because she knew that $5 \times 20 = 100$. Then she had 2 more rows which was 40 chairs. Together $100 + 40 = 140$ chairs. This is an informal use of the distributive property, $7 \times 20 = (5+2) \times 20 = (5 \times 20) + (2 \times 20)$, which Mr. Harris realized, but chose not to discuss further at this moment. His primary objective was for the students to see multiplication as an array of 7 rows of 20 chairs each.

Mr. Harris selected Kenneth to go next as his approach was similar to Jasmine's but without the diagram. Both students clearly wrote the number 20 seven times. Mr. Harris asked the students to compare and contrast the two approaches, "So, what is similar about Jasmine's and Kenneth's work and what is different?" One student observed that Jasmine had a diagram and that Kenneth did not, but both had the same answer. Another student noted that Kenneth wrote an equation, and that he started with $40 + 40$, but then added up by 20 each time after that until he got to the answer. Kenneth remarked that he was going to keep doing forties but he was getting confused so he just added by twenties so he could keep track of them all. Here the teacher wanted the students to see multiplication as repeated addition in combining 7 twenties.

Teresa presented her work next, which looked very different from the work of Jasmine and Kenneth. Mr. Harris knows that many of his students like to skip-count for multiplication, but that they easily loose track of the number of groups and get confused when writing multiplication equations. Thus, his goal with Teresa's work was to have a discussion of how skip counting relates to the concept of multiplication as combining equal groups and how it relates to writing a multiplication equation. Notice in the following dialogue how Mr. Harris first focused on how skip counting relates to the context and how it shows combining 7 twenties (lines 66–80).

Mr. Harris:	So, Teresa skipped-counted by twenties. How does this relate to the Band Concert situation?
Connor:	She counted seven times like she wrote on her paper.
Mr. Harris:	I'm not sure I understand. Can someone add on to what Connor was saying?
Grace:	Well, each time she counted it was like adding 20 more chairs, just like what Kenneth did.
Mr. Harris:	Do others agree with what Grace is saying? Can someone explain it in their own words?
Mason:	Yeah, the numbers on top are like the 7 rows and the numbers on the bottom are the total number of chairs for that many rows.
Mr. Harris:	This is interesting. So what does the number 100 mean under the 5?
Mason:	It means that altogether 5 rows have 100 total chairs, since there are 20 chairs in each row.
Mr. Harris:	Then what does the 140 mean?
Mason:	It means that 7 rows would have a total of 140 chairs.

Finally, Mr. Harris wrote the multiplication equation, 7×20, on the board. He had noticed this equation on several student papers, but not all of the papers. He wanted to ensure his students understood how the Band Concert task could be represented with a multiplication equation. He stated, "Some of you wrote this equation on your papers. How does this equation relate to each of the strategies that we have discussed so far?" (lines 81–84). Then he had the students turn and talk with a partner for a few minutes as he walked around the classroom listening in on their conversations. He asked Grace to share her thinking with the class (lines 87–90).

| Grace: | Well, we talked about how the 7 means seven rows like Jasmine showed in her picture and how Teresa showed. And the 20 is the number of chairs that go in each row like Jasmine showed, and like how Kenneth wrote down. Teresa didn't write down all those twenties but we know she counted by 20. |

Throughout the class discussion, Mr. Harris was very purposeful in the student work he selected and in how he used it to surface specific mathematical concepts, relationships, and connections for deepening his students conceptual understanding of multiplication. He also kept in mind how he was laying a foundation from which he could move his students toward procedural fluency.

Day 2 Student Work Sequence

Mr. Harris ended the first day's lesson by having his students briefly consider the work of Tyrell and Ananda, but he did not have sufficient time for a full-class discussion. He took home the student work and their responses to the exit question. This gave him time to further examine, select, and sequence student work in preparation for continuing the discussion the next day.

The class began with a discussion of Elijah's work. Elijah used repeated addition to find the total number of chairs, similar to Kenneth's work on the previous day. However, his diagram clearly showed an array of chairs arranged with a center aisle, which became the focus of the class discussion. Tyrell also clearly showed the chairs with an aisle separating groups of 10. He explained that he had counted by tens to find the total number of chairs. He decomposed each 20 into 2 tens and then skip-counted by tens to 140. The following dialogue occurred as Mr. Harris focused on combining multiples of ten and how it relates to multiplication of multiples of ten.

Mr. Harris: So, how many tens did you have?

Tyrell: 14 tens.

Mr. Harris: So, 14 tens is the same as having 140 chairs? (*Wrote 14 tens = 140 chairs.*) Can someone else explain why this is true?

Emma: Yeah, it's the same. It's like taking 14 × 10, he had 14 groups and 10 chairs in each, and that's 140. (*Mr. Harris wrote on the board, 14 groups × 10 chairs each = 140 chairs.*)

Next the class examined the work of Ananda. She explained that she counted by tens to 70 and then just knew she had 70 more chairs and added them up. Mr. Harris again emphasized how she was combining tens and wrote on the board, "7 tens + 7 tens = 14 tens = 140 chairs." He then asked the students to work with a partner to write this using multiplication. Most students wrote, "(7 × 10) + (7 × 10) = 140 chairs." Upon return to a whole-class discussion, Mr. Harris asked, "What happened to the 20?" and "Is it okay to work with tens and not twenties?" They then informally discussed the distributive property, even though he did not name it with this formal phrase as he wanted his students to focus on the mathematical ideas and not the terminology. His students agreed that it is okay to decompose the groups and then recompose them in other ways that makes it easier to work with the numbers.

Throughout the remainder of the school year, the students will continue developing their understanding of the distributive property and of multiplying by ten or a multiple of ten. The students will explore decomposing groups by building and breaking apart arrays using grid paper. They will write symbolic expressions as models of how those arrays were split and then recomposed. They will also engage in "number talks" (Parrish 2011). A number talk is a short, ongoing, daily classroom routine that asks students to compute mentally to solve purposefully selected problems, presented one at a time, and then engages students in conversations about their reasoning with number and operation relationships. For example, Mr. Harris might engage his class in a number talk on 4 × 10, 4 × 20, and 4 × 60, and surface reasoning across the set of problems that uses the distributive property as students consider how these problems can be thought of as, 4 × 1 ten, 4 × 2 tens, 4 × 6 tens. This more focused work on computation builds from earlier experiences in solving problems, like the Band Concert task.

Developing Computational Strategies along the Path to Fluency

The meaning of "fluency" is often misconstrued. This can lead to pressures on teachers to prematurely press students to commit facts or formulas to memory or to use general computational methods or algorithms without having a firm and solid foundation of conceptual understanding. NCTM (2014, p. 42), in *Principles to Actions,* defines fluency as follows:

> Being fluent means that students are able to choose flexibly among methods and strategies to solve contextual and mathematical problems, they understand and are able to explain their approaches, and they are able to produce accurate answers efficiently.

This broader view of procedural fluency builds on our growing understanding of how students best learn to understand and use computational procedures meaningfully (Fuson, Kalchman, and Bransford 2005; NCTM 2000; Russell 2000). Fluency has several components. Fluency includes students' ability to be *flexible,* meaning that students choose approaches appropriate to the numbers in the task. To solve 1003 − 998, students should realize they can easily determine that the difference is 5 by reasoning how far it is to jump from 998 up to 1003. With these numbers it is not necessary to use a more formal method, even though it is not uncommon to see students try to use a memorized algorithm and then end up with the wrong answer. Similarly, to solve $7 - \frac{1}{4}$, students should realize that they can simply rename one whole as 4 fourths and then remove 1 of these fourths, which leaves 6 wholes and 3 fourths.

Fluency also includes students' ability to *understand and explain* their approaches and strategies, including computational algorithms. For students to develop mathematical agency and believe in their own abilities to use mathematics to solve problems in the mathematics classroom and in life, conceptual understanding is essential and cannot be sidestepped or slighted. Fluency includes students' ability to be *accurate,* meaning students not only can get the right answer but can judge the reasonableness of that answer, which can only occur when fluency is integrated with understanding, which includes number sense and operation sense. Finally, fluency includes students' ability to be fairly *efficient,* meaning students do not get lost in lots of extraneous steps but see and understand a clear path to a solution.

Engage in ATL 4.2: Using an Equation Sequence to Build Toward Fluency

In this next Analyzing Teaching and Learning activity, we watch a video clip of a first-grade classroom as the teacher, Jennifer DiBrienza, works with her students in developing more advanced computational strategies as part of the journey in moving students toward fluency with addition. By "more advanced strategies," we mean using strategies that are based on reasoning with number relationships rather than counting. Given that this is first grade, the more advanced strategies involve moving students from "counting on" to "using ten."

Ms. DiBrienza is using a set of related mathematical equations that are crafted and sequenced to support students in noticing important mathematical ideas and to build toward more advanced computational strategies. These sets of related equations are usually referred to as "number strings" (Fosnot and Dolk 2011) or by the name of the specific operation, such as addition strings or multiplication strings. Turn to ATL 4.2 and investigate how the teacher builds from her students' understanding of addition and counting toward the use of more advanced strategies for adding numbers. A transcript is included in Appendix C to support your viewing of the video and its analysis.

Analyzing Teaching and Learning 4.2 more**4U**
Using an Equation Sequence to Build Toward Fluency

Begin by examining the Addition Strings task (shown below) and notice patterns in the equation sequence. Then watch the video clip of Ms. DiBrienza using the task with her first-grade students.

- How does Ms. DiBrienza use the sequence of equations to support students in moving toward more advanced strategies with addition?
- What progress do students make in their understanding and use of addition strategies?
- How does the teacher use the open number line and the hundreds chart to support students in their mathematical reasoning and to develop shared understanding of more advanced strategies?

Addition Strings Task

$$7 + 3 = \square$$
$$17 + 3 = \square$$
$$27 + 3 = \square$$
$$37 + 3 = \square$$
$$37 + 5 = \square$$

You can access this video online by visiting NCTM's More4U website (nctm.org/more4u). The access code can be found on the title page of this book.

Analysis of ATL 4.2: Taking Gradual Steps

Prior to the lesson, Ms. DiBrienza established clear goals for student learning that she used to guide her decision-making during the lesson. These goals focused not on what students would do during the lesson but rather on what students would understand about mathematics as a result of engaging with the task. Her goals included the following:

- Students will understand that advanced addition strategies use number relationships and the structure of the number system.

- Students will understand that numbers can be decomposed and added on in parts, not just by ones.

- Students will understand that noticing regularity in repeated calculations leads to shortcuts and general methods for adding numbers.

The teacher was aware of how the lesson aligned with state standards and learning progressions. Specifically, students were working toward the first-grade state standard to add within 100 using concrete objects, drawings, and strategies based on place value to add a two-digit number and a one-digit number, as well as working toward the standard to develop students' ability to mentally find 10 more or 10 less than a number without having to count and to explain one's reasoning.

Moving to More Advanced Strategies

The teacher selected and implemented a task that promoted reasoning and problem solving among her students while also supporting students to move gradually toward the use of more advanced strategies. The students entered the lesson with knowledge of how to calculate 7 + 3 and some understanding of the base-ten number system. This task, although it appeared simple because it relied on the use of prior knowledge, required students to use and extend current knowledge to solve equations that were unfamiliar as well as to look across the set of equations to find a pattern in their problem-solving strategies. The task could be considered a *procedures with connections* task (see fig. 3.1, page 41–42) because the goal was to have students notice numerical relationships and use them meaningfully to solve addition equations.

Typically in using an addition string, the teacher presents the equations one at a time, asks the students to solve the problem mentally, and then has students share and discuss their strategies. Because the equations are carefully crafted from more accessible to more challenging, students are supported in gradually considering how to apply strategies from the previous problem to the next problem in the sequence. Throughout the lesson, the teacher elicited and made use of student thinking. She began her interactions by asking students to try to understand what another student did. She consistently asked students to explain how he, she, or another student arrived at a sum, and then using what a student said, she pushed students further. For example, Destiny used the reasoning from 7 + 3 to solve 17 + 3. She explained, "Cause it was like 10 plus 10 equals 20" (line 26). The teacher encouraged the students to keep Destiny's strategy in mind to then solve 27 + 3 (lines 32–33). In this way she first assessed what it was that students were doing and then asked a question that would advance the students' thinking further toward the goals of the lesson.

After several equations are discussed in a number string, students often start to notice regularities and patterns. If not, the teacher might specifically ask students about regularities or patterns that they are noticing within and across the equations and the answers. The students in the first-grade classroom readily started noticing patterns without being prompted (lines 38–48). Ms. DiBrienza pressed this further when she asked, "So people notice that there's sevens in every column here, there's threes going down here and it's going 10, 20, 30. Why do you think that's happening?" The students were beginning to realize that each problem asked them to add 7 + 3 and then add on some more tens. As the lesson continued, the students were eventually challenged to extend their reasoning to 37 + 5. For example, a student explained, "I ah… broke up the 5 into 3 plus 2" (lines 75–89). By posing 37 + 5, the teacher establishes an opportunity to elicit student understanding of the "make a ten" strategy, which then allows other students to consider the possibility of trying out this way of reasoning. The teacher also sent a signal to students that they have the right to decompose numbers, such as 5 into 3 + 2, to form "friendly" numbers that are more compatible and thus easier to add mentally.

Throughout the lesson, the teacher supported students' ability to work through the problem without taking over the thinking for them or lowering the demand of the task. She did this by honoring students' thinking while guiding them toward more advanced reasoning. In so doing, she supported students' authority while simultaneously holding them accountable for their reasoning, hence sending the message to students that they were capable of describing how they solved the problems and of noticing patterns and relationships among a set of addition equations.

Using Representations

Visual representations are an important tool in helping students move to more advanced strategies. They serve two main purposes: representations help to clarify the reasoning of specific students, while also leaving a visible trace of the strategy, which allows other students to enter into and follow the mathematical thinking of their classmates. When several visual representations are displayed at the same time, students can also use them to compare and contrast strategies.

Ms. DiBrienza intentionally used the open number line throughout the lesson to support students in building a shared understanding of more advanced strategies. The students were familiar with using the open number line with single-digit numbers and were just beginning to use it with larger numbers. As Ms. DiBrienza represented counting on by ones on the open number line, she supported those students working on accuracy and confidence in using a counting-on approach to solve problems rather than a counting all strategy. It also reinforced using counting-on correctly in order to avoid common errors. For example, when students count on to add 7 + 3, sometimes students say the answer is 9 because they count "7, 8, 9" and think they have added on three counts. While other students might lose track of their counts and end up with answers that are too large. Showing the individual counts as jumps on the open number line was a support for accurately using counting-on as a strategy.

Towards the end of the lesson, the teacher also used the open number line to push students to consider the more advanced strategy of using 10 to solve 37 + 5. First the teacher called on a student who counted on from 37 (lines 71–73) and showed this strategy on an open number line (see fig. 4.1). Then the teacher called on a student who broke 5 into two parts and reasoned using a jump of "3" to get to 10 and then a jump of "2" to get to 42 (lines 75–89). Both of these visual representations were displayed on the board at the same time, which allowed students to compare and contrast the two approaches. Ms. DiBrienza summarized by stating, "So, instead of just making jumps of one you started at 37 and you knew the 3 more made 40 so you knew you had to add 2 more and that would give you 42" (lines 85–88).

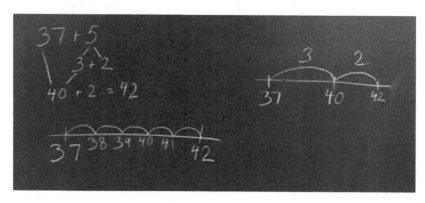

Fig. 4.1. A representational trace of student reasoning on an open number line

The teacher also used the hundreds chart to trace student reasoning (see fig. 4.2). In particular, the hundreds chart supported students in being able to mentally find 10 more than a number without having to count, which is an important goal in first grade. The student directs Ms. DiBrienza to started at 17 and count on 10 more to determine 17 + 10. Ms. DiBrienza commented, "Look, we just moved down one [row] right?" (lines 59–60). Then she continued with a curious tone in her voice, "Twenty-seven's right below it [17]. How many more do you think if I start at 17, how many more do you think I have to add to get to 27?" She pressed students to consider the generalization that moving down one row is the same as adding 10, which is an important understanding in moving to more advanced strategies.

Fig. 4.2. Discussing adding 10 on the hundreds chart

The Addition Strings task promoted students' reasoning and problem solving while allowing them to move gradually toward use of more advanced strategies. The use of visual representations became valuable tools to trace student reasoning and make a student's thinking visible to the other students in the class for consideration and discussion. Through mathematical discourse and the teacher asking often, "Okay, did anybody do it differently?" (line 73), the students were supported in gaining confidence in using counting on accurately as well as in transitioning from counting on by ones to considering the use of more advanced strategies based on number relationships, such as using ten. These young learners are already on a path toward fluency by being able to understand and explain their strategies, by considering flexible use of strategies to solve mathematics problems, and by working to produce accurate answers efficiently.

Developing Number Strings

While this ATL focused on addition strings with small numbers for these young learners, number strings can be developed for any operation and number system and be used with students throughout elementary school and beyond. The goal of number strings is to gradually nudge students toward flexible use of more efficient mental computation strategies by noticing relationships among the numbers and using properties of the operations. The general structure of a string is to have an entry problem, some helper problems, and then a challenge problem. The entry problem (such as 7 + 3 in the video) should be accessible to all or nearly all students in the class and be readily solved mentally. The helper problems (17 + 3, 27 + 3, 37 + 3) then extend the student thinking toward the target strategy, such as that in the video of making a 10 by decomposing an addend. The final challenge problem (37 + 5) prompts students to ascertain how to apply the strategy being developed through the previous problems to a new variation in the requested computation. Some sample number strings are included in figure 4.3. You might take a moment to study the strings to identify the entry problem, consider the purpose of the helper problems within the specific string, and describe how the strategy would be applied to the challenge problem.

Subtraction String Using Compensation	Subtraction String Constant Difference	Multiplication String Break Apart a Factor	Addition String Making Wholes in Adding Fractions
30 – 20	82 – 40	6 x 6	$\frac{5}{8} + \frac{3}{8}$
30 – 19	83 – 41	6 x 16	$3\,\frac{5}{8} + \frac{3}{8}$
60 – 19	81 – 39	6 x 26	$3\,\frac{5}{8} + 5\,\frac{3}{8}$
80 – 39	53 – 29	6 x 43	$7\,\frac{5}{9} + 6\,\frac{5}{9}$

Fig. 4.3. Examples of number strings

Moving Gradually to Procedural Fluency

It is important to note, especially in the elementary grades, that moving to fluency with procedures should not be rushed. Fluency develops within students over time, meaning over weeks, months, and even years of mathematical work. It does not occur in one lesson, nor even in a few lessons. NCTM (2014, p. 42) summarizes:

> Fluency builds from initial exploration and discussion of number concepts to using informal reasoning strategies based on meanings and properties of the operations to the eventual use of general methods as tools in solving problems.

This progression of student learning from exploration and discussion of concepts to the use of informal strategies to the eventual use of general methods, such as algorithms, is well documented (Carpenter, Fennema, and Franke 1996; Common Core State Standards Writing Team 2011, 2015; Griffin 2003). This pathway of learning needs to be repeated as students learn about addition and subtraction of whole numbers, and then again with multiplication and division of whole numbers. It is then repeated yet again when students move to operations with fractions and decimals.

Engage in ATL 4.3: Considering a Sequence of Tasks

In our next Analyzing Teaching and Learning activity, we examine how Ms. Cutter, who teaches fourth grade, is moving students toward procedural fluency with two-digit multiplication. She knows this is a gradual, year-long journey for her students that begins with review of single-digit multiplication, then moves to one-digit times two-digit multiplication, and now she is moving into two-digit by two-digit multiplication. Throughout the year, she has focused on ensuring students have a strong conceptual understanding of multiplication embedded in problem contexts. She is always concerned about students who seem to put their conceptual understanding to the side as they move into more symbolic work, particularly as the numbers get larger. She is determined to keep a careful eye on her students this year and integrate more connections among multiple representations into their multiplication work. By the end of the school year her district expects all of her students to be fluent in using the partial products algorithm for multiplication of two-digit by two-digit numbers. She also knows, as happens every year, her students (and their parents) will ask about the traditional algorithm for multiplication. Thus, she plans to help students understand how the traditional algorithm is just another of several mathematically valid ways of keeping track of steps in a general method for multiplication (Beckmann and Fuson 2012).

She begins her instructional sequence by building from students' prior experiences with using array and area models to solve multiplication word problems. Her students know how to use the distributive property to decompose and recompose groups using arrays on grid paper when solving one-digit times two-digit multiplication problems. Ms. Cutter now intends to build on and deepen this conceptual foundation as she moves her students toward use of informal strategies and then to more general methods for solving two-digit by two-digit multiplication problems. In ATL 4.3 we ask you to study a sequence of tasks aimed at building toward procedural fluency from and through student understanding of multi-digit multiplication.

Analyzing Teaching and Learning 4.3
Considering a Sequence of Tasks

Ms. Cutter used the tasks, shown on page 83, with her fourth-grade students. The tasks are sequential and reflect learning across a unit of instruction on multi-digit multiplication.

- What important mathematical ideas are being developed with each task?

- In what ways does the sequence of tasks support students' progression from developing conceptual understanding to using informal strategies to refining those informal strategies into more general methods and procedures?

Task A
Boxes of Crayons *Can be directly Modeled*

Ms. Weeks bought 12 boxes of crayons. Each box contains 24 crayons. What is the total number of crayons that Ms. Weeks bought?

Use base ten grid paper to represent the situation and to show your solution strategy.

Task B
Ms. Cutter's Boxes of Books

Ms. Cutter is moving and she has a lot of books to move to her new apartment. It turns out she can fit 25 books in each book box. She filled 36 boxes with books. How many books in total did Ms. Cutter pack for the move?

- Work as a group to solve the problem. *Different representation method*
- Use area model diagrams to support your solution strategies.
- Everyone in your group will need to be able to explain your group's final solution so consider that as you work. *Everyone needs to be able to explain (working toward)*

Task C
Posing Multiplication Stories *allows students to see the math from a different angle (fluency)*

Write a word problem that could be solved by using this equation: 17 × 63 = ?

Task D
Boxes and Boxes of Crayons

Mrs. Weeks needs even more crayons. She buys larger boxes of crayons with 64 crayons in each box. She buys 37 boxes. What is the total number of crayons that Mrs. Weeks bought? *→ Not the same as Task A   → Specific method   → Asking for more*

Draw an area model that shows the partial products. Write the equations that relate to each partial product. Find the total number of crayons.

Task E
Evaluating a Solution *Allows students to see it from another view*

Here is how Jessica solved 45 × 27.

$$
\begin{array}{r}
40 \quad 5 \\
\times 20 \quad 7 \\
\hline
800 \quad 35 \\
835
\end{array}
$$

Is her strategy correct or incorrect? How do you know?

Use diagrams, equations, and/or words to explain. *→ Giving options*

Analysis of ATL 4.3: The Role of Task Sequences in Building toward Fluency

The set of five tasks is just a sample of the tasks from a fourth-grade instructional unit that lasted several weeks. The task sequence provides a glimpse into a progression of students' mathematical experiences and learning expectations across the instructional unit. The sequence of tasks shows how students are building on their conceptual understanding of multiplication, beginning with arrays and area models and gradually moving toward use of a general method for two-digit by two-digit multiplication, the partial-products multiplication algorithm, which is based on the distributive property of multiplication. The progression is based on high-level tasks that promote reasoning and problem solving, as we discussed in chapter 3. Each task asks students to engage in making sense of the mathematics they are studying. Thus, students' learning of procedures is building from and remains connected to their conceptual understanding. The tasks also stand in stark contrast to what many of us as adults likely remember from our own school experiences with multi-digit multiplication, which centered on memorizing steps for a procedure to solve low-level tasks, namely multiplication equations, disconnected from understanding and sense making.

The sequence begins with tasks that *develop conceptual understanding by building on students' informal knowledge*. Task A, the Boxes of Crayons task (12 × 24), focuses on use of base-ten grid paper to represent and explore two-digit by two-digit multiplication. The grid paper is premarked to show 10 × 10 grids, thus encouraging students to consider decomposing the total quantity into groups of 100 and then some more, an important underlying understanding for working with place values when multiplying larger numbers. The size of the numbers, 12 and 24, were chosen carefully, in order to naturally build on students' prior experiences and comfort with these numbers.

Task B on Ms. Cutter's Boxes of Books (36 × 25) focuses on *developing informal strategies to solve problems* that utilize the area model. The task moves beyond grid paper but still uses a visual representation, the area model, which allows students to decompose the total quantity and visualize the relative size of partial areas. It also uses the friendly number 25, which supports students' use of informal strategies.

Task C asks students to pose their own multiplication stories for 17 × 63. This task reinforces and deepens the connection to real-world problem contexts, reminding students to not set their conceptual ideas aside as the work in the instructional unit begins to shift to more symbolic work.

Task D, Boxes and Boxes of Crayons (37 × 64), focuses on *refining informal strategies into more general methods and procedures.* This task continues to use the area model, but shows a shift to more explicit work on partial products, including writing equations for each of the partial products. The larger numbers in the problem encourage students to consider how they can refine their informal strategies from work with smaller and more friendly numbers to these larger quantities.

Task E asks students to evaluate a worked example (45 × 27), which shows a common error among students when they try to apply poorly understood strategies to larger numbers. The task checks in on students' understanding of using the partial-products multiplication algorithm and the underlying structure of the associated area it represents.

Engage in ATL 4.4: Student Learning Related to the Task Sequence

In our next Analyzing Teaching and Learning activity, we examine student work from Ms. Cutter's fourth-grade classroom. As the class progressed through the instructional unit, students' knowledge deepened and skills advanced in their work with two-digit multiplication. The student work samples provide a glimpse into students' learning as it progressed related to the task sequence.

Analyzing Teaching and Learning 4.4
Student Learning Related to the Task Sequence

Samples of student work from Ms. Cutter's classroom are shown below for each of the five tasks in the task sequence on multi-digit multiplication (see ATL 4.3).

- What are students learning to understand about multiplication, number relationships, and properties of the operations as evidenced in their work on the tasks?

- How are these understandings important for building toward fluency?

$$12 \times 24$$

$$10 \times 20 = 200$$
$$2 \times 4 = 8$$
$$10 \times 4 = 40$$
$$20 \times 2 = 40$$
$$288$$

Task A
Boxes of Crayons

Ms. Weeks bought 12 boxes of crayons. Each box contains 24 crayons.
What is the total number of crayons that Ms. Weeks bought?
Use base ten grid paper to represent the situation and to show your solution strategy.

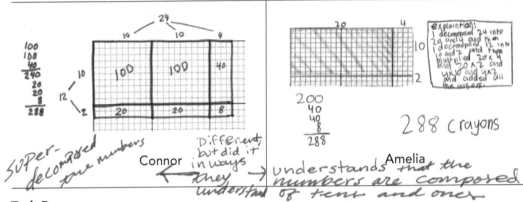

Connor

Amelia

288 crayons

Super-decomposed the numbers

Different, but did it in ways they understand

understands that the numbers are composed of tens and ones

Task B
Ms. Cutter's Boxes of Books

Ms. Cutter is moving and she has a lot of books to move to her new apartment.
It turns out she can fit 25 books in each book box. She filled 36 boxes with books.
How many books in total did Ms. Cutter pack for the move?
- Work as a group to solve the problem.
- Use area model diagrams to support your solution strategies.
- Everyone in your group will need to be able to explain your group's final solution so consider that as you work.

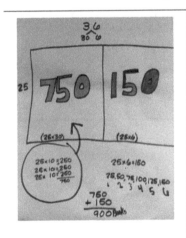

Group 1

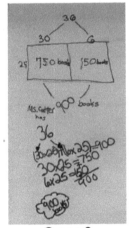

Group 2

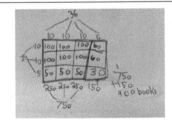

Group 3

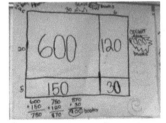

Group 4

Task C
Posing Multiplication Stories

Write a word problem that could be solved by using this equation: 17 × 63 = ?

17 groups of 63

Harry Potter had 17 couldrins. In Each couldrin, there is 63 bird wings to make a potion. How many bird wings are there in all?

Ethan

There are 17 boxes of oranges. There are 63 oranges in each box. How many oranges are there in all?

Valerie

Both did 17 groups of 63 → they understood what it meant

Task D
Boxes and Boxes of Crayons

Mrs. Weeks needs even more crayons. She buys larger boxes of crayons with 64 crayons in each box. She buys 37 boxes. What is the total number of crayons that Mrs. Weeks bought?

Draw an area model that shows the partial products. Write the equations that relate to each partial product. Find the total number of crayons.

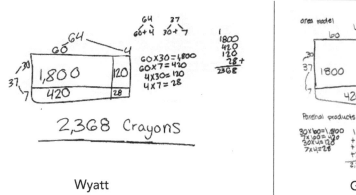

2,368 Crayons

Wyatt

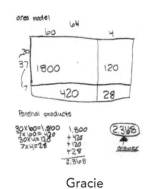

Gracie

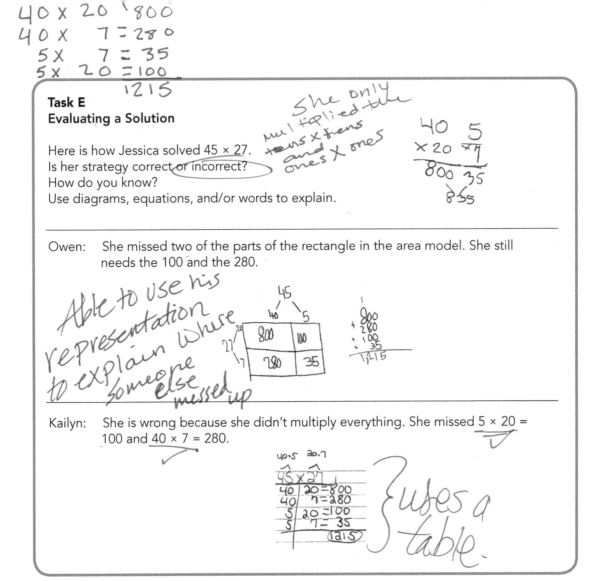

$40 \times 20 = 800$
$40 \times 7 = 280$
$5 \times 7 = 35$
$5 \times 20 = 100$
1215

Task E
Evaluating a Solution

Here is how Jessica solved 45 × 27. Is her strategy correct or incorrect? How do you know? Use diagrams, equations, and/or words to explain.

She only multiplied tens × tens and ones × ones

40 5
× 20 × 7
800 35
855

Owen: She missed two of the parts of the rectangle in the area model. She still needs the 100 and the 280.

Able to use his representation to explain where someone else messed up

45
40   5
800 100   27 {20, 7}
280   35

1
800
+ 280
100
35
1215

Kailyn: She is wrong because she didn't multiply everything. She missed 5 × 20 = 100 and 40 × 7 = 280.

40+5 20+7
45 × 27
40 20 = 800
40   7 = 280
5   20 = 100
5   7 = 35
1215

uses a table.

Analysis of ATL 4.4: Building Toward Procedural Fluency

Task A, Boxes of Crayons (12 × 24), supported students in using their conceptual understanding and prior knowledge in working on the task. Both students created 12 × 24 arrays on grid paper and decomposed the large array into smaller arrays, found the size of each smaller array, and then combined those quantities to find the total amount. The use of the base-ten grid paper served multiple purposes and supported students in their learning. The grid paper supported students in reasoning with an array interpretation of multiplication, that being 12 rows (boxes) with 24 square units (crayons) in each row. It encouraged students to consider decomposing their arrays using groups of 10, which is shown in both of the student work samples. Amelia made a 10 × 20 array. Connor marked off two 10 × 10 arrays. The grid paper also allowed the students to see and compare the actual size of each partition. For example, the students could see and talk about the size of the array with 100 units compared to the size of the array that only had 8 units. The student work shows students can represent 12 × 24 as an array, can decompose or break apart the large array into smaller arrays, and then combine those small arrays to find the total amount. Amelia also shows that she was trying to match equations to the smaller arrays with limited success. The work with decomposing arrays on grid paper continued for the next few lessons as students examined more closely how to write equations for each of the small arrays.

Task B, Ms. Cutter's Boxes of Books (36 × 25), shows that student learning has progressed to the use of area models. Students worked in small groups on the task and used each other as resources for their learning. Each group developed a poster showing their work, all of which were later posted in the hallway of the school. The area models for groups 1 and 2 show that they decomposed one factor, breaking the 36 into 30 + 6, keeping the friendly number 25 intact. Group 1 wrote the equations that match each of the subareas on the area model. Group 2 show their use of the distributive property, (30 × 25) + (6 × 25) = 90, drawing on their previous work from multiplying one-digit times two-digit numbers. The other two groups decomposed both factors, but in different ways. Group 3 broke both factors into tens and then some ones, that is, 36 = 10 + 10 + 10 + 6 and 25 = 10 + 10 + 5, and then found the size of each of the subareas. Their work most closely reflects the students' previous use of the base-ten grid paper, which helped students see the 10 × 10 arrays or groups of 100 within the larger array. Notable in their work was their ability to keep track of the 12 partial products. While group 3 reflects the prior work of the class, group 4 forecasts where the class is headed next. Group 4 broke both factors into multiples of tens and ones, 25 = 20 + 5 and 36 = 30 + 6. This solution path shows student construction of the partial-products algorithm.

Task C, Posing Multiplication Stories (17 × 63), shows that students can connect the equation to a contextual situation. Ethan created a story about 17 cauldrons with 63 bird wings in each to make a potion. Valerie created a situation about 17 boxes with 63 oranges in each box. Ms. Cutter noted that almost all the students were successful in posing word problems, but most of the stories were very similar to those they had worked on in class. She would like her students to envision other multiplication contexts, particularly those that more closely match the array and area interpretations of multiplication. This is something she will pursue further when they engage in their instructional unit on area measurement.

Task D, Boxes and Boxes of Crayons (37 × 64), shows how students are evolving in their work on multi-digit multiplication. By now most students in the class can decompose each two-digit factor into multiples of ten and ones and multiply each appropriately to obtain the four partial products. As shown in the work of Wyatt and Gracie, the students decomposed both factors into multiples of ten and ones, 37 = 30 + 7 and 64 = 60 + 4, resulting in four smaller rectangles. They also drew area models that show the relative size of the four partial products, providing evidence that they are attending to the size of the numbers and the resulting partial products. They each wrote the partial products in each of the smaller rectangles and listed the related equations for each of the partial products. Most students at this point in the instructional unit rely on drawing the area model to keep track of the partial products.

Task E asks students to evaluate a worked example (45 × 27) that does not contain a visual diagram. From their earlier work, students realize that the area represented by the expression can be decomposed into two partial products, such as shown in the work of some students for Task B, as well as into as many subareas as one chooses. Both Owen and Kailyn recognize that the worked example shows the factors decomposed into multiples of ten and ones. Owen used a visual model to show that two partial products are missing, and noted that Jessica missed the 100 and the 280, focusing on the partial products that are missing. Whereas Kailyn clearly listed the four related equations when applying the distributive property, and noted which equations were missing. This task shows how the learning of the students had further evolved into more symbolic work and meaningful use of the distributive property as the basis for multiplying multi-digit numbers.

Does the Sequence of Tasks Matter?

The progression of student learning is related to the careful selection and sequencing of high-level tasks, thus, yes the sequence of tasks matters. The tasks in Ms. Cutter's classroom were strategically sequenced to build from and through conceptual understanding and move students toward procedural fluency. This is a slow and gradual process, particularly when dealing with the complexities of multi-digit multiplication. First, students engaged with the procedure conceptually by modeling the quantities with array and area models. The sequence began with a focus on *developing conceptual understanding by building on students' informal knowledge.* Students were able to draw from their experiences with smaller numbers to consider a situation that involved a two-digit by a two-digit multiplication situation. The students were able to try out and test ways to decompose the visual diagrams (i.e., drawing array diagrams on grid paper or area models) and then see how that related to decomposing the factors. A foundation of conceptual understanding provides students with tools (other than memorization) to make sense of and reconstruct the meaning of the factors in relationship to each other within problem-solving situations.

The sequence then supported students in *developing informal strategies to solve problems* based on partitioning the area model into smaller sections to find partial products. The students made sense of when and how to use the different approaches to breaking apart the factors and how to keep track of the resulting products. The tasks gave students just enough practice at discussing and applying the strategies while still maintaining the focus on understanding. Next students began *refining informal strategies into more general methods and procedures,* that of breaking the factors based on multiples of ten and ones. This then led to moving away from direct use of the area model, while keeping those images in mind, to working more explicitly with the distributive property and the resulting equations. It is by means of this progression of task experiences that students develop meaning for multiplication procedures. Students who have multiple opportunities to explore and discuss multiplication of two-digit by two-digit factors conceptually develop an understanding of how the magnitude of the product relates to the factors. Students also have a better understanding of how and why the procedure works when they are finally using a standard algorithm. As described in *Principles to Actions* (NCTM 2014*)*, Ms. Cutter provided opportunities for students to build toward fluency by developing an understanding of the partial-products procedure and be able to demonstrate that they not only knew how to use it but could also explain how it works.

In this chapter, we examined ways to develop students' conceptual understanding through visual diagrams, story contexts, and equations that make it possible for students to draw on that understanding as they move to procedural methods that require them to work more abstractly. While it may take more time initially for students to grapple with the mathematics as they represent, discuss, and solve problem situations using their intuitive methods, the time invested up-front to develop students' understanding will pay off in time saved reteaching forgotten procedures or remedying students' lack of understanding of the quantities and the resulting answers. In addition to building conceptual foundations, we also noted the importance of *moving to* procedural fluency, where students have become so familiar with the meaning of the quantities and operations that they draw naturally on what they know to solve problems. When students are challenged to solve a problem, their confidence from working with quantities and operations conceptually makes it possible for them to evaluate which procedure would be appropriate for a particular situation, to re-create forgotten steps in mathematical procedures previously used to solve problems, and to continually think about what makes sense in working with numbers and operations in problem-solving situations. According to Martin (2009, p. 165), "mechanical execution of procedures without understanding their mathematical basis often leads to bizarre results." That is, at times students get answers that make no sense, and they have no idea how to judge correctness because they mindlessly apply a procedure that they really do not understand. The focal teaching practice to "*build procedural fluency from conceptual understanding*" places a strong emphasis on students learning to use procedures mindfully with strong connections to meaning and sense making.

What the Research Says: The Relationship of Understanding and Fluency

At the elementary level, the development of conceptual understanding needs to be a priority for instruction. These early years establish the foundation for students' learning of mathematics and that foundation must be strong. As students begin to move toward fluency with procedures, it must build from their emerging number sense and operation sense for both whole numbers and fractions (Baroody, Lai, and Mix 2006; Huinker 2002; Huinker, Freckmann, and Steinmeyer 2003). This approach was used by Ms. DiBrienza as she encouraged her students to wrestle with important mathematical ideas and relationships while moving them toward use of more advanced and more fluent computational strategies based on understanding and numerical relationships.

When students learn procedures and formulas without strong links to conceptual understanding, they are more likely to forget or mix up critical steps and apply procedures in ways that are inappropriate to the mathematical task at hand (Fuson, Kalchman, and Bransford 2005; Martin 2009). Beyond just getting wrong answers, students begin to view mathematics as isolated bits of information void of sense making (Boaler 1998). Conversely, when students build knowledge of procedures from their conceptual understanding, they are more likely to take ownership of their knowledge, adjust procedural steps for the specific numbers in the problem, reconstruct formulas and procedures if needed, and use procedures meaningfully to solve problems (NRC 2001). Shifting the emphasis from just rote learning of procedures to learning procedures from and with conceptual understanding leads, in the long run, to higher levels of mathematical proficiency and develops students with stronger agency and confidence in their mathematical abilities.

Similarly, when the focus is on memorization of single-digit addition facts or multiplication facts, rather than on understanding ways to work meaningfully with these number combinations, we undermine students' confidence in themselves as capable mathematical learners. In particular, Boaler (2014) warns about the dangers of rushing students to memorization and the use of timed tests because there is growing evidence that timed tests are a cause of early math anxiety. Students demonstrate more stress when working on the same math questions in a timed setting as compared to untimed conditions (Engle 2002). Students as young as first grade already demonstrate elevated levels of math anxiety and even display increased activity in brain regions associated with fear (Ashcraft 2002; Ramirez et al. 2013; Young, Wu, and Mennon 2012). Boaler (2014) reminds us, "Learning is a process that takes time, and it cannot be accelerated by methods that encourage speed at the expense of understanding" (p. 473).

Strong evidence supports the use of contexts and problem situations as the launching point for developing procedural skills (e.g., Carpenter, Fennema, and Franke 1996; Carpenter and Moser 1984). The mistaken view that students must learn basic skills before they are asked to solve word problems is still pervasive (Carpenter and Lehrer 1999). This is true whether it is whole numbers, fractions, or decimals. Huinker (1998) found that using a problem-solving approach to fraction instruction with fifth- and sixth-grade students established a strong conceptual foundation for then moving toward meaningful use of procedures with fractions. NCTM (1989) highlighted in its original standards document that "problem solving is not a distinct topic but a process that should permeate the entire program and provide the context in which concepts and skills can be learned" (p. 23).

Promoting Equity by Building Procedural Fluency from Conceptual Understanding

Equitable teaching of mathematics focuses on *going deep with mathematics* (Aguirre, Mayfield-Ingram, and Martin 2013), including developing a deep understanding of computational procedures and other mathematical rules, formulas, and facts. When students learn procedures with understanding, they are then able to use and apply those procedures in solving problems. When students learn procedures as steps to be memorized without strong links to conceptual understanding, they are limited in their ability to use the procedure. The NCTM (2014) position statement on procedural fluency in mathematics describes procedural fluency as the ability to—

- apply procedures accurately, efficiently, and flexibly;
- transfer procedures to different problems and contexts;
- build or modify procedures from other procedures; and
- recognize when one strategy or procedure is more appropriate to apply than another.

Equitable classrooms place a high premium on learning with understanding and developing students' agency and ownership of mathematical knowledge. Unfortunately, too many students rely heavily on memorization in mathematics rather than engaging in reasoning and sense making, and it is these students that often have greater anxiety toward mathematics (OECD 2016). The Program for International Student Assessment (PISA) found that students in high-performing countries, such as China and Japan, report less reliance on memorization as a learning strategy than students in lower-performing countries, such as the United States. Unfortunately, students in the U.S. too often learn procedures through memorization, thus limiting and depriving them of the deeper mathematical knowledge that will serve them more powerfully throughout their lives. The development of richly connected mathematical ideas, including that of developing procedural understanding (Star 2005), is essential for engaging every student fully as a member of mathematical communities of practice.

Many students are labeled as struggling learners in mathematics (Gersten et al. 2009). While some of these students are identified as having special needs or being at-risk, many are struggling due to conceptual gaps in their knowledge that continue to widen and leave them farther and farther behind in mathematics as compared to their peers. Response-to-intervention programs, while well-intentioned, are sometimes poorly implemented and leave students further behind (Balu et al. 2015). In mathematics, intervention programs are sometimes misguided in placing too much emphasis on memorizing and then practicing procedural skills rather than filling conceptual gaps in students' knowledge. For example, Fuchs and colleagues (2013) found that an intervention program for at-risk fourth-grade students that focused on a measurement interpretation of fractions and the number line, rather than a traditional part-whole paradigm, lead to greater mathematical proficiency and narrowed the achievement gap between at-risk and low-risk students. This study shows how going more deeply with the mathematics benefits students identified as struggling in mathematics.

Taking Action in Your Classroom

Throughout this chapter, you have examined and considered ways that teachers can help students develop meaningful use of procedures by building from conceptual understanding in moving toward procedural fluency. Here we summarize some of the key messages for you to keep in mind as you take action in your own classroom.

- Instruction begins with a focus on conceptual understanding of concepts, number relationships, and operations as a basis for learning to use procedures meaningfully.

- Without a strong conceptual underpinning, students often confuse procedural steps or misapply procedures, and are unable to judge the reasonableness of their solutions.

- Fluency includes the ability to use procedures with flexibility, understanding, accuracy, and efficiency in solving contextual and mathematical problems.

- Fluency develops gradually over time and needs to emerge from a solid foundation of conceptual understanding.

- Rushing students to fluency with procedures undermines their confidence in their own mathematical agency and their interest in mathematics, as well as causing mathematics anxiety.

- Fluency builds from initial exploration of number concepts to informal strategies based on meanings and properties of the operations to the use of general methods and algorithms.

- Conceptually focused instruction promotes student understanding and skill development, as well as the ability to use procedures meaningfully to solve problems.

We now invite you to take action as you consider what implications the ideas discussed in this chapter have for your own professional setting. We suggest you select a specific operation and develop an equation string to use with your students. The string should move your students toward the use of more advanced strategies on their path to fluency and build upon their current conceptual understanding of operations and number relationships.

Taking Action in Your Classroom
Developing and Using Equation Strings to Build Toward Fluency

Develop an equation string to use with your students that would support movement toward more advanced use of procedural strategies.

- Select an operation and a specific type of number, such as whole numbers, fractions, or decimals, in which your students need to move toward more advanced use of strategies.

- Identify the mathematics learning goals that will be supported by your equation string.

- Develop a sequence of three to five equations that will build toward student fluency connected to conceptual understanding and reasoning.

- Reflect on the following questions as you plan to facilitate a discussion of the equation string with your students.

- What strategies do you anticipate students using for each equation in your string, including those you hope they will use as examples of more advanced strategies?

- How will you record each strategy using visual models, number bonds, or equations?

- What questions will you ask to probe students' conceptual understanding as your progress through the equation string?

CHAPTER 5

Pose Purposeful Questions

Teacher questioning is the main instructional tool educators have to surface student reasoning and understanding so they can build from what students know to develop deeper knowledge and the ability to make important mathematical connections. In this chapter, you will explore the effective mathematics teaching practice, *pose purposeful questions*. According to *Principles to Actions: Ensuring Mathematical Success for All* (NCTM 2014, p. 35):

> Effective teaching of mathematics uses purposeful questions to assess and advance student reasoning and sense making about important mathematical ideas and relationships.

The chapter includes three Analyzing Teaching and Learning (ATL) activities.

- ATL 5.1: Examine excerpts from a lesson transcript for the types of questions posed by a first-grade teacher and consider the purpose of her questions.

- ATL 5.2: Compare and contrast teacher-questioning patterns in two different first-grade classrooms and consider how each pattern impacts the opportunities for student learning.

- ATL 5.3: Study student work from a third-grade classroom on the Brownie task and consider the difference between questions that assess student understanding and questions that advance student learning.

For each ATL, we encourage you to note of your responses, and if possible, share and discuss your ideas with colleagues. Once you have shared or written down your thoughts, continue reading the analysis of the ATL in which we relate the activity to the chapter's focal teaching practice. After the ATL activities, the chapter includes research findings on formulating and posing questions and examines how the focal teaching practice promotes equity for students. We end the chapter with suggestions for applying the ideas on questions in your own classroom.

Examining the Purpose of Teacher Questions

In effective teaching of mathematics, teachers are aware of not only the types of questions they pose to students but are also conscious of their interaction patterns in questioning students. In our first Analyzing Teaching and Learning activity in this chapter, we enter a first-grade class working on the Caterpillar task (based on the children's book, "The Very Hungry Caterpillar" by Eric Carle [1969]), shown in figure 5.1. The teacher selected the task because it was well aligned with her learning goal for the lesson: to see and model the mathematical elements in a contextual problem, to understand addition as putting together sets of objects, and to understand that counting can be used to answer "how many" questions. Take a moment to work through the Caterpillar task and jot down at least three different solution paths you would envision being used by first-grade students.

On Monday, the hungry caterpillar ate through one apple, but he was still hungry. On Tuesday he ate through two pears, but he was still hungry. On Wednesday he ate through three plums. On Thursday he ate through four strawberries. On Friday he ate through five oranges. How many pieces of fruit did the hungry caterpillar eat during the week?

Figure 5.1. A first-grade task on combining sets

Engaging in ATL 5.1: Noticing the Effect of Teacher Questions

We begin by joining Ms. Bouchard's first-grade classroom. Her students worked independently using physical materials and drawings to represent and solve the Caterpillar task. If a student used manipulatives, they were told to also draw a picture that showed how they solved the problem. We ask you to turn to ATL 5.1 and examine the teacher's questions as the class discusses student solution paths. Consider how the questions help move the students toward the mathematics learning goals for the lesson.

Analyzing Teaching and Learning 5.1

Investigating the Effect of Teacher Questions

An excerpt from Ms. Bouchard's classroom discussion is shown below. The transcript excerpt includes two segments. Segment 1 occurred at the beginning of the whole-class discussion and Segment 2 occurred toward the end of the class discussion. Read through the segments, paying close attention to the teacher's questions, and consider the following:

- What do you notice about the questions the teacher asked?

- What purpose did each question appear to serve?

- Which questions reveal insights into students' understanding and strategies for addition?

- Which questions orient students to each other's reasoning?

Ms. Bouchard's Class Discussion of Solution Paths for the Caterpillar Task

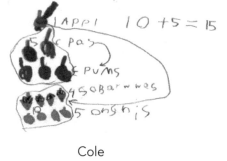

Cole

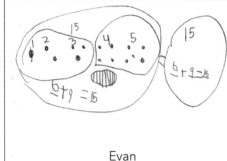

Evan

Segment 1

We enter the whole-group discussion after Cole has shared his solution path with the class.

1	Ms. B:	How did you solve for the total number of pieces of fruit?
2	Cole:	I counted the 4, 5, and 1 because that makes 10. Then I added 5 more
3 4	Ms. B:	How many students understand what Cole did? (Five students raise their hands.) Rosa, can you say back what Cole did in your own words?
5 6	Rosa:	He knows that 4 + 5 and 1 makes 10 and he likes to make 10, because it is easier, and then Cole adds 5 more.
7	Ms. B:	Can anyone else tell us what you heard?
8	Earth:	10 + 5 is 15 pieces of fruit.
9 10	Sengi:	When you make 10 you don't even have to count 5 more because it just goes on the end.
11	Ms. B:	What did Sengi mean when he said, "It [the ones] just goes on the end?"
12 13	Julia:	Like 10 + 5 = 15, 10 + 4 = 14 and 10 + 2 is 12. The 10 is always there and then you add the ones on.
14 15 16 17	Ms. B:	(*The teacher records 10 + 5, 10 + 4, 10 + 3, and 10 + 2.*) So the equations show us that with total amounts such as 15, 14, 13, or 12. We see that we have one ten, in the ten's place, and then some extra ones, in the one's place. (*Mrs. B underlines the tens and circles the ones.*)

The same pattern of conversation is used to discuss Evan's solution path of 6 + 9.

Segment 2

Next we share the discussion of the comparison between 10 + 5 (Cole) and 6 + 9 (Evan).

18 19 20 21	Ms. B:	Thank you for sharing your ways Cole and Evan. Cole wrote 10 + 5 and he got 15 pieces of fruit. Evan said he solved 6 + 9 and he got 15 pieces of fruit too. How can both Cole and Evan each get 15 pieces of fruit when they each wrote and solved a different equation?
22		(*10 + 5 = 15 and 6 + 9 = 15 is recorded on the board.*)
23	Irene:	I know, 10 + 5 = 15.
24	Ms. B:	How did you know the sum was 15?
25 26	Irene:	I did 10 and then went 11, 12, 13, 14, 15. (*Uses her fingers to keep track of counting on.*)
27 28	Ms. B:	You counted on 5 more from 10 and got 15. 10 + 5 = 15 pieces of fruit. Who can use what you know about 10 + 5 to think about the sum of 6 + 9?

29	Irene:	I did 10 and then went 11, 12, 13, 14, 15. (*Uses her fingers to keep track of counting on.*)
30 31	Ms. B:	You counted on 5 more from 10 and got 15. 10 + 5 = 15 pieces of fruit. Who can use what you know about 10 + 5 to think about the sum of 6 + 9?
32 33 34	Marcus:	Can I show you? (*Marcus proceeds to the display of counters*) You take one off of 10 and it is 9. Then you put the extra one with the 5 so now it is 6. So instead of 10 + 5 now he wrote 6 + 9. They both equal 15.
35	Ms. B:	Who agrees with and understands what Marcus just said?
36	Maya:	He just moved them around but he didn't get any more.
37	Ms. B:	Can someone else add on?
38 39	George:	Marcus starts at 9 and counts 6. If you start at 10 you have to only count 5 because the other one is in the 10.
40 41 42	Ms. B:	You can add either 10 + 5 or 6 + 9. Cole counted 10 so he only had to add on 5 more. Evan counted 9 so he had to add on 6. Can we write 10 + 5 = 6 + 9? Why or why not? Turn and talk with your partner.
43	Juan:	Both are 15 so they are the equal.
44	Ms. B:	Who agrees or disagrees with Juan?

Fig. 5.2. Excerpts from Ms. Bouchard's class discussion

Analysis of ATL 5.1: Five Types of Teacher Questions

Before delving into an analysis of Ms. Bouchard's question, it is worthwhile to consider what students know and what we can learn about their thinking. The students in Ms. Bouchard's classroom can solve and justify solution paths flexibly; they make tables and lists and combine subsets as a means of combining multiple addends. Marcus (lines 32–34) used the counters to show how you can transform 10 + 5 into 6 + 9. He knows that he can move an amount from one set to another set and he recognizes that the total amount remains the same. Both Maya (lines 36) and George (lines 38–39) get to the underlying reason why the two expressions are equivalent when they indicate that items in each amount are just moved around, that no additional items are added to the sets, and that a difference of one exists between each addend. It is evident that the students in Ms. Bouchard's classroom can decompose and recompose quantities flexibly.

In *Principles to Actions*, NCTM (2014, pp. 36–37) synthesized key aspects of several questioning frameworks and identified four types of questions that are particularly important for mathematics teaching: (1) questions for gathering information, (2) questions for probing thinking, (3) questions for making the mathematics visible, and (4) questions for encouraging reflection and justification. The four types of questions are shown in figure 5.3, along with a fifth category we added on engaging students with the reasoning of others. This new category underscores the role of teacher questions in building collective thinking among a class of students by engaging them in talking about and understanding each other's solution strategies and mathematical insights (Chapin, O'Connor, and Anderson 2013; Michaels et al. 2010). Take a moment to review the question types, purposes, and examples before we take a closer look at Ms. Bouchard's questions. We include examples of questions that pertain to the Caterpillar task lesson and were pulled from various points throughout the entire lesson as the teacher interacted with students individually, in pairs, or during the whole-class discussion and which pertain to other student work beyond the two samples presented in this ATL.

Question Type	Purpose	Examples
Gathering information	These questions ask students to recall facts, definitions, or procedures.	• How many pieces of fruit did the caterpillar eat on Friday? • Can you show me how you counted the fruit?
Probing thinking	These questions ask students to explain, elaborate, or clarify their thinking, including articulating the steps in solution methods or completion of a task.	• I see you wrote 10 + 5 on your paper. Where did the 10 come from? • Tell me about your picture. I see you wrote the days of the week and then drew squares.
Making the mathematics visible	These questions ask students to discuss mathematical structures and make connections among mathematical ideas and relationships.	• Marisa wrote 1 + 2 + 3 + 4 + 5 = 15. Is that okay to write an equation with all those plus signs? • What pattern do you see in the equations 10 + 2 = 12, 10 + 3 = 13, 10 + 4 = 14, and 10 + 5 = 15?
Encouraging reflection and justification	These questions reveal deeper insight into student reasoning and actions, including asking students to argue for the validity of their work.	• I see you put a circle around the 1, 4, and 5. Why did you put these pieces of fruit together? • What makes 10 + 5 equal to 9 + 6?
Engaging with the reasoning of others	These questions help students gain understanding of each other's solution paths and thinking, and lead to the co-construction of mathematical ideas.	• Who understands Shyanne's explanation and can say it back in your own words? • Can you add on to what Nate said? • Do you agree or disagree with Anne? Why?

Fig. 5.3. Five types of questions

Returning to Ms. Bouchard's discussion, notice how her questions made it possible for us to learn so much about student thinking. Ms. Bouchard gathers information and then uses five probing questions in the short excerpt, which was her typical interaction pattern during the class discussion.

- How did you solve for the total number of pieces of fruit? (line 1)
- How many students understand what Cole did? (line 3)
- Rosa, can you say back what Cole did in your own words? (line 5)
- Can anyone else tell us what you heard? (line 7)
- What did Sengi mean when he said, "It [the ones] just goes on the end?" (line 11)

Probing in this way proved to be beneficial because each additional probing question raised new ideas among the students. We learn that Rosa views addition with ten as an easier addition combination, Earth knows the sum of $10 + 5$ is 15, and Julia recognizes a pattern when adding ten (lines 5–6, 8, and 12–13 respectively). As the teacher probes student thinking she assesses the ideas raised and decides which to pursue further. Her knowledge of the trajectory of learning helps her decide to ask additional questions about combining the numbers based on number relationships.

Making the mathematics visible is now possible because of the knowledge of student thinking that Ms. Bouchard has gained. With this knowledge and her own understanding of the importance of making a ten and using ten in solving addition problems because it relates to understanding place value ideas of our number system, she challenges students to consider the pattern in the equations of $10 + 5 = 15$, $10 + 4 = 14$, $10 + 3 = 13$, and $10 + 2 = 12$. This move makes the mathematical ideas more visible and open for discussion (lines 14–17).

Later in Segment 2 of Ms. Bouchard's lesson (see fig. 5.2), she uses the same cycle of posing a probing question, surfacing the mathematical ideas, and pressing for a justification. Of particular note in this excerpt is how the teacher focused students' attention on equivalence, a big mathematical idea, when she asked, "How can both Cole and Evan each get 15 pieces of fruit when they each wrote and solved a different equation?" (lines 19–21). Later the teacher presses further by asking, "Who can use what you know about $10 + 5$ to think about the sum of $9 + 6$?" (lines 27–28) and "Can we write $10 + 5 = 9 + 6$?" (line 41). By setting the two expressions equal to each other and pressing students to explain how they are equivalent, students must analyze and discuss the relationship between the expressions (Falkner, Levi, and Carpenter 1999). Ms. Bouchard uses questions to focus the discussion on this important mathematics by making those mathematical ideas visible for students to consider and discuss. This also gives mathematical authority to students as they are now the one's who must do the work to make sense of the mathematics and engage in a collective co-construction of equality in this instance. Here students must build an argument for why you can write $10 + 5 = 9 + 6$, which leads to some very lively discussion and debate among students as they present their own reasoning and consider or critique the reasoning of others.

One other question type that is noteworthy is a move to orient and engage more students with the reasoning of their peers. This is our fifth type of question in figure 5.3. These questions are intended to help students collectively gain understanding of other's solution paths and mathematical reasoning and lead to the co-construction of mathematical understanding (Hufferd-Ackles, Fuson, and Sherin 2014). Ms. Bouchard used this type of questioning throughout the lesson. She would ask a student to share his or her strategy, and then the other students were expected to make sense of and talk about that student's solution path. Within each cycle of a discussion, Ms. Bouchard was careful to involve between three and five students.

Keeping everyone in the class involved, together, and focused during lessons with multiple solution paths and several mathematical ideas is not easy, but is certainly important. Ms. Bouchard consistently used engaging questions toward this purpose: "Who understood what…? Who can put the ideas into their own words? Who agrees or disagrees with…?" Maintaining this type of questioning and student accountability is particularly important as the lesson progresses and students are asked to respond to more challenging questions, such as the comparison between solution paths or the discussion of key mathematical ideas. Think about it as making sure you bring all students along on the journey.

For teachers just beginning to use these type of engagement questions, it is helpful to put the question stems for teachers listed in figure 5.4 on a card and hold them in your hand for reference as you facilitate pair, small-group, or whole-class discussions. We also recommend that you post on chart paper a selection of the sentence stems for students as a model and reference for them so that eventually they can be heard during the lesson, whether in whole-group, small-group, or pair discussions, saying I can add on to that, I respectfully disagree, or I can say more about that (Wagganer 2015).

Question Stems for Teachers	Sentence Stems for Students
• That seems really important, who can say that again? • Who can say that back in your own words… ? • What does she mean when she says…? • Who can add on to that explanation…? • Do you agree or disagree with ____? Why? • Turn and talk with a partner about …. Who can tell the class what your partner said? • Let's all try using ____'s approach on this new problem. • Who has a similar way of looking at that? • Who has a different way? • Let's look at these two approaches. How are they similar? How are they different?	• I agree with ____ because … • I respectfully disagree with that because… • I still have questions about… • I'm confused by … • I have a different perspective because … • I connected with what ____ said because … • I chose this method because … • Can I add on to what ____ said about …? • I thought about it the same way because… • When you said … that really helped me understand it so much better. • I was wondering… • Could we try that strategy on a new problem?

Fig. 5.4. Question stems for engaging students with the reasoning of others

Studying Teacher Questioning Patterns

Beyond just the types of questions that teachers ask, another aspect of posing purposeful questions concerns the interaction patterns of teachers and students. Teachers must make numerous "in-the-moment decisions on how to respond to students with questions and prompts that probe, scaffold, and extend student thinking" (NCTM 2014 p. 56). After a student response is elicited, the teacher must interpret the response and then decide how to use this information. This is a critical instructional decision. Should the teacher turn the response back to the student for further consideration or ask other students to respond? Should the teacher probe further into the student's understanding? Should the teacher move on with a new question? These are difficult decisions and some interaction patterns are not as effective as others in deepening and furthering student learning.

Engaging in ATL 5.2: Noticing How Teachers Respond to Students

We now turn to a discussion in the first-grade classroom of Ms. Chong, who also engaged students in solving the Caterpillar task (see fig. 5.1). She used the same lesson routine as Ms. Bouchard. Students worked on the task independently using physical materials and drawings to represent and solve the problem, followed by a whole-class discussion of students' solutions. Turn to ATL 5.2 and study the class discussion in Ms. Chong's classroom and consider how it compares to that of Ms. Bouchard.

Analyzing Teaching and Learning 5.2
Noticing How Teachers Respond to Students

An excerpt from Ms. Chong's classroom discussion is shown below. The transcript excerpt includes two segments. Segment 1 occurred at the beginning of the whole-class discussion and Segment 2 occurred toward the end of the class discussion. Read through the transcript of the segments, as you consider the following:

- What do you notice about the types of questions asked by Ms. Chong?

- What do students seem to understand about addition and the use of addition strategies?

- How do the interactions between the teacher and students in Ms. Chong's classroom compare to those of Ms. Bouchard?

- In what ways might the differences in how the two teachers interact with and question their students affect student learning?

Ms. Chong's Class Discussion
of Solution Paths for the Caterpillar Task

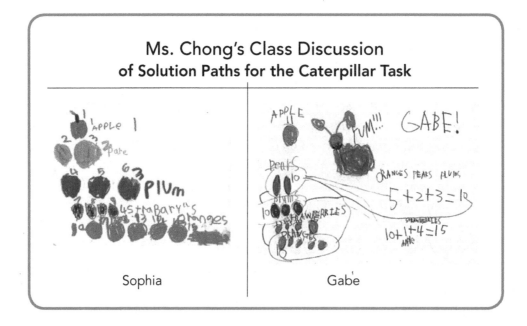

Sophia | Gabe

Segment 1

We enter the whole group discussion as Sophia shares her solution path with the class.

1	Ms. C:	Sophia, how many total pieces of fruit did the caterpillar eat?
2	Sophia:	15.
3	Ms. C:	How did you figure out that the answer was 15?
4	Sophia:	I counted.
5	Ms. C:	Let's all try that. Everyone count with me. (*Teacher points to each piece of fruit*
6		*as the students count in unison.*)
7	Students:	1, 2, 3, 4, 5, 6, 7, 8, 9, 10, 11, 12, 13, 14, 15.
8	Ms. C:	Nice. So, does everyone understand how Sophia figured out the answer
9		was 15?
10	Students:	(*Some students nod their heads.*)
11	Ms. C:	Thumbs up if you get what Sophia did.
12	Students:	(*Some students put up their thumbs.*)
13	Ms. C:	Okay let's hear from Landon.

The same pattern of talk is used to discuss Landon's solution who also counted the fruit by ones.

Segment 2

Next we share the discussion of Gabe's solution.

13	Ms. C:	Tell us how you solved it, Gabe.
14	Gabe:	I counted 5 + 2 + 3 and that's 10. Then I added 1 + 4.
15	Ms. C:	So you first added 5, 2, and 3, and got 10. Then you added on 1 + 4, which is 5 more?
16	Gabe:	Yeah.
17	Mrs. C:	So how many total pieces of fruit did you get?
18	Gabe:	15.
19	Ms. C:	So everyone count with me to check Gabe's work. He had 10 and then added on 5 more. So, let's start counting at 10. (Teacher holds up one hand showing how to keep track of the counts as the students count on in unison.)
20	Students:	Ten... 11, 12, 13, 14, 15. (Most students also use one hand to track their counting.)
21	Ms. C:	Nice job. So we can use counting all to find the answer or a faster way would be to use counting on to find the answer.
22		on 5 more. So, let's start counting at 10. (*Teacher holds up one hand showing*
23		*how to keep track of the counts as the students count on in unison.*)
24	Students:	Ten... 11, 12, 13, 14, 15. (*Most students also use one hand to track their counting.*)
25	Ms. C:	Nice job. So we can use counting all to find the answer or a faster way would
26		be to use counting on to find the answer.

Fig. 5.5. Excerpts from Ms. Chong's class discussion

Analysis of ATL 5.2: Teacher-Student Interaction Patterns

Even though Ms. Bouchard and Ms. Chong used the same task and had the same class routine of problem exploration by students followed with a whole-class discussion, the opportunities for deepening student understanding as well as the outcomes for student learning were very different. Little is really known about student thinking and understanding in Ms. Chong's classroom. The teacher gathered some information from students, but did not probe into their reasoning nor surface some of the mathematical opportunities apparent in their work. Sophia said she counted (line 4) and looking at the way she numbered the fruit in her drawing, it appears she counted all the fruit by ones. Gabe seems to recognize that $5 + 2 + 3 = 10$ and that $1 + 4 = 5$, but we are not sure (line 15). The teacher asked students "how" they solved the problem, which could have lead to a focus on justification and reflection, but she merely acknowledged their response by restating it herself and, it seems, interpreting it in the manner she wanted. It might appear that Ms. Chong tried to orient students to each other's work, but any involvement, such as asking for thumbs-up (line 11), was at a very superficial level of engagement.

The class discussion in Ms. Chong's classroom is clearly directed by the teacher who seems to have a predetermined outcome for the whole-class discussion, that of engaging students in counting on as an addition strategy. Consequently, rather than probing into the thinking of Sophia and Gabe, Ms. Chong leads the class discussion down a desired pathway. She has the class practice counting all, starting at one (lines 5–7), on the basis of Sophia's response that she counted (line 4), even though we cannot be sure that this was really her strategy or merely how she marked her drawing. Later in the discussion of Gabe's work, we do not know whether Gabe counted on or just knew that combining 10 and 5 totals 15. It was Ms. Chong's decision to go down the pathway of having all students practice counting on from ten (lines 21–24).

Ms. Chong's pattern of interaction with the students could be characterized as an I-R-E talk pattern in which a question is initiated by the teacher, a response is given by a student or students, the teacher evaluates the response, and the cycle repeats (Mehan 1979). Another way to characterize her interaction pattern with students is that of "funneling." Herbel-Eisenmann and Breyfogle (2005) observed this interaction pattern of teacher-student talk in many mathematics classrooms. A teacher with this pattern steers the lesson toward his or her desired outcome and pays little attention to student thinking and reasoning. While counting on as a strategy is an important step in children's learning in first grade, it is not enough. The learning trajectory is to advance students to the use of number relationships and the decomposing and recomposing of numbers. As a result of the funneling, Ms. Chong missed several opportunities to surface important mathematical ideas and engage her students in the potential high-level demands of the task. It was clear that Ms. Chong was the mathematical authority in the classroom not the students, as she determined what was valued and examined in the class. The purpose of facilitating class discourse (as discussed in chapter 7) is to "build shared understanding of mathematical ideas by analyzing and comparing student approaches" (NCTM 2014, p. 29). Rather, the class discussion in Ms. Chong's class seemed to be not much more than providing students with counting practice. The teacher even summed up the intent of the lesson from her perspective when she stated, "So we can use counting all to find the answer or a faster way would be to use counting on to find the answer" (lines 25–26).

In contrast, Ms. Bouchard listened carefully to her students, determined how to press students to communicate their solution paths, and then engaged all students in building on one another's ideas as they examined and made connections among the various approaches. This pattern of questioning is referred to as a "focusing pattern" (Herbel-Eisenmann and Breyfogle 2005). In this pattern, the teacher engages students in a whole-class discussion with the goal of learning about students' thinking and using the information in ways to engage all students toward shared understanding as well shared authority of the mathematics.

In what ways do the differences in how the teachers interact with and question the students affect student learning? The questions do matter. The questions convey to students what is valued in the class and what it means to learn mathematics. A funneling talk pattern conveys to students that the goal of the lesson is to get to the answer and that the teacher's solution path is the one of importance. In classrooms such as Ms. Bouchard's, students know that their solution paths are valued because their ideas are shared and probed. They also know that they are expected to collectively work together on this mathematical journey, sharing their thinking and reasoning and striving together to make sense of and understand other students' solution paths and mathematical reasoning.

Using Questions to Assess and Advance Student Learning

Effective teaching of mathematics makes intentional use of questioning to both assess student understanding and to advance student learning (NCTM 2014). Teaching involves asking lots of questions. The main reason for questioning is to surface students' understanding and reasoning. For example, what do students understand about a specific mathematical idea, such as three-ninths, and how would they reason through its representation with an area model or on a number line? Questions of this type are referred to as *assessing* questions because they allow the teacher to probe student thinking, ask for clarification, and gather more information related to the student's understanding of problem-solving strategies, key mathematical ideas, or the meaning inherent in representations. A question that follows-up on the assessing question is an *advancing* question. An example of an advancing question would be, "Using the diagram you drew for three-ninths, how would you explain why three-ninths is equivalent to one-third?" These questions build on students' present knowledge and move students beyond where they currently are toward the mathematics learning goals of a lesson or further along on a specific learning trajectory.

The characteristics of assessing and advancing questions are shown in figure 5.6. Take a moment to read through the characteristics and reflect on which type might be more prominent in your own teaching practice. Also make note of and consider the interplay of whether the teacher stays and listens to a student's response to the question or walks away.

Assessing Questions	Advancing Questions
• Based closely on the student's current work and approach. • Clarify aspects of the student work and approach and what the student understands about that work or approach. • Provide information to the teacher about what the student understands about the mathematical ideas and relationships. **Teacher STAYS to hear the answer to the question.**	• Use student work as a basis for making progress toward the target goal of the lesson or to move further on a learning trajectory. • Move students beyond their current thinking by pressing students to extend what they know to a new situation. • Prompt students to think about a mathematical idea they are not currently considering. **Teacher WALKS AWAY, leaving students to figure out how to proceed.**

Fig. 5.6. Characteristics of assessing and advancing questions (Bill and Smith 2008)

Engaging in ATL 5.3: Posing Assessing and Advancing Questions

In this analyzing teaching activity, we shift to using student work on the Brownie task (see fig. 5.7). Take a few minutes and work through the Brownie task from the perspective of students. Record several approaches that you would anticipate within a class of third-grade students.

The Brownie Task

There are 7 brownies. Four friends are sharing the brownies so that everyone gets exactly the same amount. How much of the brownies will each friend get? What do you call that amount?

Fig. 5.7. A third-grade task on making fair shares

Ms. Palmer, a third-grade teacher, used the Brownie task with her students early in their unit on fractions. She wanted them to understand that fair shares of a group of discrete objects may require partitioning one or more objects into smaller parts, so that each person gets the same-size share, and that all of the sharing material is exhausted or used up. In addition, she wanted her students to begin using fraction language and symbols meaningfully. Turn to ATL 5.3 in which you are asked to formulate some assessing and advancing questions for students in Ms. Palmer's classroom.

Analyzing Teaching and Learning 5.3
Posing Assessing and Advancing Questions

Imagine you are the teacher in this third-grade classroom. Your students produce the four work samples shown below.

- Study the four student work samples on the Brownie task.

- Formulate one assessing question and one advancing question related to Ms. Palmer's learning goals for the lesson that you might ask each of the students.

The Brownie Task
Examples of Third-Grade Students' Work

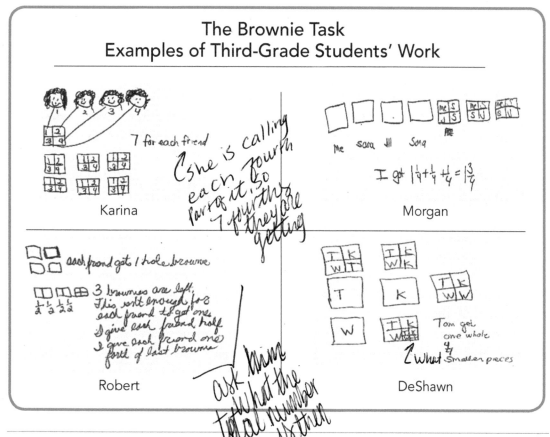

Karina

Morgan

Robert

DeShawn

Analysis of ATL 5.3: Stay-and-Listen or Ask-and-Walk-Away

The Brownie task work shows that each student understands something about the fair-sharing situation and about partitioning discrete objects. The work also shows that each student has not fully met the teacher's learning goals for the lesson. Both assessing and advancing questions can be posed to the students. Reflect on the questions you posed for each student and compare them with those posed by the teacher as discussed in the following analysis.

Karina successfully partitioned the seven brownies into fourths, but wrote down that each person gets "7." She told the teacher that each friend gets "seven pieces" in response to the assessing question, "What share of the brownies did each friend get?" The teacher then posed an advancing prompt, "Each person did receive seven small pieces. Can you figure out the size of each piece as it relates to one whole brownie? Then try writing a number sentence using fractions that shows how you are keeping track of the number of small pieces each person gets." This question challenges the student to name the size of each piece as one-fourth of a brownie. The question also provides the student with a gentle nudge, but the prompt still requires that the student problem solve and share her thinking and reasoning. Then the teacher walked away and moved on to the next student with the intent to return and check on Karina later.

The teacher asked Morgan, "Can you tell me about the share of brownies that you got?" Because this student has already written an equation to describe one person's share of the brownies, the advancing question needs to challenge the student further. The teacher asked, "You received $1\frac{3}{4}$ brownies. What share of the brownies do the other three friends receive? How do you know $1\frac{3}{4}$ is the correct share of the brownies?" This prompts Morgan to realize that each friend gets the same-size share and that this is the correct answer because 4 groups of $1\frac{3}{4}$ brownies totals 7 brownies.

Ms. Palmer paused for a moment when she looked at Robert's work and then asked, "What share of the brownies will each person receive?" Robert explained that each person gets one whole brownie, one-half of a brownie, and one-fourth of a brownie. She then prompted, "What is one whole brownie plus one-half of a brownie plus one-fourth of a brownie? What might be one name you can give for that total amount?" As the teacher walked away, she noticed that Robert was starting to partition some of the brownies further.

With DeShawn, the teacher asked, "So, what do the letters mean?" As the student explained, it became apparent that DeShawn was sharing the brownies among three not four students. Next the teacher asked the student to retell the problem in his own words. Upon the retelling, he realized he needed to include himself as one of the friends who got some of the brownies. Ms. Palmer did not need to say anything else, because DeShawn started to redraw and partition the brownies.

By asking assessing questions such as, "Can you tell me about your work?, Can you tell me about the share of brownies that each friend would get?, and How did you pass out the brownies?," the teacher had the opportunity to learn about each student's current understanding of the mathematics within the task. Because each student was at a different place in his or her level of understanding, the next "doable" question for each student differed. In this manner the teacher was differentiating her instruction to meet each student where the student was at in his or her understanding; then through her purposeful questioning, she advanced or pressed each student to think further about specific mathematical aspects of the task and potential solution paths.

The teacher also gave careful consideration to which question in the trajectory of learning was the next appropriate question for each student. Ideally the question should be one that a student will be able to take off and run with on his or her own. Questions that build on existing work are often the best method for advancing student learning because the student already has a natural link to the ideas. It is important to first ask an assessing question because you need to know where a student is currently in his or her learning. Then by asking an advancing question you not only scaffold the student's understanding but also convey to each student that you believe in him or her as a learner.

What the Research Says: Teacher Questioning

Teacher questioning is viewed as a critical aspect of effective mathematics teaching and shows strong links to gains in student achievement (Redfield and Rousseau 1981; Samson et al. 1987). Examination of teacher questioning has a long history, including identification of the types of questions that teachers ask, as well as the culture of asking questions in classrooms. As Martino and Maher (1994) noted, "The art of questioning may take years to develop for it requires an in-depth knowledge of both mathematics and children's learning of mathematics. Once acquired, the teacher has available a powerful tool to support students in their building of mathematical ideas" (p. 54). In fact, questions are often seen as the main tool that teachers have to prompt and scaffold student learning in mathematics (Holton and Clarke 2006).

The inclusion of posing purposeful questions as an effective teaching practice (NCTM 2014) has brought attention back to the importance of skillful teacher questioning in order to achieve the expectations of rigorous and challenging mathematics standards (NGA Center and CCSSO 2010). Unfortunately, the types of questions posed by teachers, particularly in the United States, may not be supporting the deep levels of student understanding needed. Perry, VanderStoep, and Yu (1993) found that primary grade teachers in Japan and China asked significantly more questions about conceptual knowledge and problem-solving strategies than U.S. teachers. These questions ask students "to transcend the problem at hand" (p. 34) and discuss underlying mathematical principles, much like Ms. Bouchard and Ms. Palmer did earlier in this chapter. Stigler and Hiebert (2009) also observed that teachers in the U.S. pose fewer high-level questions in middle school mathematics classrooms than teachers in other countries. It is important to note that it is not just the asking of questions that makes the difference in student learning but rather the verbalization by students in response to those questions (Brown and Kane 1998). It is that verbalization which causes students to pause in their thinking and to reorganize, as needed, their mental knowledge structures resulting in deeper and more robust learning (Fuson, Kalchman, and Bransford 2005).

In addition to the types of questions that teachers pose, the pause between those questions often makes the difference in student learning. Teachers are impatient and do not like silence. Often one of hardest tasks for teachers during instruction is to simply wait after asking a question and allow students time to process the ideas mulling in their heads and to formulate a response. Rowe (1974) found that teachers tend to leave no more than one second of silence before calling on a student to answer their questions or addressing an unanswered question by restating it or answering it themselves. In her research, she identified two types of wait time. Wait time is most often thought of as the lapse of time that occurs between a teacher's question and a student's answer; this is wait time one. Another important moment to pause is the interval between the response by the student and the acknowledgment of that response by the teacher; this is wait time two.

When teachers wait for three or more seconds after their questions (wait time one) and after students complete their responses (wait time two), profound benefits, related to changes in teacher and student discourse, including higher levels of cognitive learning (Rowe 1974, 1986; Tobin 1986, 1987), are observed for student learning. Most notably, more students volunteer to respond, the number of "I don't know" responses decrease, the length of students' responses increase, and students react more to each other's statements. The pause also impacts teacher behaviors in that they ask more probing and higher-level questions and fewer recall or information-gathering questions. Stahl (1994) recommended the use of the term "think-time" with students because it names the academic purpose and activity of this period of silence—time to think. For example, teachers might state the following:

- "Before you raise your hand, think carefully about what you want to say."
- "No hands until I give you the signal…(wait 5 to 10 seconds)…Raise your hand now if you would like to share your response to my question."
- "No hands at all. I'm going to ask you a question, give you some time to think, and then I'll call on someone" (or draw a name from the deck of name cards).

The culture of asking questions is seen through patterns of interactions among teachers and students in mathematics classrooms. Too often these patterns restrict rather than provide students with opportunities to engage in mathematical reasoning and sense making (Herbel-Eisenmann and Breyfogle 2005; Stein et al. 2009). The I-R-E talk pattern (Mehan 1979) is still far too common in mathematics classrooms. With this approach, the teacher initiates a question (usually a recall question), a student gives a response (or the class responds in unison), the teacher evaluates the response, and the cycle repeats. The teacher is clearly the person with the mathematical authority in the classroom and controls the exchange of knowledge.

As teachers shift to the use of more high-level mathematics tasks and questions, they need to be conscious of one's own talk patterns with students. Herbel-Eisenmann and Breyfogle (2005) observed that well-intentioned teachers would begin with high-level mathematics tasks and questions, but then proceed to funnel the discussions to specific pathways, such as rehearsal of specific strategies. Similarly, Stein and colleagues (2009) examined the pattern of talk in middle school classrooms and noted that students' opportunities to engage in high levels of thinking and reasoning diminished as the emphasis shifted to a discussion of procedures and how to get the correct answer. This emphasis on funneling also appears more common in the United States than in other high-achieving countries. Stigler and Hiebert (2009) found that U.S. teachers in mathematics rarely posed higher-level tasks and questions to their students, and when they did, they would often reduce the cognitive demand by funneling student thinking.

An alternative is the "focusing" pattern of questioning (Herbel-Eisenmann and Breyfogle 2005). In this approach, teachers begin with and are able to sustain high-level thinking and reasoning among students while advancing student knowledge toward the intended learning. To keep students focused on the important mathematics, teachers must be clear on the mathematics learning goals for the lesson. In addition, teachers who have anticipated student approaches and planned potential questions to ask students related to specific solution paths are more successful in maintaining the higher cognitive demand in whole-class discussions (Henningsen and Stein 2011).

Teaching mathematics includes developing students' ability to think mathematically, that is, to develop the habits of mind of mathematical thinkers (Goldenberg, Shteingold, and Feurzeig 2003; NGA Center and CCSSO 2010). Through purposeful questioning, teachers send important messages to students that learning mathematics includes reasoning quantitatively and abstractly, constructing explanations and justifications, examining the reasoning of others, and making sense of mathematics. This necessitates that teachers pose more higher-level questions that surface and make visible important mathematical structures and connections, that probe students' mathematical understanding and reasoning, and that encourage justification, reflection, and generalizations. Purposeful questioning is a critical tool for effective teaching. Teachers need to pause more frequently and longer—both after asking a question and before replying to a student's response—and insist that students slow down and stop their rush to provide answers. In other words, teachers can strategically and intentionally ask questions and use pauses to give students time and space to acquire those mathematical habits of mind and focus on developing deep and lasting understanding of important mathematical ideas and relationships.

Promoting Equity by Posing Purpose Questions

Equitable teaching of mathematics requires the intentional use of teacher questioning to ensure that each and every student not only progresses in his or her learning of important and challenging mathematical ideas but also develops a strong mathematical identity (Aguirre, Mayfield-Ingram, and Martin, 2013). Teacher questioning and positioning of students influence how students view themselves as potential members of the mathematics learning community in the classroom. Positioning includes the way that students are "entitled, expected, and obligated to interact with one another as they work on content together" (Gresalfi and Cobb 2006, p. 51). Are all students' ideas and questions heard, valued, and pursued in the mathematics classroom? Who gets called on to answer questions? What mathematical ideas are examined and discussed? Whose thinking is selected for further inquiry and whose thinking is disregarded among students in small-group and whole-class discussions?

As discourse patterns change in mathematics classrooms toward building collective and deeper understanding, new sociomathematical norms must be established (Yackel and Cobb 1996). Students are not accustomed to teacher questioning that asks them to talk about mathematics and to openly share their emerging and partially formed thoughts and strategies. The idea of discussing a problem, listening to different points of view, and building on each other's ideas is a new experience for many mathematical learners, particularly for those from historically marginalized groups (Civil 2007). Putting one's mathematical ideas and strategies into public view for examination can put students in vulnerable positions as related to issues of power and status structures among students in the classroom (Civil and Planas 2004). Students become anxious in revealing their reasoning for fear of mistakes and not looking smart (Ashcraft 2002; Maloney and Beilock 2012). The recent focus on the role of mistakes as opportunities for learning (Carter 2008; Steuer, Rosentritt-Brunn, and Dresel 2013) and brain growth (Moser et al. 2011), employing praise and feedback for using effective strategies (Dweck 2007; Hattie and Timperley 2007), and attention to growth and fixed mindsets (Dweck 2006) also support changing norms in mathematics classrooms toward giving more students a voice in mathematical conversations.

Teachers make numerous decisions in their classrooms every day and need to be more aware of which students are called upon in whole-class discussions with particular attention to including students from marginalized populations. Not only must teachers carefully consider what questions to ask their students about mathematics but they must also be conscious of which students are given voice and authority in those mathematical conversations (Civil and Planas 2004; Heinz 2010). By eliciting and valuing the thinking of each and every student, teachers can work toward building identity and agency within students as capable individuals in learning and using mathematics to solve problems (Aguirre, Mayfield-Ingram, and Martin 2013; Schoenfeld 2014).

Taking Action in Your Classroom

Throughout this chapter, you have examined the types of questions posed by teachers and analyzed the interaction patterns of class discussions. Here we summarize some of the key messages for you to keep in mind as you take action in your own classroom.

- A balance of question types—gathering information, probing student thinking, making the mathematics visible, and encouraging reflections and justifications—should be used to surface different aspects of students' mathematical understanding and reasoning.

- Teachers need to be cautious in their interaction patterns with students to ensure that discussions do not erode into funneling student thinking down a particular pathway, often the teacher's pre-expected solution, and should be diligent in focusing discussions and conversations on students' ideas and ways of reasoning.

- Questions that ask students to add on to other's ideas, to say back an idea in their own words, or to agree or disagree ensure that students are listening and participating in the lesson and share in the co-construction of a solution path, as well as shape students' views of what it means to do mathematics.

- Assessing and advancing questions are important teacher tools for gaining insight into students' current ideas and understanding and for moving students closer to the mathematical goal of the lesson.

We now invite you to take action in your own professional setting. We suggest you examine the questions you ask your students by recording an upcoming lesson and then plan a lesson by formulating purposeful questions to both assess and advance student learning about important mathematical ideas and relationships.

Taking Action in Your Classroom

Analyzing Your Questions for a Lesson

Teach a lesson using a high-level task. Video- or audio-record the lesson. Consider the extent to which the questions you asked—

- revealed students' current understandings;

- probed students' decisions by asking them to explain, elaborate, or clarify their thinking;

- made the mathematics more visible and accessible for student examination and discussion; and

- engaged students with the reasoning of each other.

Then consider the discussion from an equity perspective:

- Did historically marginalized students have equal opportunities to answer questions that probed their mathematical decisions and made their mathematical ideas visible, accessible, and valid for examination by other students?

- Did some students only get asked information retrieval questions?

Posing Assessing and Advancing Questions for a Lesson

Select an upcoming lesson that uses a high-level task. Identify the mathematics learning goal and anticipate student solution paths, including both productive and unproductive ways that students might approach the task.

- Formulate both assessing and advancing questions aligned to your goals and the anticipated solution paths to ask students as they work independently or in small groups.

- Teach the lesson and reflect on the ways the assessing questions gave you greater insights into student thinking and how the advancing questions moved student learning forward.

CHAPTER 6

Use and Connect Mathematical Representations

Representations play an important role in deepening student learning of mathematics, as well as providing students with multiple entry points and access to the study of mathematics. The National Research Council (2001) noted, "Mathematics requires representations. In fact, because of the abstract nature of mathematics, people have access to mathematical ideas only through the representations of those ideas" (p. 94). In this chapter, you will examine the effective teaching practice, *use and connect mathematical representations*. According to *Principles to Actions: Ensuring Mathematical Success for All* (NCTM 2014, p. 24):

> Effective teaching of mathematics engages students in making connections among mathematical representations to deepen understanding of mathematics concepts and procedures and as tools for problem solving.

Mathematical representations include ways to convey or envision mathematical ideas. The diagram in figure 6.1 highlights important connections for students among five modes of representations of number—contextual, visual, verbal, physical, and symbolic (adapted from Lesh, Post, and Behr 1987). Note that the arrows go in both directions indicating that students should be able to alternate directionality in using representations. For example, students should not only be able to solve a given word problem, they should be able to do the reverse, given an equation such as $9 + 5$, 4×26, or $6 \div {}^3/_4$, they should be able to pose their own problem situation. Student flexibility in moving between representations is a hallmark of competent mathematical thinking and understanding because each representation highlights critical features or reveals different structural aspects of a mathematical concept or action.

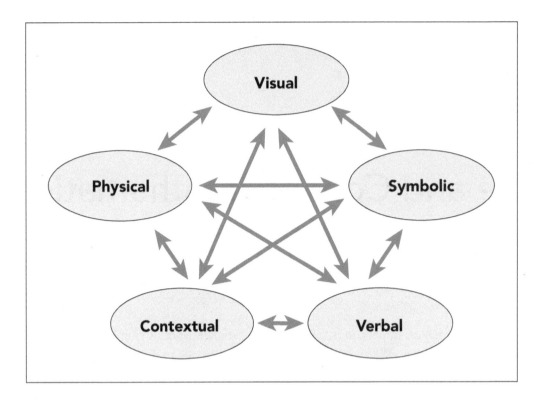

Fig. 6.1. Important connections among representations (NCTM 2014, p. 18)

The chapter includes three Analyzing Teaching and Learning (ATL) activities.

- ATL 6.1: Examine student responses on an assessment check-in aimed at surfacing understanding of connections among multiplication representations.

- ATL 6.2: Study student work for evidence of flexibility in using representations to understand and solve a subtraction word problem.

- ATL 6.3: Read two vignettes and identify ways the teachers are developing the representational competence of their students.

For each ATL, we encourage you to make note of your responses, and if possible, share and discuss your thoughts and ideas with colleagues. Once you have shared or written down your thoughts, continue reading the analysis of the ATL in which we relate the activity to the chapter's focal teaching practice. After analyzing the teaching activities, the chapter includes research findings on using mathematical representations and examines how the focal teaching practice promotes equity among students. We end the chapter by offering suggestions for applying the ideas on using and connecting representations in your own classroom.

Deepening Understanding through Representations

Effective teaching of mathematics includes a focus on representations in order to deepen students' mathematical understanding. When students perceive mathematics as a rich web of interconnected ideas, as opposed to a collection of disconnected facts and rules, they have the underpinnings to develop their confidence and agency in mathematics. However, oftentimes it appears that students are understanding the mathematics when, in fact, their knowledge is limited and only partly developed. To acquire a richer understanding of a mathematical concept, relationship, or procedure, it is important that students are able to view that mathematical idea through all five modes of representation and be able to translate, or move fluidly and easily, from one mode of representation to another.

Engage in ATL 6.1: Assessing Knowledge of Representations

We begin by examining a formative assessment task for our first Analyzing Teaching and Learning activity in this chapter. The intent of the assessment (see fig. 6.2) is to check in on students' conceptual understanding of multiplication by asking them to not only solve a given equation (symbolic representation) and explain their reasoning but to also generate visual and contextual representations. Familiarize yourself with the assessment and consider what types of pictures or diagrams students might draw and what types of stories they might write, and also predict what student mistakes and faulty conceptions might appear in student responses.

Multiplication Check-In

1. Find the answer to 4 × 7.

2. Explain how you figured out the answer.

3. Draw a picture that shows what 4 × 7 means.

4. Write a story problem for 4 × 7.

Fig. 6.2. Assessment task of understanding representations for multiplication

The multiplication assessment was given to a class of third-grade students during the first semester of the school year. While most students in the class arrived at the correct answer of 28, their responses for drawing a picture and writing a story problem reveal a range of understanding from faulty ideas about multiplication to limited knowledge of representations to stronger interconnected ideas about multiplication. We ask you to engage in ATL 6.1 and examine representative responses from four students on the multiplication assessment.

Study the four student work samples (shown below) for the multiplication assessment task (fig. 6.2).

- What does each reveal about the student's understanding of multiplication?

- Considering this representative sample of student responses, what might be some implications for instruction?

Olivia

1. Find the answer: 4 x 7 = ?

Answer 28
4x7= 28

2. Explain how you figured out the answer.

I counted 4's up to seven like
this. 4,8,12,16,20,24,28
    1 2 3 4 5 6 7

3. Draw a picture that shows what 4 x 7 means.

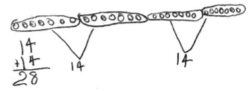

You count by 4's up to
Seven.

4. Write a story problem for 4 x 7.

The class went on a trip.
4 people did not go. How many
people was going?

Mateo

1. Find the answer: 4 x 7 = ?

4x7= 28

2. Explain how you figured out the answer.

4X7=28 Because 7+7=14
and another 7+7=14 so I add
the to 14's together

3. Draw a picture that shows what 4 x 7 means.

14
+14
28   14   14

4. Write a story problem for 4 x 7.

4 x 7 = 28   4
              x7
              28

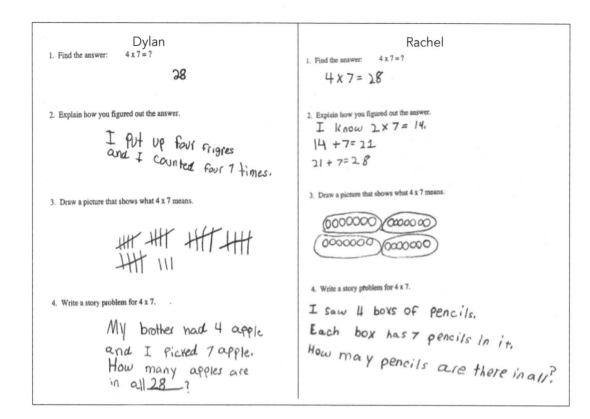

Analysis of ATL 6.1: Translations among Representations

The multiplication check-in examines students' ability to translate among representations. It specifically targets the connections from a symbolic representation to a visual representation and to a contextual representation. The assessment reverses the directionality from which students are accustomed to being asked. It is more common for students to be presented with a story problem to solve than to pose their own story or problem situation. Similarly, it is more common to begin with physical objects or pictures and then write an equation that models the visual representation. Reversing the directionality provides the teacher with new insights into what students really understand, and surfaces misunderstandings and confusions that can then be addressed.

Individual Student Ability to Translate and Connect Representations

The multiplication check-in revealed strengths among some students, particularly those who were able to find the correct answer, explain their reasoning, and make translations to visual and contextual representations. It also revealed that while students have strategies to figure out the answer (e.g., skip counting, doubling a known fact, and repeated addition), they might have only limited understanding of the meaning of the operation. Some individual students appear to have glaring gaps in their understanding of multiplication as demonstrated in their inability to translate among the representations.

Rachel demonstrated a strong understanding of multiplication with accurate translations from the equation to both visual and contextual representations. Her diagram clearly shows 4 groups with 7 objects in each group. Her story problem about boxes of pencils is clearly a multiplication situation with intentional wording that "each box" has 7 pencils in it. Rachel is ready to start working with other visual representations such as arrays, tape diagrams, or number lines.

Mateo drew a clear diagram of 4 groups with 7 objects in each group, very similar to Rachel's drawing. He also shows in his visual representation that he knows he can combine 2 groups to get 14, repeat this with the other 2 groups, and then add them together to get the answer, 14 + 14 = 28. Knowing that he can double 14 to get the answer shows an advanced reasoning strategy, which was not a common approach among the students in the class. Mateo was not able to pose a story problem. When the teacher asked him about it, he said he was not sure what to write. Mateo is adept at working with quantities and numerical relationships, so the teacher was surprised that he struggled to link his numeric work to a real-life, contextual situation.

Olivia and Dylan both said they used skip counting to find the solution to the equation; they worked with "four 7 times" rather than reasoning about 4 groups with 7 objects in each group. Interestingly, they both were not able to make translations to contextual and visual representations. Dylan wrote, "I put up 4 fingers and counted 4 seven times." It is not clear whether he skip-counted or counted on by ones, nor how he knew when to stop counting, but he did arrive at the right answer. His picture shows a total of 28 tally marks with no indication of equal groups. It is likely that Dylan has memorized a procedure for finding the answer and does not understand multiplication as combining equal groups. His lack of understanding multiplication is further demonstrated by his story problem, which describes adding two unequal groups of apples, even though he states that the answer to the story problem is 28.

Olivia wrote, "I counted 4s up to seven" to explain how she figured out the answer. Her written explanation verifies that she did skip-count because she wrote, "4, 8, 12, 16, 20, 24, 28." Olivia also wrote the numbers from 1 to 7 above the skip-count numbers. This likely helped her keep track of the number of times she needed to skip-count. Her visual diagram shows 7 hearts, which might represent groups, but it does not show 4 as a quantity in each of those groups. It is more likely that Olivia represented her seven skip counts because her story problem shows no connection to understanding multiplication as combining sets of objects. It is likely that Olivia has also memorized a procedure, skip counting, to find the answer to multiplication equations.

Overall Class Results and Instructional Implications

Beyond just assessing the understanding of individual students, the multiplication check-in allowed the teacher to identify overall trends in the use of representations among her class. She also used the evidence to reflect on her own instructional practice and identify implications for strengthening her teaching with representations. She first noted that almost all the students got the right answer. Most students explained that they had used skip counting or repeated addition; some just said, "I knew it"; and only a few, like Mateo, had doubled a known fact. She specifically selected "4 × 7" because she had hoped students would use the "double a known fact" strategy, which they had examined as a class. One implication for her instruction is to provide students with more structured work on exploring and discussing this advanced reasoning strategy.

In the past, before learning about the importance of representations, the teacher would have only asked the first two questions, solve the problem and explain one's reasoning, and she would have been fairly happy with the results. She now wants more for her students. She wants them to have a deeper and richer understanding of multiplication that includes the ability to fluently and flexibly translate among representations. Only about half of the class had a visual representation that clearly showed 4 equal groups with 7 objects in each group, and all of the visual representations were similar to Rachel's and Mateo's pictures in that they showed discrete equal group situations. Her students did not draw arrays, even though they had some experience with them. Additional implications for her instruction are to engage students in explicit discourse on mapping equations to representations and to provide more experiences for students to generate visual representations for multiplication, including specific work with arrays. In other words, a long-term learning goal for her students is to be able to generate, not just one, but multiple types of visual representations for a given multiplication equation. To that end, she will also bring in additional visual displays, including tape diagrams and number lines.

The most problematic translation was that of posing a story problem to match 4 × 7. About a fourth of the class had an accurate story problem. Far too many stories were like Dylan's word problem in which the stories did not describe equal groups of objects. The students took the numbers 4 and 7, named them both as specific objects, for example apples or cars, and then said the answer was 28. Now that the teacher has evidence of her students' thinking, she plans to start her lesson the next day by displaying two story problems, that of Dylan and Rachel, and engage the class in a discussion of which story problem is modeled by the equation. The teacher also concludes from the assessment that her students need more encounters with contextual situations for multiplication and more experiences posing their own multiplication stories. In addition, the teacher wants to move beyond just discrete equal-group situations and include, at first, more array situations, and then move to problem situations that involve continuous quantities as linear and area measures.

Using Representations as Tools in Problem Solving

Representations can support the learning goal of deepening students' knowledge of mathematical concepts and procedures. Another important goal is to help students learn to use representations as tools for solving problems. "Students should be able to approach a problem from several points of view and be encouraged to switch among representations until they are able to understand the situation and proceed along a path that will lead them to a solution" (NCTM 2014, p. 26).

Engage in ATL 6.2: Flexibility in Using Representations

In ATL 6.2 we observe Ms. Shea's second-grade classroom and consider the representations her students use to solve the Swings task (see fig. 6.3). The task presents the students with a missing part (addend) word problem. Take a moment and read through the task. What representations might students use to understand the situation? What representations might students use as tools to find a solution to the word problem?

The Swings Task

At recess, 13 children were playing on the swings. Then some more children joined them. Now there are 21 children on the swings. How many children joined the first group?

Make sure you show your thinking, write an equation, and record your answer.

Fig. 6.3. Second-grade missing part word problem

Ms. Shea teaches with a focus on representations. She expects her second-grade students to use physical, visual, and symbolic representations to make sense of word problems, that is, to discern the relationships among the quantities in the problem situation. She also expects her students to use representations in flexible ways to find answers to word problems. Read ATL 6.2 and study how six students used representations to solve the Swings task.

Analyzing Teaching and Learning 6.2
Flexibility in Using Representations

Ms. Shea gave the Swings task (see fig. 6.3) to her second-grade students. Study their use of representations as shown below in the six student work samples.

- How do students use visual and symbolic representations to understand the problem situation and discern the relationships among the quantities in the story?

- How do students use visual and symbolic representations as tools to help them solve the word problem?

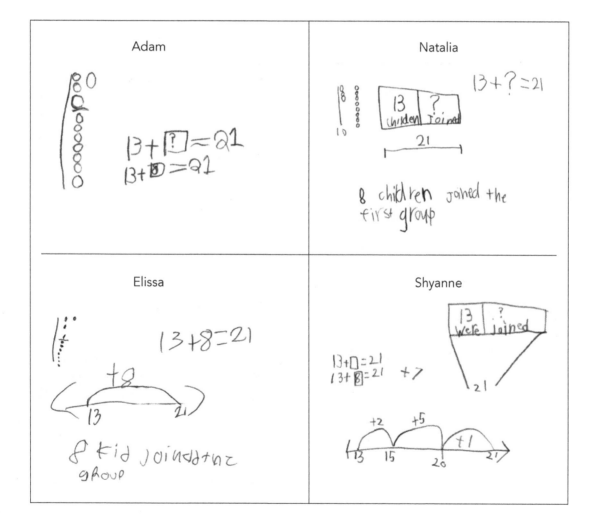

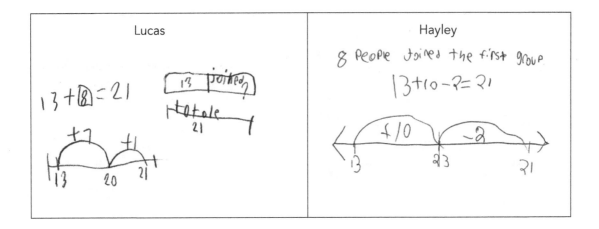

Analysis of ATL 6.2. Student Choice in Use of Representations

The student work displays a variety of visual representations. The students used tape diagrams, open number lines, and sticks and dots (to represent tens and ones). The students also used symbolic representations in the form of equations in a variety of ways. Some students indicated the unknown added in their equations with a box, a question mark, or both. Studying the work closer, we can see that the students used the representations for two purposes. Some representations helped students make sense of the problem situation while other representations were used as tools for finding solutions to the word problem.

Representations for Understanding Word Problems

One purpose for using representations is to understand or discern the mathematical relationships among the quantities in problem situations. Students can generate representations to mathematize, that is, "to organize and interpret their world through a mathematical lens" (Fosnot and Dolk 2001, p. 10). Tape diagrams are one means for organizing and depicting relations among quantities. In this particular example, some teachers would call them part-part-whole diagrams, given that the situation only describes two parts of a total amount. Ms. Shea calls them tape diagrams with her students. She knows that her school district expects students to grow in their sophistication of using tape diagrams across the grades. She is starting her students on a journey of using tape diagrams beginning with addition and subtraction word problems, which will be extended to multiplication and division situations in later elementary grades, and then to ratio, proportional relationship, and algebra problems in the middle grades.

Three students used tape diagrams to represent the problem situation and discern the relationships among the known and unknown quantities in the word problem. Natalia wrote "13 children" in one part of her tape diagram and wrote "? joined" in the other part. Shyanne wrote "13 were" in one part indicating that 13 children were on the swings and wrote "? joined" in the other part. Lucas wrote "13" in one part and then wrote "joined ?" in the other part. All three students indicated that the total amount in the tape diagram was 21. Natalia and Lucas drew a line segment horizontal and equal in length to the base of the rectangle and wrote 21 by it. Lucas even wrote the word "totale" on the line. Shyanne also showed in her picture that the total was 21.

The tape diagram helped these students consider the relationships among the quantities in the word problem as well as to identify the relationship of the unknown amount to the other quantities. Specifically, the students realized the total amount was 21, that the known part (addend) was 13, and that they needed to figure out the size of the unknown part (the missing addend). Natalia, Lucas, and Shyanne also wrote missing addend number sentences (e.g., 13 + ? = 21) that matched their tape diagram. While Adam did not draw a tape diagram, it is likely that writing an equation that matched the structure of the problem situation helped Adam understand the relationships among the quantities because he showed the unknown amount as both a box and a question mark. It is not as evident how Elissa and Hayley came to discern the relationships among the quantities, and it might be worth a follow-up question from the teacher asking, "How did you know you had to find the missing part rather than just add the two numbers together?" or "Can you put something on your paper to show me how you knew you had to find the missing part?"

Representations as Flexible Tools for Solving Word Problems

Another purpose for using representations is that they serve as tools for solving problems. To broaden student access and success in problem solving, students need to learn that they can use representations flexibly to solve problems. From the set of student work from Ms. Shea's classroom, we can see that her students are already learning to use both visual and symbolic representations as tools to mediate their understanding, reasoning, and problem solving.

Three students, Adam, Natalia, and Elissa, drew sticks and dots to visually represent tens and ones. The students are accustomed to representing quantities using connecting cubes to form sticks of ten. The drawings reflect their internal representations of this previous work with the cubes. Natalia even labels her stick as "10." Ms. Shea observed all three students drawing one ten stick and three dots, and then counting on by ones until they reached 21, drawing one dot for each count. Adam and Elissa drew a line to separate the dots that represented the students on the swings from those who joined them, as well as carefully organized the dots so no more than ten dots would be in a column. Natalia used the sticks and dots differently. She started a new column of dots to separate the known and unknown number of children.

Four children drew open number lines on their paper. Elissa, however, did not use it as a tool to solve the problem. In fact, Elissa drew the open number line after she had already found the answer using the sticks and dots representation. She showed the relationship among the numbers on the open number line and, perhaps, was beginning to explore how she might use the open number line as a tool in her math work. On the other hand, Shyanne, Lucas, and Hayley each used the open number line as a tool for finding the answer to the Swings task and each used it in a different flexible manner. Shyanne made a jump of 2 to get to 15, then a jump of 5 to get to 20, and then a jump of 1 to get to 21. Then she must have added up her jumps to get an answer of 8 children. Lucas made a jump of 7 to get to 20 and then a jump of 1 to get to 21. Hayley's work is very interesting. While her use of the open number line is unconventional, it clearly shows her reasoning. She made a jump of 10 from 13 to 23, and knew she had made 2 jumps too many and needed to subtract 2. Her equation also clearly supports her reasoning, as she wrote, "13 + 10 – 2 = 21." In time, Hayley will learn other ways to represent her reasoning on the open number line that maintain an ordinal sequence. For now, Ms. Shea was proud of Hayley in using 10 as part of her strategy and proud of her perseverance in figuring out a way to represent her reasoning with both visual and symbolic representations.

These students' reasoning and representations matched the structure of the problem. As adults, we recognize the underlying structure of subtraction within missing addend problems, but these young learners more naturally follow the story line of the problem situation. Through their flexible use of several different representations, the students are already beginning to abstract and model numerical relationships found in problem situations and could benefit from further discussion of how their representations are similar and different. It is important that learning about representations does not become the end product but rather that students come to view representations as tools for solving problems (Greeno and Hall 1997). Teaching with a focus on representations includes providing students with regular opportunities to make choices about which forms of representation to use in approaching problems, as well as facilitating class discourse that examines and compares the advantages or suitability of using various representations for different types of problem situations.

Teaching for Representational Competence

Representations play an important role in the development of students' mathematical understanding and proficiency, and the use of representations has long been advocated in the teaching of mathematics (Bruner 1966; NCTM 1989, 2000). In fact, Collins (2011) argued that "the teaching of representational competence should lie at the center of classroom practice in math and science" (p. 105). In essence, representational competence in mathematics is students' ability to work successfully with and move flexibly among varied representations. This includes creating, evaluating, and refining a variety of representational forms (diSessa and Cobb 2004).

Three specific instructional strategies to support students' development of representational competence are suggested by Marshall, Superfine, and Canty (2010, p. 40). They include—

- engaging in dialogue about the explicit connections between representations;
- alternating directionality of the connections made among representations; and
- encouraging purposeful selection of representations.

Engage in ATL 6.3: Shifting Instruction to a Focus on Representations

In ATL 6.3, you examine vignettes of two teachers, Ms. Robinson, a first-grade teacher, and Mr. Martinez, a fourth-grade teacher, who are both making a shift to teaching with representations as a central component of their instructional practice. These teachers now allow their students more choice of representations in solving problems. Ms. Robinson remarked, "Now I let students select and use their own representations. I think one of the biggest changes for me is the idea of students being able to show diverse representations and how that starts with me allowing them to use different representations." Mr. Martinez noted, "I want to see students be flexible in using multiple representations, so I often let them decide what representations they want to use. I've also noticed that when students get stuck, they don't give up as easily but often go to another representation, usually from symbolic to something more visual or concrete, especially when we work with fractions." Both teachers display the representation diagram (see fig. 6.1) as a poster in their classrooms. The poster serves, not only as a reminder to the teachers but also to their students that making connections among representations is a valued aspect of learning mathematics.

Analyzing Teaching and Learning 6.3

Shifting Instruction to a Focus on Representations

Read the two following vignettes. Each vignette illustrates how teachers are shifting their instruction to focus on teaching for representational competence.

- In what ways does the increased focus on representations strengthen each teacher's instructional practice and deepen students' mathematical understanding?

- Which of the three instructional strategies are evident in each vignette—engage in dialogue on explicit connections, alternate directionality, or student selection of representations?

Vignette 1: What Is the Same? What Is Different?

Ms. Robinson teaches first grade. One day she posed the following problem to her students, "Clare has 12 bears and 8 chairs. If all the bears want to sit on a chair, how many bears won't get a chair?" This problem is aligned with her learning goal for students to understand and represent comparison problem situations. Some students chose to use bear counters and chairs, whereas others used connecting cubes, number paths, or ten frames. A few students decided to draw pictures on paper.

After some work time, the students were told to explain their thinking and use of the math tools to a partner. For example, Ashley explained to her partner, "I made a train of 12 cubes and a train of 8 cubes and matched them up." Her partner, Samuel, explained, "I set out 8 chairs and then I put the bears on the chairs and 4 didn't get a chair." Next Ms. Robinson asked the partners to compare what they did and talk about "what was the same" and "what was different."

The teacher monitored the conversations and selected some pairs to present their work in the whole-class discussion. She first gathered the students around Ashley and Samuel who explained their reasoning strategies. Then the class compared their approaches. One student observed, "They both showed 8 and 12 but they used different things." Another student noted, "They both found that 4 bears didn't get a chair." After a few more observations, the class moved to another pair of students.

Shown below is the work of Donell and Jayla, who shared their thinking with the class. Then Ms. Robinson asked her students to discuss what was the same and what was different in the drawings. Some student observations included the following: "They both made jumps." "They both counted 1, 2, 3, 4." "Donell drew all the chairs and bears and Jayla didn't." "Jayla had a tape diagram." "Jayla wrote the numbers 8, 9, 10, 11, 12. Donell used the number path."

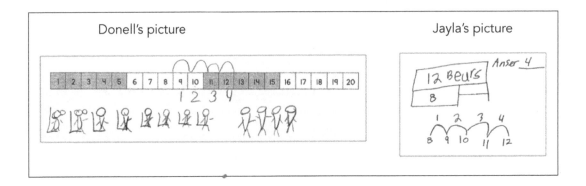

Ms. Robinson closed the lesson by asking, "So, I'm wondering how did you decide what math tool to use to help you solve the problem?" After some sharing, she also asked her students whether they would use the same tool or might try a different math tool the next time they solved a similar problem and why. Overall Ms. Robinson is pleased with the progress of her students in making sense of comparison problem situations by using a variety of representations.

As Ms. Robinson reflected on the shifts in her teaching with representations, she commented, "I've made a big change this year from simply having my students share their strategies and representations to actually having them compare their work with each other. In the past it was really just more show and tell; now I ask students to tell what is similar and different about their representations."

Vignette 2: Tell a Story; Show a Picture

Mr. Martinez teaches fourth grade. In the past he did not place much emphasis on contextual or visual representations, but now they play a central role in his teaching. One approach he often uses is to reverse directionality. He explained, "I ask students to create a context that would fit the number problem. Oftentimes this will cue me into whether or not the student understands the operation or is just trying to memorize a procedure." For example, he recently asked his students to "tell a story" to match $5 - \frac{2}{3}$ and then to "show a picture" of the situation. Below are responses from two students.

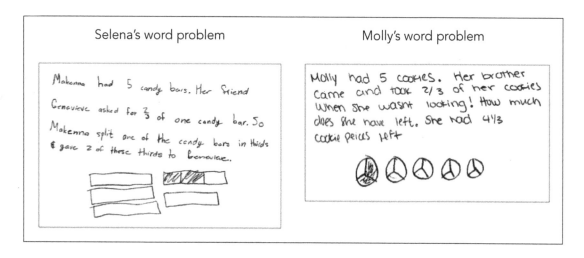

Selena's word problem	Molly's word problem
Makenna had 5 candy bars. Her friend Genevieve asked for $\frac{2}{3}$ of one candy bar. So Makenna split one of the candy bars in thirds & gave 2 of these thirds to Genevieve.	Molly had 5 cookies. Her brother came and took 2/3 of her cookies when she wasn't looking! How much does she have left. She had 4¹/₃ cookie peices left

Selena showed she has a clear understanding of the meaning of $\frac{2}{3}$ in the equation, that it represents part of one referent whole. Whereas Molly could find the correct answer to the equation using her picture, she did not show understanding of the meaning of $\frac{2}{3}$ in context as she states her brother took "$\frac{2}{3}$ of her cookies" implying $\frac{2}{3}$ of all 5 cookies rather than taking $\frac{2}{3}$ of just 1 cookie.

Mr. Martinez wonders how many students left his classroom with this misunderstanding about the referent whole in previous years. He also realized that most stories were about candy bars and cookies and that the diagrams rarely included number lines; something he definitely needs to address. Now he is planning to bring in more linear measurements and contexts. A simple request to alternate directionality, connecting from the equation to a context or story, is now a common task in Mr. Martinez's classroom whether students are working with whole numbers, decimals, or fractions.

As he thought about the shifts he has made in his teaching with representations, he remarked, "I am now a firm believer that students have to use multiple representations. I even keep a poster of the representations up in my classroom and we refer to it almost every day. If students are only able to use one of the types of representation, they just do not know the topic as deeply as needed."

Analysis of ATL 6.3. Development of Representational Competence

Teaching for representational competence includes developing students' knowledge of specific representations while fostering students' ability to move flexibly among varied representations as tools to make sense of and successfully solve problems (Huinker 2015b). This involves creating teaching and learning environments that value the central role of representations in learning mathematics. Both Ms. Robinson and Mr. Martinez are shifting to teaching with representations and would say that representations now permeate their mathematics instruction. We now look more closely at how these teachers are developing students' representational competence by encouraging them to make purposeful selection of representations, asking them to alternate directionality in translating between representations, and engaging them in dialogue on explicit connections between representations.

Student selection of representations

Let's begin with the vignette of Ms. Robinson. She often allows her first-grade students to make choices about which forms of representation to use as tools for solving problems. She notices that her young learners are very flexible in their use of representations. The students know they can use more than one type of representation, as well as switch among representations, when solving problems. Her students also know that they have to be able to explain their thinking to the teacher and to the other students. The teacher's new focus on also having the students compare their work with each other is more challenging for these learners who are usually very eager to talk about their own thinking and ideas. Ms. Robinson is pressing them regularly to consider the work of their peers as she often asks them to talk about "what is the same" and "what is different" in their problem representations.

The vignette describes the lesson in which the students were solving a word problem about Clare's 12 bears and 8 chairs. The teacher allowed the students to choose whether they wanted to use physical representations, such as bear counters and chairs, connecting cubes, number paths, or ten frames, or whether they wanted to create a visual representation and draw pictures on paper. Many students chose the bears and chairs or connecting cubes, while other students chose to use a number path or to draw on paper.

Ms. Robinson expects her students to share their thinking, and she is working to hold them more accountable for listening to and trying to understand the thinking of their classmates. One way she does this is by having partners explain to each other how they used the various math tools or representations to solve the problem. For example, Ashley explained to her partner Samuel how she "made a train of 12 cubes and a train of 8 cubes and matched them up." Then Samuel explained, "I set out 8 chairs and then I put the bears on the chairs and 4 didn't get a chair." This partner talk also gives the students a chance to try out and rehearse their explanations in preparation to share them with the class.

To press students to compare their use of strategies and representations with each other requires teacher facilitation and questioning. In the lesson, Ms. Robinson first had the students gather around Ashley and Samuel as they explained their thinking. Then the teacher asked the students to describe what was the same and what was different in how they solved the problem. One student observed, "They both showed 8 and 12 but they used different things." Another student noted, "They both found that 4 bears didn't get a chair." After a few observations, the class moved to examine the work of Donell and Jayla.

Donell first drew the chairs and then put bears on them in his drawing, and then also marked the number path. Jayla used a tape diagram and then showed how she counted on from 8 to 12. While the representations were different, classmates observed that both students used the same strategy of counting on and that they both wrote out the numbers to show how they counted. The students are slowly making strides in beginning to orient themselves a bit more to the reasoning and work of their peers and becoming more astute at noticing what is the same and what is different. Ms. Robinson has also begun to ask students to consider and talk about the advantages and suitability of various representations when solving problems. For example, many students thought using the bears and chairs was a good idea because it was easy to see the bears and chairs, but it took a while to set it all up. They seem to favor the connecting cubes because they could be snapped together in two trains and then matched up, but you couldn't tell which train of cubes was the bears and which was the chairs because they were all just cubes. Most students were less sure of using the number path, which was a fairly new tool for them.

Student ability to alternate directionality

Now let's look more closely at the vignette of Mr. Martinez. He places strong emphasis on developing and assessing his students' ability to move back and forth between representations. He feels this is particularly important for his fourth-grade students so that he can probe into the depth of their mathematical understanding and address any knowledge gaps or faulty ideas. He often gives students an equation and then prompts, "Tell a story" or "Show a picture." This has become a core expectation in his classroom throughout the school year as students are presented with addition, subtraction, multiplication, and division equations for whole numbers, fractions, and decimals.

In particular, Mr. Martinez knows that students often confuse contextual situations for subtraction with fractions to that of multiplication with fractions. He wants to make sure his students understand the meaning of each fraction in an equation for a specific operation and how it relates to the referent whole. He also wants to see if his students are clear and precise in their language when describing contextual situations for fractions. Thus, he asked his students to tell a story for $5 - \frac{2}{3}$.

Selena is very explicit in her word problem about the meaning of each fraction in relation to both the operation and the referent whole. She clearly states, "Genevieve asked for $\frac{2}{3}$ of one candy bar" indicating that the $^2/_3$ refers to the referent whole, in this case, a candy bar. She goes on to state, "Makenna split one of the candy bars in thirds and gave 2 of these thirds to Genevieve." Again she is very precise about the meaning of $^2/_3$—that it refers to 1 candy bar— and that it was this part of 1 candy bar that is subtracted. Selena's picture also closely matches the story context and illustrates 5 whole candy bars and the removal of 2 parts of size $^1/_3$ of 1 candy bar.

Molly draws a picture that clearly shows 5 whole objects, cookies in this case, with each cookie cut into three, approximately equal parts, and then shades 2 pieces of size $^1/_3$ of a cookie. If Molly had just been asked to draw a picture, the teacher might have concluded that she understands subtraction with fractions as she successfully translated from the equation to the visual representation. By also asking her to tell a story, her tentative understanding of the referent whole emerges. In her story, the $^2/_3$ refers to the set of 5 cookies, not to just 1 cookie when she writes, "Her brother came and took $^2/_3$ of her cookies." Thus, she is telling a story about $^2/_3 \times 5$, which would result in her brother taking 3 $^1/_3$ cookies. Her question, "How much does she have left" is appropriate for a subtraction context, but would result in a multi-step problem for the multiplication context, that is, if her brother ate 3 $^1/_3$ cookies, then Molly would have 1 $^2/_3$ cookies remaining. Molly again loses track of the referent whole as she wrote her answer as "She had 4 $^1/_3$ cookie pieces left" now referring to pieces rather than whole cookies.

By alternating the usual directionality of connections between representations, Mr. Martinez surfaced evidence of what his students understood well and what was muddled in their thinking that might otherwise have stayed hidden. The teacher knows he needs to spend more instructional time on the referent whole and ensure his students can articulate the meaning of each number in an equation. He will also have students solve and pose more word problems for situations with fractions. Mr. Martinez also made several additional observations that have implications for his instruction. He noticed that most of the story problems were about candy bars and cookies and that the diagrams rarely included number lines. Thus, he intends to bring in more contextual examples that include linear measurements and have his students work more with number lines.

Engage students in dialogue on explicit connections

An important aspect of representational competence is students' ability to translate from one representational form to another. Both Ms. Robinson and Mr. Martinez engaged their students in dialogue on explicit connections that included connections between different modes of representation and connections within modes of representation. The distinction of the words "between" and "within" is intentional (Huinker 2015a). Teaching with representations focuses on two types of translations, as depicted in the modified diagram in figure 6.4. The first type of translation, between representational modes, is the one that we more commonly associate with the diagram. This is shown by the orange arrows between different modes of representations, such as moving from a visual diagram to a symbolic equation. The second type of translation is shown by the curved gray arrows and depicts moving within a specific mode of representation. For example, comparing an array model to a set model for 7 × 35 is an example of making an explicit connection from one visual representation to another visual representation. Another example of within connections is comparing equivalent expressions and equations, such as 7 × 35 = 7 × (30 + 5) = 7 × 30 + 7 × 5.

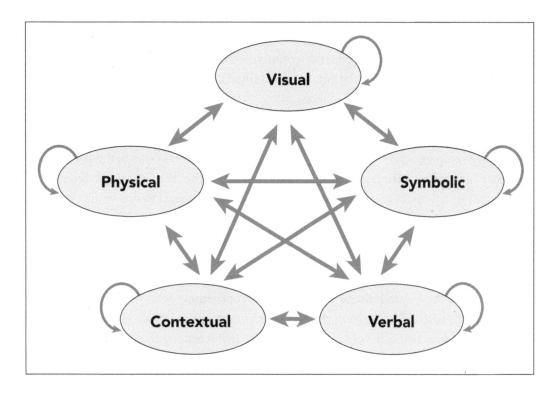

Fig. 6.4. Connections within modes of representation (Huinker 2015a)

Let's return to the vignette of Ms. Robinson. She asked students to explain how their representation showed 12 bears and 8 chairs, making a connection *between* the context of the story and their physical or visual representations. She also asked students to translate *within* specific modes of representations. For example, she asked students to identify how Ashley showed 12 bears (with the bear counters) and how Samuel showed 12 bears (with the connecting cubes). This comparison involved translating from one physical representation to another physical representation. She also asked the students to explain how Donell showed the answer of 4 on his number path diagram and how Jayla showed the answer of 4 bears in her picture. This engaged the students in dialogue on explicit connections *within* visual representations. The focus on explicit connections between and within representations focuses students' attention on the underlying structure of the mathematical ideas. Tripathi (2008) noted that discussing connections among "different representations is like examining the concept through a variety of lenses, with each lens providing a different perspective that makes the picture [concept] richer and deeper" (p. 439).

Mr. Martinez also firmly believes in the importance of viewing a concept through multiple lenses because each representation brings a distinctive perspective that deepens and enriches students' understanding. His vignette presents the work of Selena and Molly. In a class discussion, Mr. Martinez began by asking his students to talk about how each picture shows the $5 - \frac{2}{3}$, explicitly translating *between* symbolic and visual representations. He then also asked the students to translate *within* visual representations by asking his students to compare the two visual depictions (the rectangular candy bars and the circular cookies) to each other. The students noticed that both showed 5 objects, either rectangles or circles. However, Selena only partitioned one rectangle into thirds, whereas Molly partitioned all the circles into thirds. The class concluded that it was not necessary to partition all the circles.

Next they compared the two story problems, translating *within* contextual representations. The students noticed how the 5 was clear in both stories, but that the $\frac{2}{3}$ seemed different across the two situations. Selena clearly indicated that the $\frac{2}{3}$ referred to one whole, in her case one whole candy bar. Molly realized from this discussion that her $\frac{2}{3}$ referred to all of the cookies and that she needed to revise her story. Students also noticed that Selena did not have a question or answer in her story problem, whereas Molly had a question that would work for a subtraction situation, but her answer of "She had $4\frac{1}{3}$ cookie pieces left" did not seem appropriate. The focused discussions on explicit connections *between* and *within* modes of representations surfaced underlying mathematical structures and made essential features of mathematical ideas visible for examination and discussion leading to deeper and richer mathematical understanding.

What the Research Says: Representations and Student Learning

Representations play an important role in the development of students' mathematical understanding. It is through representations that students come "to understand the abstract concepts that are central to mathematics learning" (Pape and Tchoshanov 2001, p. 118). Students use representations to learn new mathematical concepts, deepen understanding of existing concepts, and to support sense making when they are solving mathematical or contextual problems. Thus it is important for teachers to emphasize representations in their teaching (Collins 2011) because their instruction, in turn, influences students' own knowledge of and ability to use representations.

All of mathematics is abstract because it is about relationships that humans use to quantify, describe, and make sense of their world. Kamii and colleagues (Kamii, Kirkland, and Lewis 2001), on the basis of the work of Piaget, describe our mental constructs of these relationships as logical mathematical knowledge. The key idea to keep in mind is that relationships do not exist in the external world, but must be constructed by each individual inside his or her own mind. For example, the fraction $5/4$ is not something that just exists but is a relationship we impose on an object or an event, such as has walking $5/4$ miles. Thus, when we use the term *representations* in teaching mathematics, we are usually referring to external representations, such as contextual, physical, visual, verbal, and symbolic representations (see fig. 6.1). These external representations give us greater access to our internal mental representations and allow us to examine, discuss, and explore mathematical ideas with others. Asking students to describe their mathematical thinking with multiple representations allows us as their teachers to gain a better sense of the internalized understandings, as well as faulty ideas or misunderstandings, that students hold about abstract mathematical ideas (Goldin and Shteingold 2001).

Dreyfus and Eisenberg (1996) argued that flexibility in moving across or between representations is a hallmark of competent mathematical thinking and understanding as each representation highlights critical features or reveals different structural aspects of a mathematical concept or action. This use of multiple representations can be generally defined as providing the same information in more than one form of external representation (Goldin and Shteingold 2001). Consider further the fraction "$5/4$." Physical and visual representations allow students to see the meaning of this fraction symbol and express it verbally as "5 parts of size $1/4$" or perhaps as "5 lengths with each length being $1/4$ mile long." Contextual representations deepen understanding even more as students relate the mathematical idea to their everyday lives and realize it can be used in many different settings, such as to quantify or operate with discrete or continuous measures (e.g., $5/4$ meters of rope or the amount each person receives when 5 cookies are shared equally among 4 people).

Not only should students be able to understand and translate between modes of representations but they should also translate within a specific type of representation (Lesh, Post, and Behr 1987). For example, connections from one symbolic representation to another, such as comparing equivalent expressions, are extremely valuable in extending understanding. When students understand that "$5/4$" is equivalent to "$4/4 + 1/4$," as well as to "$1/4 + 1/4 + 1/4 + 1/4 + 1/4$" or "$10/8$" or "1.25" or even "125%," their understanding becomes stronger, deeper, and more accessible in solving problems. As another example, consider which visual representations your students might use to show a multiplication relationship, such as 5×27. Students might draw groups of discrete circles or tally marks, arrays, area models, tape diagrams, or number lines. Each visual representation reveals some aspect of the underlying structure of the mathematical idea and each contributes to deepening student understanding.

Representational competence in mathematics includes the ability to use representations meaningfully to understand and solve problems (Marshall, Superfine, and Canty 2010). In the literature, this ability is sometimes referred to as "representational flexibility" (Greer, 2009), "representational fluency" (Nathan et al. 2010), or "representational thinking" (Pape and Tchoshanov 2001). Regardless of the term, each emphasizes the value of students' ability to work proficiently with varied representations and how that ability supports students' success in learning mathematics. Collins (2011) argued that teaching to develop representational competence among students should be central to mathematics instruction. He even suggested, "Mathematics education focuses a lot of time and effort on teaching algorithms, which technological artifacts are able to carry out for them. The time might be better spent in helping students build a strong representational competence" (p. 108).

Unfortunately, teaching for representational competence is not a focus nor goal in many mathematics classrooms. Cross-national analyses of mathematics curricula and textbooks show that U.S. students have less systematic exposure to multiple representations than Asian students (Mayer, Sims, and Tajika 1995). Brenner and colleagues (1999) also found that students in high performing countries were more skilled in using and translating among representations than students in the United States. They examined the representational skills of sixth-grade students in different countries and found Chinese and Taiwanese students were nearly five times and Japanese students were nearly three times as likely as U.S. students to correctly respond to items in which they were asked to translate between (e.g., from a diagram to symbols) and within (e.g., from one symbolic expression to an equivalent expression) modes of representation. The focal teaching practice discussed in this chapter, "use and connect mathematical representations," highlights and elevates the need for a stronger focus on teaching for representational competence in our mathematics classrooms as an important and high-leverage teaching practice for raising student success in mathematics.

Promoting Equity by Using and Connecting Mathematical Representations

Equitable teaching of mathematics includes a focus on multiple representations. This includes giving students choice in selecting representations and allocating substantial instructional time and space for students to explore, construct, and discuss external representations of mathematical ideas. As students use and translate among external representations—contextual, physical, visual, verbal, and symbolic—their mathematical knowledge becomes stronger, deeper, and more usable in solving problems (Greeno 1987; Lesh, Post, and Behr 1987; Webb, Boswinkel, and Dekker 2008). This focus on multiple mathematical representations supports the equity-based practice to *go deep with the mathematics* (Aguirre, Mayfield-Ingram, and Martin 2013). Too often students see mathematics as isolated facts and rules to be memorized. In classrooms such as those of Ms. Robinson and Ms. Shea, students are expected to develop deep and connected knowledge of mathematics and are engaged in learning environments rich in use of multiple representations. Mathematics learning is not a one size fits all approach in their classrooms, meaning not every child is expected to engage in the mathematics in the same way at the same time. Their students are allowed choice in mathematical tools (physical representations), such as cubes, number paths, or ten frames, and in visual representations; the diversity of their sense-making approaches is reflected in the diversity of their representations. In addition, the teachers check in regularly, like Mr. Martinez, on their students' abilities to translate between and within representations so that shallow or faulty ideas are identified and addressed rather than allowing students to move on with limited ideas and gaps that are more likely to widen as students progress in their study of mathematics.

This use of multiple mathematical representations allows students to draw on multiple resources of knowledge, another of the five equity-based practices (Aguirre, Mayfield-Ingram, and Martin 2013). For example, asking students to pose their own contextual examples of mathematical concepts and operations, such as describing examples of using fractions and percentages in their lives, recognizes and positions students as a source of knowledge and as authors and owners of mathematical examples. In equitable classrooms teachers regularly "recognize and intentionally tap students' knowledge and experiences—mathematical, cultural, linguistic, peer, family, and community—as resources for mathematics teaching and learning" (Aguirre, Mayfield-Ingram, and Martin 2013, p. 43). Embedding mathematics in a cultural context that matters to students (Ladson-Billings 2009) not only allows students to see themselves as part of a mathematical world outside of school it also brings their world into the mathematics classroom and curriculum.

For example, Leonard and Guha (2002) describe how they created a culturally relevant learning experience for students in Grades 2 to 5. During a walk around the children's neighborhood, the students took pictures of sites and people in their community, and then the students used the photos to write word problems. Some of the pictures included the church marquee, an individual carrying groceries, a history marker about the church, and a local street. The students were highly motivated to engage in the mathematical work and they wrote word problems that placed mathematics in their everyday cultural context or that involved community problems or issues. This powerful example shows students how mathematics learning activities and tasks can affirm students' cultural experiences (Ukpokodu 2011), uphold their identities (Wlodkowski and Ginsberg 1995), and develop student agency (Schoenfeld 2014) to engage mathematically by examining real problems that affect issues and situations in students' lives.

Taking Action in Your Classroom

Throughout the chapter you have examined and considered ways that teachers focus on teaching with representations to deepen students' understanding and support their flexible use of representations in problem solving. Here we summarize some of the key messages for you to keep in mind as you take action in your own classroom.

- Teaching for representational competence needs to be a priority in mathematics classrooms.

- Students should often engage in explicit dialogue on connections among representations, be asked to alternate directionality between representations, and make decisions on which representations to use in solving problems.

- Instruction needs to focus on interconnections among all five modes of representations—contextual, physical, visual, verbal, and symbolic.

- Task implementation that provides multiple entry points differentiates instruction by allowing students to select and use varied representations to make sense of the mathematics.

- Comparing multiple representations helps students discern underlying mathematical structures and essential features of mathematical ideas that persist regardless of the form of representation.

- Student flexibility in moving between and within all five modes of representation is a hallmark of competent mathematical thinking and deep understanding of mathematics.

- Learning to use representations is not the end goal, but rather it is to empower students to use varied representations as tools to understand mathematical ideas and to solve problems.

We now invite you to take action as you consider what implications the ideas discussed in this chapter have for your own professional setting. We suggest you select a topic that you are currently teaching and check in on students' ability to translate proficiently among different representations. Then consider the implications for your own teaching and how you might deepen student understanding of that topic by teaching for representational competence.

Taking Action in Your Classroom
Assessing Proficiency to Translate Among Representations

Select a mathematics topic that you are currently teaching and design an assessment to check in on your students' ability to translate between specific modes of representations. Below are some translation suggestions to keep in mind as you design your assessment.

- From a tape diagram, array, or open number line (visual) to telling a story (contextual)

- From an array (visual) to describing it (verbal)

- From an array or open number line (visual) to writing an equation (symbolic)

- From an equation (symbolic) to explaining the meaning of each number (verbal)

- From an equation (symbolic) to telling a story (contextual)

- From an equation (symbolic) to drawing a picture or diagram (visual)

- From an equation (symbolic) to acting out the operation using objects (physical)

Then give the assessment to your students, analyze it, and determine implications for your teaching of that topic.

- Which translations were solid for your students as a class?

- Which translations were problematic for many students?

- What else did you notice as strengths or limitations in your students' representations?

- What are some next steps you can implement now to strengthen your students' representational competence?

CHAPTER 7

Facilitate Meaningful Mathematical Discourse

Instruction focused on mathematical discourse engages students as active participants in making sense of mathematical ideas and reasoning about mathematical relationships. NCTM (2014) defines discourse as "the purposeful exchange of ideas through classroom discussion, as well as through other forms of verbal, visual, and written communication" (p. 29). In this chapter we will explore the effective teaching practice, *facilitate meaningful mathematical discourse*. According to *Principles to Actions: Ensuring Mathematical Success for All* (NCTM 2014, p. 12):

> Effective teaching of mathematics facilitates discourse among students to build shared understanding of mathematical ideas by analyzing and comparing student approaches and arguments.

Mathematical discourse is the vehicle by which students express their ideas about mathematical topics and clarify mathematical understanding. It is through discourse that students internalize new mathematical ideas as they connect prior knowledge to new knowledge, as well as recognize the need to reorganize or reconceptualize certain ideas as they determine what they do not understand clearly (Fuson, Kalchman, and Bransford 2005). It is through whole-class discussions as students engage in discourse related to their mathematical observations, ideas, and strategies that students build shared mathematical understanding and develop into mathematical learning communities.

The chapter includes four Analyzing Teaching and Learning (ATL) activities.

- ATL 7.1: Revisit "The Case of Robert Harris and the Band Concert Task" and identify ways in which the teacher engaged his students in mathematical discourse throughout the lesson.

- ATL 7.2: Read a transcript excerpt of a first-grade lesson and look closely at the role of the teacher and the role of the students as they engage in a whole-class discussion.

- ATL 7.3: Anticipate student approaches to solving a fraction task and consider how the preparation to teach the lesson supports a teacher's ability to facilitate meaningful discourse during this lesson.

- ATL 7.4: Examine student work from the fraction task, select and sequence student work for a whole-class discussion, and identify important mathematical connections for student learning.

As you engage in each ATL, we encourage you to make note of your responses, and if possible, share and discuss your ideas with colleagues. Once you share or write down your thoughts, continue reading the analysis of the ATL in which we relate the activity to the chapter's focal teaching practice. After the Analyzing Teaching and Learning activities, the chapter includes research findings related to mathematical discourse and then examines how the focal teaching practice promotes equity among students. We end the chapter with some suggestions for applying the ideas related to mathematical discourse in your own classroom.

Examining Mathematical Discourse

Discourse entails making sense of mathematical ideas, including making connections among varied representations and comparing student approaches in solving mathematical tasks. Most often discourse entails verbal communication, that is, students talking about mathematics with other students or the teacher. Discourse as written mathematical communication includes writing sentences and even paragraphs, as well as other representational means to communicate students' sense-making attempts, such as drawing diagrams, making tables, graphical displays, or writing equations. In essence, mathematical discourse entails the ways humans attempt to communicate their thoughts and observations with each other with the goal to build a shared understanding of mathematical ideas.

Engage in ATL 7.1: Discourse in the Case of Robert Harris

As you engage in ATL 7.1, you will revisit "The Case of Robert Harris and the Band Concert Task" presented in chapter 1 and examine the various opportunities for students to engage in mathematical discourse throughout the lesson. The case, as you may recall, presents a lesson on multiplication with third-grade students. The students are tasked with making sense of a problem situation involving 7 rows of chairs with 20 chairs in each row.

Reread "The Case of Robert Harris and the Band Concert Task" (see ATL 1.1, page 10). Read through the case with the objective of identifying ways in which students engage in mathematical discourse.

- What opportunities did students have to work with a partner during the lesson? What was the mathematical purpose of the partner interactions?

- What opportunities did students have to engage in whole-class discussions? What appeared to be the teacher's intended mathematical purpose in each of these class discussions?

- What opportunities did students have to write about or represent on paper their mathematical understanding, justifications, observations, or ponderings? What was the likely intent of the written communication?

Analysis of ATL 7.1: Building Shared Understanding of the Mathematics

Discourse takes many forms during a lesson. Robert Harris used three ways of engaging his students in mathematical discourse—partner discussions, whole-class discussions, and written mathematical work.

Partner Discussions

Mr. Harris was very intentional in his use of pair work during the lesson. The case notes five instances in which the teacher asked students to talk with a partner (lines 23–24, 46–48, 56–57, 83–84, 93–95). Interestingly, in all of these instances the students did not work together on the task, but rather the teacher used the pair discussions for students to clarify and share their ideas and work. For example, he stated, "Before you begin working on the task, think about a representation you might want to use and why, and then turn and share your ideas with a partner" (lines 23–24). This allowed students to clarify their understanding of the problem situation in the task, as well as provided an opportunity for students to get ideas from a peer on how one might represent the situation. You can imagine students weighing options with each other about how to represent it and why. This partner talk also caused students to slow down their thinking and processing of the task. Students are often eager to jump into a task without fully examining its parameters, so the partner discussion forced them to pause and consider aspects of the task a bit further before beginning to tackle it.

Similarly, before holding the whole-class discussion, the teacher asked the students to find a classmate who had used a representation different from their own and directed them to take turns explaining and comparing their work as well as their solutions (lines 46–48). This partner discussion had multiple purposes. It allowed students to check the accuracy of their work, and in Molly's case, get assistance from a peer. It gave all students a chance to share their work on the task, allowing everyone to voice their ideas and have their work valued given that not all students can present during the whole-class discussion. It provided a rehearsal for those students who would be presenting, which is particularly important for students for whom English is not a first language or who might be nervous or anxious to present their work to the class. Most important, it engaged students with the mathematical ideas that were the goal of the lesson as peers compared their work with each other. It is clear that Mr. Harris valued this peer sharing of their solutions as he asked them to find a new partner and repeat the process once more (lines 56–57).

In the midst of the whole-class discussion, Mr. Harris had his students turn and talk to a partner after he wrote the equation $7 \times 20 = 140$ on the board, "Some of you wrote this equation on your papers. How does this equation relate to each of the strategies that we have discussed so far? Turn and talk to a partner about this equation" (lines 81–84). Mr. Harris had noticed that many students had not written a multiplication equation on their papers, and given that this was one of his learning goals for the lesson, this brief partner discussion allowed all students a chance to talk about this important mathematical idea. It again also provided a quick rehearsal and voicing of ideas, which usually results in more students being willing to speak up during the whole-class discussion.

The final partner discussion occurred close to the end of the lesson (lines 93–95). Tyrell and Ananda had just presented their work, and Mr. Harris knew the decomposition of 20 into 2 tens and their informal use of the distributive property were important ideas for his students. He also knew that the approaches of these two students were not common within the class. The quick turn and talk marked their approaches as important and caused the students to pause and consider these representations a bit further.

Whole-Class Discussions

An important component of any lesson is the whole-class discussion as the teacher and students engage in discourse, building a shared understanding of the intended mathematics. While Mr. Harris held brief discussions with the whole class to launch the Band Concert task (lines 15–21) and consider potential representations (lines 22–25), the main class discussion occurred after the students worked on the task individually and shared their solutions in pairs. The purpose of the main class discussion was not merely to have students "show and tell" about their work but to engage students in making sense of the solution paths and ideas put forth by their peers in ways that highlight and connect mathematical ideas. Mr. Harris selected particular approaches used by students, and had them present their work in a specific order. He began with Jasmine and then Kenneth, comparing how they represented and then combined the 7 twenties (lines 59–62). Next, Teresa presented how she used skip counting, at which point Mr. Harris pressed the students to explain connections among skip counting, the context, and the meaning of multiplication in order to surface the underlying mathematical structure of multiplication (lines 63–80). Specifically, he wanted the students to explain how skip counting relates to having 7 groups with 20 objects in each group, which relates to 7 × 20. Throughout the class discussion, Mr. Harris engaged many students, pressing them to compare and connect the student approaches to important mathematical ideas.

Robert Harris was very intentional in how he structured his lesson. In fact, he based it on the five practices for orchestrating productive class discussions described by Smith and Stein (2011). As shown in figure 7.1, these practices begin by *anticipating* student solutions to a specific task and foreseeing questions to ask students related to each of the solutions. Although we have no direct evidence in the case regarding Mr. Harris's planning related to student thinking and preparing questions, without this information he would not have been able to interact with students as effectively as he did nor engage in the subsequent practices. During the student work time, we see Mr. Harris *monitoring* student struggles and successes, keeping track of who was doing what, and asking questions as needed to assess what students knew and advance them toward the goals of the lesson (lines 27–32). When the whole-class discussion begins, we see Mr. Harris *selecting* specific solution strategies that will be presented because of the mathematics they make available for discussion (lines 59–63, 91–93). Furthermore, the *sequencing* of those solution paths is intentional. Mr. Harris wanted to engage the entire class in the discussion and move them through a coherent mathematical storyline, which flows from the analysis of a visual diagram, to repeated addition, to skip counting, to the multiplication equation, and finally to a discussion of the distributive property. Throughout the lesson, Mr. Harris is continually pressing students to compare solution paths, *connecting* students' approaches to each other and to the key mathematical ideas of the lesson.

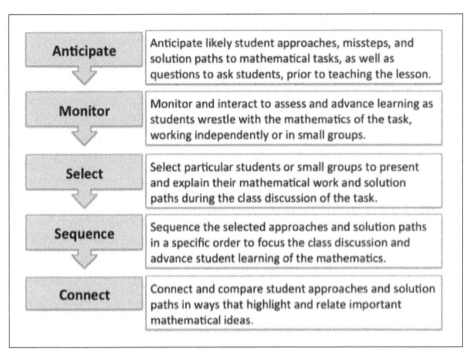

Fig. 7.1. Five practices in orchestrating productive class discussions

Written Communication

Another way that Robert Harris engages his students in discourse is by having them write about their mathematical thinking (lines 22–23, 94–95). Although it was not stated in the case, the students were expected to put their thinking on paper, even those who chose to use physical materials to represent and solve the problem. By pressing students to produce a written product, they must slow down their thinking and reflect on their ideas. This expectation holds every student accountable and makes it possible for each of them to contribute equally to partner, small-group, and whole-group discussions.

The written work provides formative information for the teacher to use as he interacts with individual students and in shaping the path he will take throughout the lesson. As the students worked, Mr. Harris made his way around the classroom making note of his students' written work (lines 32– 34). This gave him initial insights into his students' thinking, which then positioned him either to probe deeper into his students' understanding or to push his students ideas further, thus using purposeful questions in assessing and advancing student learning, as discussed in chapter 5. For example, on the basis of what he saw on students' papers, he asked students, "How does your drawing show the seven rows?" "How does your drawing show that there are twenty chairs in each row?" "Why are you adding all those twenties?" "How many twenties are you adding and why?" (lines 37–39).

The written work serves as a record of thinking and reasoning. In this way it is an artifact that students can discuss with each other in pairs and small groups as well as become a focus for the whole-class discussion. For example, when Mr. Harris asked the students to find someone in the class who had a different representation than they had used with whom to partner, the written work made it possible for students to find an individual who thought differently from themselves, which would likely lead to a richer peer conversation (lines 49–51, 58–59). The student written work, in essence, becomes a written dialogue, making it possible for students and the teacher to keep track of their thinking over the course of the lesson so that both can determine ways in which student understanding is evolving and deepening.

Toward the end of the lesson, Mr. Harris requests one more piece of written communication from his students in the form of a reflective response to a writing prompt (lines 93–95). After Tyrell and Ananda had presented their work, he asked his students to first "turn and talk" with a partner and to then put into writing their thoughts about whether or not it was okay to work with tens rather than twenties in solving the problem. Asking students to "talk then write" allows students to find words to express their thoughts and test out their ideas prior to writing, which then results in more elaboration in their written work (Huinker and Laughlin 1996). The meaning that is constructed through talk finds its way into students' writing and the writing further contributes to construction of meaning and understanding of the mathematics. This final piece of written discourse also served as an "exit ticket," providing Mr. Harris with insight into his students' evolving understanding that he used in planning subsequent lessons.

Teacher and Student Roles in Mathematical Discourse

When teachers and students engage in mathematical discourse, teachers can gain insight into students' thinking and provide them with opportunities to clarify, refine, and deepen their mathematical understanding. In our next Analyzing Teaching and Learning activity, we go into the classroom of Ms. Chavez where first-grade students are working on the Class Attendance task (see fig. 7.2). Take a moment to work through the task and make note of the mathematical ideas that are likely to emerge as students engage in making sense of the task.

Class Attendance Task

In our class, there are 17 students. Four students are absent today.

How many students are in attendance today?

Fig. 7.2. A missing-part problem situation for first grade

Ms. Chavez selected this task as an opportunity for students to use problem-solving strategies to solve a subtraction word problem and to wrestle with the meaning of subtraction as separating a whole amount into two parts, one known amount and one unknown amount. The task allows the teacher and students to engage in discourse on the relationship between addition and subtraction.

Engage in ATL 7.2: What is the Teacher Doing? What are Students Doing?

Several times each week Ms. Chavez and her first-grade students begin the day working with the attendance data for their class, so this is a familiar routine for the students. On this particular day, students first worked independently and then with a partner on the Class Attendance task (see fig. 7.2). As you engage in ATL 7.2, consider both the role of the teacher and the role of the students in meaningful mathematical discussion.

Analyzing Teaching and Learning 7.2
What is the Teacher Doing? What are Students Doing?

Read the excerpt of the class discussion (shown below) as the first-grade students examine various approaches to solving the Class Attendance task (see fig. 7.2).

- What is the role of the teacher in the class discourse and how does she engage students in thinking about the mathematics?
- Who asks the questions? Who provides the explanations?
- How are mathematical representations, specifically visual, physical (concrete objects), and verbal (specific language) supports, used during the discussion?
- What is the role of the students during the class discussion and to what extent are their ideas central to the mathematical discourse?

Ms. Chavez's Class Discussion of the Classroom Attendance Task

1	**Cameron:**	There are 13 students here today because I counted them *(points to his*
2		*counters).*
3	**Teacher:**	Say more. Can you show us what you did with the counters?
4	**Cameron:**	I said 4 students are absent *(child puts four counters in one section of a part-*
5		*part-whole mat)* and then I counted 5, 6, 7, 8, 9, 10, 11, 12, 13, 14, 15, 16, 17
6		*(he counts on 13 more and puts one counter for each count into the other section of*
7		*the mat.)*

8
9
10
11
12 **Students:** I agree. Me too. That's what I did.
13 **Teacher:** So we know 4 students are absent, that's the part we know, and we have to
14 find out how many are here today, that part is unknown or missing. How
15 many students are here today?
16 **Cameron:** Thirteen because I counted how many were in that other part.
17 **Shawn:** I got 13 too.
18 **Teacher:** So Cameron counted on. Can someone show us another way to solve the
19 problem? Kyra?
20 **Kyra:** I did 17 take away 4. I thought in my head 7 minus 4 is 3, and then I just
21 knew it was 13.
22 **Teacher:** Who thinks they understand what Kyra did and can use counters to explain
23 her thinking?
24 **William:** She started with 17 *(student shows 17 counters)*. And then she counted back
25 four *(removes 4 counters while counting back)*. She did 17, 16, 15, 14, and said
26 there were 13 left.
27
28
29
30
31
32
33
34 **Kyra:** I see what William did, but that's not what I said. I knew that 17 has 10
35 and 7 so I took the 4 away from the 7 and that left 3 and the 10 that I never
36 touched. *(Shows 10 and 7 counters, removes 4 from the group of 7, and then
37 points to the remaining 10 and 3.)*
38
39
40
41
42
43 **Teacher:** Who understands how Kyra's strategy is different from what William did?
44 Would anyone like to ask Kyra a question?
45 **William:** I see what you did. You just knew 7 minus 3 was 4, so then you added 10 and
46 3. Hmm. I counted back from 17. I like your way.
47 **Jordan:** I have a question. Why did you do it that way?
48 **Kyra:** I know 7 minus 4 is 3 so it was easier to just subtract that and then add
49 back 10.
50 **Jordan:** Oh, so it was just easier.

51	**Teacher:**	So some of you started with the whole amount 17 and removed the known
52		part, the 4. We could write the equation as 17 minus 4. (*Writes 17 – 4 = ___.*)
53		Some of you started with the known part and added on until you got to 17.
54		(*Records 4 + ___ = 17.*)
55	**William:**	I did it that way. I did 4 and counted until I got to 17. Then I counted those
56		up and got 13.
57	**Teacher:**	So Jordan and Cameron did 4 + __ = 17 and Kyra and William solved
58		17 – 4 = __. Can both of these equations be used to figure out the number of
59		students here today?
60	**Luis:**	You can do it either way.
61	**Shanica:**	They both have 17 and 4.
62	**Jenna:**	One is minus and one is adding. They both work.
63	**Fin:**	You get the same answer so it doesn't matter.
64	**Jenna:**	But they are different. My mom told me one is subtraction and one is
65		addition.
66	**Teacher:**	So why are we able to figure out how many students are in attendance by
67		either adding on or by removing some?
68	**Jason:**	Because you know we have 17 kids in our class and you know 4 kids are
69		absent so you remove them and it is 13. (*Ms. Chavez shows Jason's reasoning*
70		*on the part-part-whole mat; starting with 17 counters, she moves 4 into the*
71		*known part and moves the rest into the unknown part.*)
72	**Alisha:**	Or you can start with the 4 and say if they were here with the 13 we would
73		have all 17 of us. (*The teacher uses the part-part-whole mat to show Alisha's*
74		*reasoning.*)
75	**Teacher:**	So we can start with 4 in the part we know and add on counters to figure out
76		the missing part (*the teacher points to the part-part-whole mat*). Or the other
77		way is to start with the whole amount, then separate out the part we know,
78		and then put the rest into the unknown or the missing part.

Analysis of ATL 7.2: Components of a Math-Talk Community

Ms. Chavez and her students were engaged as a "math-talk community" in making sense of the various approaches for solving a missing-part problem, the two different ways to write equations, and the relationship between addition and subtraction. Hufferd-Ackles, Fuson, and Sherin (2015) identify five components for consideration when analyzing the mathematical discourse or "math-talk community" of a classroom: (1) teacher role, (2) questioning, (3) explaining mathematical thinking, (4) mathematical representations, and (5) building student responsibility within the community. For each component they describe four levels of moving from teacher-centered to student-centered discourse (see fig. 7.3). Take a few moments and read through the progression of levels for each of the five components. We use these components as a lens for examining the mathematical discourse in Ms. Chavez's classroom.

	Teacher role	Questioning	Explaining mathematical thinking	Mathematical representations	Building student responsibility within the community
Level 0	Teacher is at the front of the room and dominates conversation.	Teacher is only questioner. Questions serve to keep students listening to teacher. Students give short answers and respond to teacher only.	Teacher questions focus on correctness. Students provide short answer-focused responses. Teacher may tell answers.	Representations are missing, or teacher shows them to students.	Culture supports students keeping ideas to themselves or just providing answers when asked.
Level 1	Teacher encourages sharing of math ideas and directs speaker to talk to the class, not to the teacher only.	Teacher questions begin to focus on student thinking and less on answers. Only teacher asks questions.	Teacher probes student thinking somewhat. One or two strategies may be elicited. Teacher may fill in an explanation. Students provide brief descriptions of their thinking in response to teacher probing.	Students learn to create math drawings to depict their mathematical thinking.	Students believe that their ideas are accepted by the classroom community. They begin to listen to one another supportively and to restate in their own words what another student has said.
Level 2	Teacher facilitates conversation between students, and encourages students to ask questions of one another.	Teacher asks probing questions and facilitates some student-to-student talk. Students ask questions of one another with prompting from teacher.	Teacher probes more deeply to learn about student thinking. Teacher elicits multiple strategies. Students respond to teacher probing and volunteer their thinking. Students begin to defend their answers.	Students label their math drawings so that others are able to follow their mathematical thinking.	Students believe that they are math learners and that their ideas and the ideas of their classmates are important. They listen actively so that they can contribute significantly.
Level 3	Students carry conversation themselves. Teacher only guides from the periphery of the conversation. Teacher waits for students to clarify thinking of others.	Student-to-student talk is student initiated. Students ask questions and listen to responses. Many questions ask "why" and call for justification. Teacher questions may still guide discourse.	Teacher follows student explanations closely. Teacher asks students to contrast strategies. Students defend and justify their answers with little prompting from the teacher.	Students follow and help shape the descriptions of others' math thinking through math drawings and may suggest edits in others' math drawings.	Students believe that they are math leaders and can help shape the thinking of others. They help shape others' math thinking in supportive, collegial ways and accept the same.

Fig. 7.3. Components and levels of a math-talk learning community (from Hufferd-Ackles, Fuson, and Sherin 2015, p. 127)

What is the teacher's role?

Ms. Chavez is active in the lesson at critical points and plays an important role in engaging students in discourse and making their ideas central to the class discussion. She selects students to explain their solution paths, and prompts the students to ask each other questions and make comparisons between solution paths. The teacher role in this excerpt is clearly at level 2 as she facilitates conversations among the students and encourages the students to ask questions of one another. Throughout the discussion, the teacher is careful to monitor her own participation in order to convey to students that they are responsible for listening and responding to each other. Some specific examples of ways the teacher prompts students to engage with each other's ideas include the following:

- The teacher opens the door for more contributions: "Say more." (line 3) "Who understands how Kyra's strategy is different from what William did?" (line 43).
- The teacher challenges students to make sense of the approaches of their classmates: "Who thinks they understand what Kyra did and can use counters to explain her thinking?" (line 22–23).
- The teacher pulls together several ideas by summarizing and juxtaposing them to draw attention to the underlying mathematical structure of subtraction, that is, knowing the whole amount and one part (lines 51–54, 75–78).

Who asks the questions?

Throughout the lesson, Ms. Chavez prompted students to engage with the mathematical thinking of their classmates. While Ms. Chavez asked most of the questions in the excerpt, her questions served to guide rather than direct or funnel the discussion. It is not easy to get young learners (or older learners for that matter) to ask each other questions about one's mathematical thinking. This might be due to the fact that they are so focused on the formation of their own evolving understanding, or perhaps they do not perceive the "role of the student" as one in which questions are asked and curiosity about the thinking of their peers is expected. In moving toward a math-talk community, one goal is to foster more student-to-student communication with students talking, actively listening, responding, and questioning. Thus, this component is not really just about questions, but about how students respond to each other, which can also include their observations, restatements (e.g., revoicing, paraphrasing), or summaries of each other's work and ideas. For example, in the class discussion, Ms. Chavez encourages students to ask each other questions, "Would anyone like to ask Kyra a question?" (line 44). Then William responds by commenting and restating what Kyra did, "I see what you did. You just knew 7 minus 3 was 4, so then you added 10 and 3. Hmm. I counted back from 17. I like your way." Next Jordan speaks up, "I have a question. Why did you do it that way?" (line 47).

Ms. Chavez judiciously and purposefully asks questions throughout the lesson. Her questions were strategically placed to link student's contributions, engage students in active listening, request explanations, and encourage comparisons. The questions served to signal to students that they have the "right" to respond to each other's interpretation of their work (e.g., Kyra, line 34), to question each other (e.g., Jordan, line 47), and to comment on each other's work (e.g., Luis, Shanica, Jenna, and Fin, lines 60–65). In regard to the levels of math-talk, the questioning component seems to be mainly at level 2. The teacher needs to prompt students to orient and engage themselves with the thinking and reasoning of their peers, and facilitates the student-to-student talk.

Who provides the explanations?

Another component of math-talk communities asks us to consider who talks during the lesson, who provides the explanations and justifications, and whose ideas are valued. In essence, "Who owns the learning?" Throughout the discussion, student explanations and ideas were central to the discourse. The teacher elicits multiple strategies as the class considers the solution paths of Cameron, Kyra, and William. The teacher probes deeper into the student's approaches, such as asking Cameron, "Can you show us what you did with the counters?" (line 3). The teacher prompts students to contrast strategies, "Who understands how Kyra's strategy is different from what William did?" (line 43). Through the discussion, the teacher closely follows the students' ways of viewing and making sense of the task. In regard to the levels of math-talk, the class discussion seems to be a mixture of level 2 and level 3. The discourse focuses more on explanations and the teacher summarizing than on students defending and justifying their answers, however, Kyra does defend her solution path when she states, "I see what William did, but that's not what I said" (line 34).

How do mathematical representations support discourse?

The students in Ms. Chavez's class had access to counters and part-part-whole mats to support their problem solving. These were critical tools in examining and surfacing an underlying mathematical structure and relationship of addition and subtraction as being comprised of a total amount that is composed from or decomposed into two parts. Even though this component of the math-talk community emphasizes math drawings, we broaden it to include physical and visual representations (as discussed in chapter 6), particularly for these young learners. In this lesson, students were learning to use the counters and mats to "depict" or rather demonstrate their mathematical thinking, so we would consider this to be at level 1 for mathematical representations of a math-talk community. We also acknowledge the important and critical work of helping students "put their thinking on paper" by making visual records showing their use of physical objects to represent and solve problems. Unfortunately, no written record was made during this lesson so students had to rely on their visual images of the various student approaches. However, in other lessons, the students are moving toward level 2 in learning to put their thinking on paper by creating and labeling their math drawings.

The focus on mathematical language as a "verbal representation" was essential in the class discussion, another of the five representational modes discussed in chapter 6. The part-part-whole mat and the consistent use of part-part-whole language and missing-part language by the teacher and students signal the meaning of the quantities in relationship to each other. This provides verbal support to students, enabling them to not only participate in the lesson but also challenging them to ponder and examine the underlying mathematical structure. As the work progresses with these students, they will be expected to make a math drawing showing their thinking, as well as write an equation as a symbolic representation to describe how they are thinking about the students in attendance compared to those who are absent.

How are students sharing responsibility for learning?

The culture of Ms. Chavez's classroom is clearly well beyond level 0 in building student responsibility within the math-talk community. Students do not keep their mathematical ideas to themselves nor see mathematics as just recalling answers. The students readily shared their solutions paths and their ideas. For example, students readily used the counters to represent their solution paths as a means of helping others understand their thinking and reasoning (Cameron, lines 4–7; William, lines 24-26; Kyra, lines 34–37). Students share solution paths with each other. They actively listen to each other, both questioning and refuting claims. Students did not develop these mathematical habits of thinking on their own; they have been nurtured over time by Ms. Chavez. She consistently demonstrates student thinking with counters and other physical objects, as well as with drawings, making student reasoning visible and more accessible to each other. She hoped, and expected, that students would follow in her footsteps, which we can see in the class discussion as Cameron, William, and Kyra used the counters to show their reasoning along with their verbal explanations. In building shared responsibility, the class is at a level 3. The class discussion leaves a strong impression that her students believe their own ideas and the ideas of their classmates are valued and accepted by the classroom community.

Establishing norms for mathematical discourse

Rich class discussions in mathematics classrooms, such as that in Ms. Chavez's room, do not just happen, but must be nurtured and developed as well as negotiated and re-negotiated over time. This entails establishing socio-mathematical norms (Yackel and Cobb 1996), that is, norms for how students interact and respond to each other as a mathematics community of learners. The chart of "Talk Expectations" shown in figure 7.4 was developed, or negotiated, by Ms. Chavez and her first-grade students, but only after several months of the teacher intentionally fostering a math-talk community. One day, Ms. Chavez showed her students a video of one of their class discussions. She then invited the students to make observations about the ways in which they were working and talking with each other. She charted students' responses, as shown in the figure, and gave students credit for their contributions to its development. The list of talk expectations now serves as a guide and a reminder for the class in regard to how they should behave and respond as part of a math-talk community. As a result of posting these talk norms, Ms. Chavez remarked that *more* of her students are now *more* engaged in their discussions, both as a class and in pairs and small groups, because students know what is expected, not only of themselves but of each other.

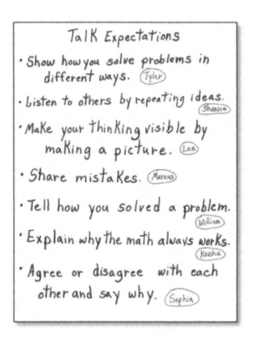

Fig. 7.4. An example of classroom norms for mathematics discourse

Planning for Mathematical Discourse

Meaningful mathematics discourse does not just happen; it requires prior planning and preparation. In planning for a lesson, teachers make critical decisions that affect the implementation of the lesson and, thus, student learning. Intentional planning allows the mathematics discourse to be more manageable for the teacher and assists the teacher in being more strategic in moving students toward the mathematics learning goals. In addition, it informs the many decisions teachers must make in the moment during instruction, and helps teachers resist taking over the thinking and reasoning for their students.

Ms. Chavez, in the previous Analyzing Teaching and Learning activity, was able to engage students in meaningful mathematical discourse because of the thoughtful lesson planning process in which she engaged prior to teaching the lesson. Rather than having to make in-the-moment decisions about how to respond to student contributions, she had anticipated possible student approaches and prepared potential questions and supports prior to the lesson. She even thought about how she might structure the whole-class discussion of anticipated student approaches in a manner that would likely further student understanding toward the mathematical agenda of the lesson. Her planning process was based on the five practices of orchestrating productive class discussions introduced in ATL 7.2. Here we examine the first of these practices, that of anticipating likely student approaches, missteps, and solution paths to mathematical tasks prior to implementing the lesson.

Engage in ATL 7.3: Anticipate Student Approaches

Turning to ATL 7.3, we ask you to consider a specific approach to lesson planning that focuses on mathematics learning goals and anticipates student solution paths. Ideally, teachers would work with colleagues to identify the mathematics learning goals for the upcoming lesson(s), select a high-level mathematics task(s) that aligns with the goals, anticipate likely student solution paths, and consider how to best respond to students as they engage in the task. The anticipated student approaches should include appropriate use of representations and solution paths, as well as likely student missteps, misconceptions, and errors. With anticipated solution paths in hand, teachers can envision observing students enacting them and prepare questions to assess and advance student learning as we did in chapter 5.

As you engage in ATL 7.3, focus on just one aspect of the planning process, that is, anticipate the ways in which students might approach solving a specific task. Because it is not always easy to generate a range of student approaches, we suggest you work with colleagues to conceive likely student solution paths. The value of doing this with colleagues is that a group of teachers, when asked to solve a task, will almost always generate and use a variety of solution paths.

Analyzing Teaching and Learning 7.3
Anticipate Student Approaches

The Walking from School task, shown below, is appropriate for fourth-grade students learning to compare fractions in a linear measurement context.

- Solve the task yourself using visual representations, such as number lines, and make note of the mathematical ideas embedded in the task.

- Brainstorm a list of student solution paths among a class of fourth-grade students, including some with correct reasoning and others that contain errors and misconceptions. Consider a variety of visual representations, such as number lines and area models.

- Which of the approaches on your list do you think are most likely and least likely to be used by students in a typical fourth-grade class?

Analysis of ATL 7.3: Anticipating Solution Paths with Correct Reasoning and with Errors

The Walking from School task is rather ambitious in that it requires students to compare five different fractions that represent linear distances, that is, the distance in miles that each student walks home from school. This high-level task can be solved in several different ways, using a variety of representations and strategies, thus offering students multiple entry points. The task demands that students draw on their conceptual understanding of fractions, which if lacking or weak, will also result in solution paths with probable errors and misconceptions. As you solved the task yourself, we asked you to make note of the mathematical ideas embedded in the task. Some of the mathematical concepts include the following:

- Students need to understand fractions as numbers, that is, they must understand a fraction $^a/_b$ as the quantity formed by a parts of size $^1/_b$ For example, in this task, $\frac{2}{3}$ is the quantity formed by 2 parts of size $\frac{1}{3}$ of a mile).

- Students need to accurately partition wholes into halves, thirds, fourths, and sixths. The tasks suggests that students use number lines, but does not require it. It is likely that some students will use rectangles and circles.

- If students choose to use number lines, they need to understand and represent a fraction as a number on the number line. This requires students to define the whole as the interval from 0 to 1, partition it into the required number of equal parts, recognize how to mark off the needed number of lengths from zero, and recognize that its endpoint locates the specific fraction on the number line.

- Students must understand and be able to explain that two fractions (i.e., $\frac{2}{3}$ and $\frac{4}{6}$) are equivalent (equal) if they are the same size or name the same point on a number line.

- Students must be able to compare fractions with different numerators and different denominators by reasoning about their size, use diagrams to explain and justify those comparisons, and most important, they must recognize that comparisons are valid only when the two fractions refer to the same whole.

- Students should notice that they can compare some fractions by relating them to a benchmark fraction such as $\frac{1}{2}$ or by considering their distance from 1 whole. Some students might consider comparing fractions by considering those that have common numerators (i.e., $\frac{2}{3}$ and $\frac{2}{6}$) or common denominators (i.e., $\frac{2}{6}$ and $\frac{4}{6}$) or rename fractions so that they have common numerators or denominators.

As noted, the mathematical demands of this task are ambitious but within the capabilities of fourth-grade students. The complexities of the task are played out in the many options and choices available to students for approaching the task, such as choice of visual representations and choice in ways to reason about the size of the fractions in relation to each other. Anticipating students' responses goes far beyond just considering whether they will get the "right answers" or "wrong answers." It involves considering how students might mathematically interpret a task, which mathematical understandings they draw upon, and the array of strategies—both correct and incorrect—which students might put into play as they tackle the task.

We asked you to brainstorm a list of student solution paths, those that utilize correct reasoning and those paths which might contain errors and misconceptions. Figure 7.5 displays some examples of anticipated solution paths for the Walking from School task. Our list is not exhaustive, but rather it is representative of our own experiences in using similar tasks with students as well as our knowledge of common errors and approaches found in the research literature. If students have limited experiences with number lines, it is likely that they will use rectangles or circles to represent and compare the fractions (Strategies 3, 5, 6, 8, 9). To do so accurately, students must realize, for example, that the rectangles must be the same size because comparisons are valid only when the two fractions refer to the same-size whole. We should note that the wholes need not have the same shape, but must have the same area. For students that use number lines (Strategies 1, 2, 4, 7), they can decide whether to put all or some of the fractions on the same number line. If students use one number, the whole unit is the same for all fractions. If students use two or more number lines, the interval defining one whole must be the same size on all number lines. Comparing fractions, particularly five fractions as in this task, requires very accurate representation of them in visual diagrams. It is hoped that students draw upon both their knowledge of how to represent fractions with diagrams as well as their knowledge of fraction compositions and relationships (e.g., $\frac{4}{6} = \frac{3}{6} + \frac{1}{6} = \frac{1}{2} + \frac{1}{6}$) including consideration of fractions that might be equivalent, such as $\frac{2}{3}$ and $\frac{4}{6}$.

Strategy	Solution Paths with Correct Reasoning	Examples of Student Reasoning
1	**Compares fractions as distances by drawing and aligning five number lines.** Student compares by looking at the distance from 0 or the closeness to 1 whole. Student draws five aligned number lines, accurately defines same-size whole units, partitions each number line corresponding to a specific fraction, and shades lengths from 0 or marks endpoints to indicating the size of the fraction as a distance from 0.	 Student might say: *Shelia is incorrect cause I looked at my number lines and it seems to be Derrick is the one that walks the farthest. And Maria walked the nearest. I also know Shelia and Harold walked the same amount of miles.*
2	**Compares fractions as distances by marking all five fractions on one number line.** Student compares fractions by considering distances from 0 or closeness to 1 whole. Student draws one number line, defines the whole unit, partitions it repeatedly corresponding to each fraction, and marks the location of each fraction. The student clearly shows that $2/3$ is equivalent to $4/6$.	 Students might say: • *It's Derrick. He is the farthest on the number line. Shelia and Harold were the same at the second farthest.* • *Derrick is closest to 1 whole mile, so he walked the farthest.*
3	**Compares fractions as areas by drawing same-size shapes, such as five rectangles, circles, or squares.** Student draws and aligns five same-size (or nearly same) rectangles. Partitions each and shades area corresponding to each fraction. Student draws five same-size circles, partitions them, and is able to determine which circle has the most area shaded.	Students might say: • *Derrick did because he has the most filled in, more than Shelia.* • *Derrick walked the farthest because his is closest to being 1 whole, more than any other person.*
4	**Compares fractions to the benchmark fraction $1/2$.** Student represents fractions with diagrams, realizes you only need to compare those three fractions that are greater than $1/2$ ($2/3$, $3/4$, $4/6$), either looks at distance to $1/2$ or closeness to 1 whole to determine who walked the farthest.	 Student might say: *I know it's not Suzy or Maria because the others are already over $1/2$. Derrick is closer to 1 whole mile than Shelia or Harold.*

Fig. 7.5. Anticipated solution paths for the Walking from School task
(*Continued on next page*)

Strategy	Solution Paths with Correct Reasoning	Examples of Student Reasoning
5	**Compares each fraction to Shelia's $^4/_6$ mile.** Student represents fractions with diagrams, compares each fraction to Shelia's, and uses a process of elimination to find which fraction is the largest.	Student might say: *Maria walked half as much as Shelia. Shelia walked more than Suzy. Harold and Shelia walked the same. Shelia walked less than Derrick.*
6	**Compares fraction size by using a common denominator for some or all fractions to assist with reasoning.** Student represents fractions with diagrams, but still uses a common denominator, such as 6 or 24, for all or some fractions to support reasoning and explanation.	Student might say: *I found a common denominator so the fractions would be easier to compare.*
7	**Puts all five fractions on one or more number lines but does not realize that $^2/_3$ and $^4/_6$ are equivalent.** Student is fairly accurate in placing fractions on a number line, knows Derrick walked the farthest, but does not have $^2/_3$ and $^4/_6$ as equivalent, just close to each other.	Student might say: Derrick walked the farthest because he is the most away from 0. Shelia walked the second farthest, then Harold, then Suzy, then Maria.
8	**Draws five shapes but the wholes are not the same size, or places fractions incorrectly on a number line(s).** Student uses different size wholes or does not use proportional spacing to place fractions on a number line.	Student might say: *Shelia is right; she walked the farthest because she has the most shaded in.*
9	**States that the bigger the number the bigger the fraction or that fractions are opposite and smaller means bigger.** Student reasons by looking at individual numbers and does not consider the relative size of the fraction.	Student might say: *Shelia walked the farthest because there is **four** sixths and that's the biggest number of miles.*

Fig. 7.5. Anticipated solution paths for the Walking from School task

Additional approaches that students might use are to consider the relationship of some fractions to a benchmark fraction such as $^1/_2$ (Strategy 4) or to compare all fractions to Shelia's $^4/_6$ mile (Strategy 5) since the task specifically asks students to examine her claim. Some students might also find a common denominator (Strategy 6) for some or all of the fractions and use this knowledge to assist with, but not replace, their reasoning and sense making. Given that the task asks for diagrams and an explanation, it is critical to look a bit more closely at the work of students who might find common denominators to ensure they are using this procedure with connections to conceptual understanding. We also added one more additional path to our list (Strategy 9), knowing that some students are likely to use erroneous reasoning by comparing the individual numbers in the fractions. They might agree with Shelia by comparing numerators to numerators and conclude that 4 is the largest number on top so it must be the largest fraction. Conversely, students might also erroneously reason that smaller means bigger when it comes to fractions, as did this student, *"No, Shelia did not walk the furthest. Suzy did because she walked a half mile and Shelia walked* $^4/_6$ *of a mile. Half is way more! Shelia thinks she walked more because her numbers are higher but its opposite in fractions."*

With this list in hand, the next step in the planning process would be to develop assessing and advancing questions for each strategy (as discussed in chapter 5). The table could be extended with two more columns. In one column, list assessing "stay and listen" questions that probe deeper into what the student understands. In the second column, list advancing "ask and walk away" questions that press students to make progress toward the learning goals or to go beyond their current thinking. To evolve the table just a bit further into a monitoring tool that you could use during implementation of the lesson, you could add a column to keep track of which students used which strategies. We would suggest you also leave some blank rows at the bottom of the table to jot down unanticipated strategies used by students. Teachers that have developed such a monitoring tool express how valuable it is in managing the dynamics of teacher-student interactions during the lesson. It provides reminders of how the teacher might respond to individual or groups of students as they work, it documents which students used which strategies, and it helps in the selecting and sequencing of student work for the whole-class discussion. Additionally, teachers can save the monitoring tool to review and update the next time they plan to use the same task. Anticipating student solution paths, including errors and misconceptions, in advance of a lesson, as part of a monitoring chart with assessing and advancing questions, is an important step in preparing to facilitate a meaningful and productive mathematical discussion among students toward building a shared understanding of important mathematical ideas.

Orchestrating a Whole-Class Discussion

Orchestrating a whole-class discussion that maintains students' engagement in thinking and reasoning and that advances student learning toward the goals of the lesson is a challenging and complex task of teaching (Boerst et al. 2011; Franke, Kazemi, and Battey 2007). The five practices for orchestrating productive discussions—anticipate, monitor, select, sequence, and connect (see fig. 7.1) are designed to support teachers in planning, managing, and facilitating meaningful mathematics discourse as a part of ambitious teaching practice (Smith and Stein 2011).

In the Case of Robert Harris and the Band Concert task (see ATL 1.1, page 10 and ATL 4.1, page 68), as well as Ms. Chavez in ATL 7.2, we saw the teachers selecting specific solution paths, sequencing those selections in a particular way, and asking questions aimed at connecting those solutions paths in a storyline that built toward an understanding of the mathematics goals of the lesson. The success of these lessons did not occur by chance, but instead resulted from careful planning that allowed for purposeful facilitation of mathematical discourse on high-level tasks. Students became empowered owners and authors of mathematical ideas and took shared responsibility for their learning within the math-talk community.

Engage in ATL 7.4: Select, Sequence, and Connect

In ATL 7.4, you engage in a process of selecting, sequencing, and connecting student work from the Walking from School task for a whole-class discussion. Considering the anticipated student solution paths for the task discussed in ATL 7.3, you will study a set of student work and make decisions on which approaches you would select and in what order for a whole-class discussion as well as consider potential mathematical connections among the solution paths. The overall purpose of the whole-class discussion is to build shared mathematical understanding among a class of students while moving them toward the intended mathematics learning goals.

In fact, keeping the mathematics learning goals "front and center" (Meikle 2016) is essential to the success of this process in ensuring a productive class discussion. Imagine that the following set of learning goals was established for a lesson featuring the Walking from School task.

Goal A. Students will understand that comparison of fractions involves reasoning about the relative size of fractions and is only valid when the fractions refer to the same-size whole.

Goal B. Students will understand that fractions with different numbers of parts and different size parts (i.e., unlike denominators and unlike numerators), within the same-size whole, can be compared by partitioning a number line(s) to represent the size of each fraction.

Goal C. Students will understand and begin using comparative reasoning strategies based on the relative size of fractions, within the same-size whole, including fractions which have same-size parts (i.e., common denominators) or the same number of parts (i.e., common numerators), respectively, by reasoning about the same-size parts (e.g., $4/9$ and $7/9$) or having the same number of parts but parts of different sizes (e.g., $7/6$ and $7/5$).

Goal D: Students will understand and begin comparing fractions, within the same-size whole, by using known benchmark quantities (e.g., $\frac{1}{2}$ or 1 whole) to determine the relative size of fractions, such as reasoning whether a fraction is larger, smaller, or the same size as a benchmark quantity (e.g., $\frac{2}{5}$ is smaller than $\frac{1}{2}$; $\frac{7}{4}$ is larger than 1 whole).

With these learning goals in mind, turn to ATL 7.4 and try your hand at selecting and sequencing a set of student work. You might want to use the list of anticipated solution paths from the previous Analyzing Teaching and Learning activity (see ATL 7.3) to help with this process. We also ask that you consider and make note of connections to important mathematical ideas that you would want to highlight for each selected solution path during the class discussion.

Analyzing Teaching and Learning 7.4
Select, Sequence, and Connect

Imagine your class working on the Walking from School task and you observed the set of six student work samples shown below. Keeping your learning goals in mind, you need to make some decisions in preparation for the whole-class discussion.

- Which samples of student work would you select for a class discussion and why? Assume you only have time remaining in the class session to discuss three to five pieces of student work.

- How would you sequence your selected student solution paths and why?

- What mathematical connections would you surface through the analysis and comparison of your selected approaches that would move students toward the intended learning goals?

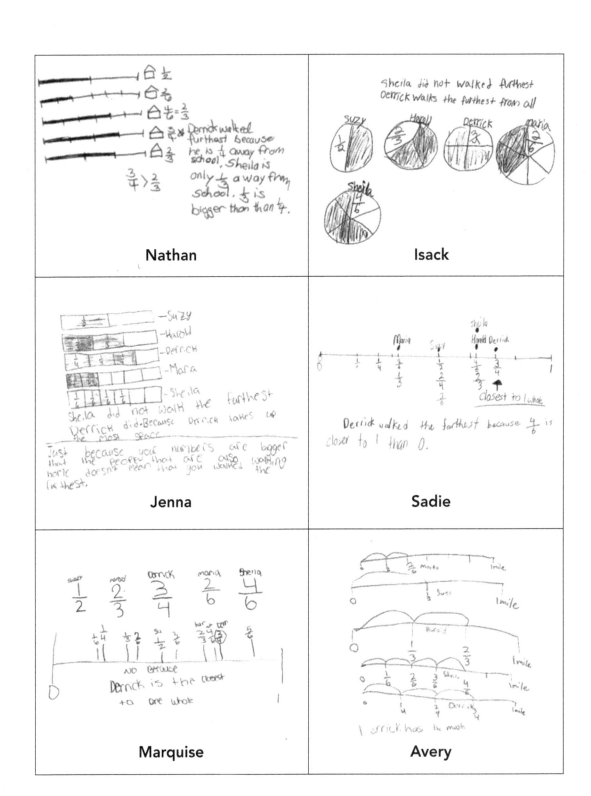

Nathan

Isack

Jenna

Sadie

Marquise

Avery

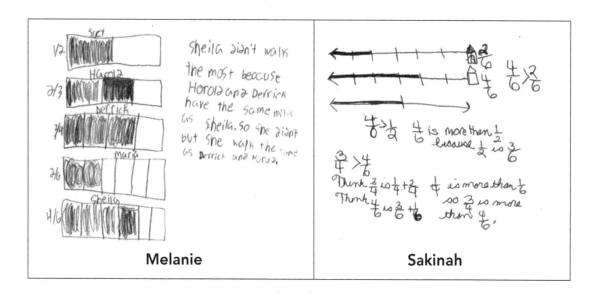

The handwritten student work shows:

Melanie (left panel): Fraction bars labeled 1/2 (Sici), 2/3 (Harold), 3/4 (Derrick), 2/6 (Maria), 4/6 (Sheila) with a written explanation:

> Sheila didn't walk the most because Harold and Derrick have the same mile as Sheila. So she didn't but she walk the same as Derrick and Harold.

Sakinah (right panel): Number lines with fractions, showing:

$$\frac{4}{6} > \frac{1}{2} \quad \frac{4}{6} \text{ is more than } \frac{1}{2} \text{ because } \frac{1}{2} \text{ is } \frac{3}{6}$$

$$\frac{3}{4} > \frac{4}{6}$$

> Think $\frac{3}{4}$ is $\frac{4}{4} + \frac{3}{4}$ $\frac{4}{6}$ is more than $\frac{1}{6}$ so $\frac{3}{4}$ is more than $\frac{4}{6}$. Think $\frac{4}{6}$ is $\frac{3}{6} + \frac{1}{6}$

Analysis of ATL 7.4: More than "Show and Tell"

Upon inspection of the set of student work samples on the Walking from School task, you obviously noticed a wide range of student approaches, some correct and some that contained errors or faulty reasoning. This work is from the fourth-grade class of Ms. Balistreri. Her class has twenty-eight students, so she had to make some critical decisions about which student work to highlight in the whole-class discussion of the task. She narrowed it down to the eight work samples in figure 7.6, as she thought each contained important mathematical ideas that she would like to examine more closely with her students and that would support student progress toward her mathematics learning goals. However, looking at the clock, Ms. Balistreri realized the class only had time to discuss a subset of these work samples. Selecting and sequencing student work samples is demanding work and must often be accomplished within a class session while teaching the lesson. Having thought about potential student approaches as part of the lesson planning, as well as keeping the learning goals front and center, was essential to making this aspect of instruction more manageable for the teacher. Based on the mathematics goals articulated for the lesson, a few criteria present themselves that could inform these decisions:

- To meet goal A, at least one piece of student work should focus on the need for the wholes to be the same size, perhaps using a work sample that shows an error in a visual representation.

- To meet goal B, at least one or two student work samples should represent fractions as distances on number lines and make connections to the linear measurement context and to the placement of equivalent fractions as showing the same distance on a number line.

- To meet goal C, discussion of the student work should make connections between comparing fractions with the same numerators or denominators and their visual representations.

- To meet goal D, at least one approach should focus on the use of a fraction benchmark, such as one-half or one whole, to compare the distances.

Beyond consideration of the mathematics learning goals, your decisions about sequencing the student work should also be done in a manner that makes the mathematics accessible to each and every student in your class. Returning to our metaphor of a storyline, consider beginning with a student approach that establishes the setting for the discussion and draws all learners into the mathematics being examined. Thus, it might be best to begin with a visual representation that shows the problem context and was a common approach among the students in the class. Then the plot develops with each subsequent student work sample, adding new elements to the story, thus deepening students' understanding of the mathematics while building toward meaningful and more fluent use of strategies and procedures.

Making purposeful choices about the selection of student approaches and the order in which to have students share and analyze specific solution paths can maximize the chances that students will make steady progress toward the goals for the lesson. Meikle (2016) also reminds us, "If a solution strategy does not seem to have the potential to promote any of the underlying concepts of the mathematical learning goal, then do not select this solution strategy for the whole-class discussion" (p. 232). Some suggestions to consider when selecting and sequencing student solution strategies for a whole-class discussion include the following (Stein et al. 2008):

- Start with a strategy used by the majority of students before examining those that were used by only a few students, or start with a particularly easy-to-understand strategy so that the beginning of the discussion is accessible to all or nearly all students.

- Work in a strategy based on a misconception held by several students to clear up that misunderstanding as well as to acknowledge and validate errors and mistakes as a normal and important part of learning mathematics.

- Sequence related or contrasting strategies consecutively to make it easier for students to compare them mathematically.

Using the mathematics learning goals and considering how to build a mathematical story line that builds and deepens student understanding, Ms. Balistreri selected and sequenced the student work as shown in figure 7.6. The column on the left shows the selected student work in the order presented. The column on the right includes questions for the teacher to ask that support students in making connections between the selected solution paths and the important mathematical ideas.

Sharing, Comparing, and Discussing the Task	
Sequence	**Questions for Connecting to the Mathematics**
1. Jenna compares areas represented by each fraction using rectangles as a visual diagram. 	How did you approach comparing the distances that the five students walked home from school? What is one whole in the word problem? How did you show that in your picture? What does each rectangle represent? How did you go about deciding how to partition the rectangles? Who walked the farthest and how do you know? What observations can you (the class) make about Jenna's work? How is Jenna's strategy similar to what we have done in class before for fractions?
2. Nathan compares distances or lengths on number line diagrams using a benchmark fraction of 1 whole. 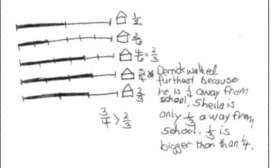	How does Nathan show the whole in his picture? How is that similar or different than how Jenna showed one whole mile? Who walked the farthest and how can you tell just by looking at Nathan's picture? Who understands and can try to explain in their own words what Nathan means when he says Derrick is $1/4$ away from school? Is Derrick really $1/4$ mile away from school? I thought the problem said he lived $3/4$ mile from school? What is Nathan really thinking about here when he says Derrick is $1/4$ away, away from what? How can Shelia only be $1/3$ away from "walking a whole mile" when she walked $4/6$ of a mile? *Continued on next page*

Sharing, Comparing, and Discussing the Task	
Sequence	**Questions for Connecting to the Mathematics**
3. Marquise makes an error in locating fractions on a number line diagram. 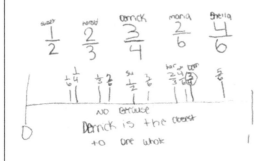	How do we know with this picture who walked the farthest? He said that "Derrick is the closet to one whole," to one whole what? This looks confusing, who can make some observations about Marquise's picture? Is it okay to put all those different kinds of fractions on the same number line? Some of you mentioned that some fractions are not in the right spot. How might we use Jenna's or Nathan's diagrams to help us figure out where to put some of these fractions? How might we show that some of these fractions are just different names for the same amount or the same spot on the number line?
4. Sadie compares relative size and position of fractions on a number line diagram. 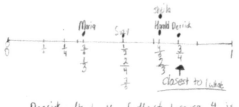	What strategies did you use to figure out where to put the fractions on your number line? How does Sadie show that some fractions are equivalent? What does it mean again to be equivalent when we are talking about fractions? That's a good question, should we shade the distance from 0, like Nathan did, or is it okay to just put a dot on the number line to show the location of the fractions? She said that ³/₄ is closest to 1 whole? One whole what? What does this have to do with walking home from school? Is ³/₄ really closer to 1 than to 0? Convince me. How far away are the other fractions from 1? From 0?
	Continued on next page

Sharing, Comparing, and Discussing the Task	
Sequence	**Questions for Connecting to the Mathematics**
5. Sakinah compares fractions by reasoning with a benchmark fraction of 1/2. 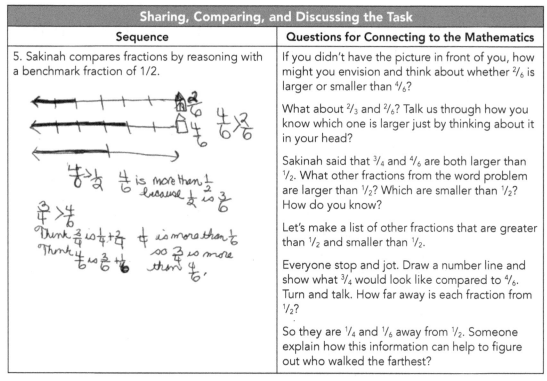	If you didn't have the picture in front of you, how might you envision and think about whether $^2/_6$ is larger or smaller than $^4/_6$? What about $^2/_3$ and $^2/_6$? Talk us through how you know which one is larger just by thinking about it in your head? Sakinah said that $^3/_4$ and $^4/_6$ are both larger than $^1/_2$. What other fractions from the word problem are larger than $^1/_2$? Which are smaller than $^1/_2$? How do you know? Let's make a list of other fractions that are greater than $^1/_2$ and smaller than $^1/_2$. Everyone stop and jot. Draw a number line and show what $^3/_4$ would look like compared to $^4/_6$. Turn and talk. How far away is each fraction from $^1/_2$? So they are $^1/_4$ and $^1/_6$ away from $^1/_2$. Someone explain how this information can help to figure out who walked the farthest?

Fig. 7.6. A sequence of student work for a class discussion

Ms. Balistreri asked Jenna to describe her thinking and reasoning first. The students have experiences folding and using paper fraction strips to compare fractions, so the visual representation of fractions was accessible and familiar to the students in the class. The discussion drew students' attention to the care in which Jenna made the rectangles the same size (or nearly the same) so that the comparison would be valid (Goals A and C). It also noted how she very carefully aligned the rectangles, shading from the left to the right, so it would be easier to compare the five fractions and determine which was the largest. Her reasoning focused on the area shaded as she stated, "Derrick takes up the most space."

Nathan was next to describe his approach to the task. The class discussion began with a comparison to Jenna's work as both students had taken care to have same-size wholes and to align their visual diagrams. Nathan reasoned with the linear measurement context in the task as he talked about the fractions as being distances and lengths (Goals B and D). His work also pushed the thinking of the students in the class to not only consider which fraction length was the longest but to also consider how far away it was from one whole mile.

Then Marquise shared his work. While he had a correct answer, he struggled to put the fractions on a single number line (Goal B). He commented that it was confusing and hard to keep track of the spacing. He did eventually position the fractions in approximately the right places, but not as mathematically precise as needed. The class made some comparisons to the work of both Jenna and Nathan and examined the alignment of the various fractions. For example, students noticed that $\frac{1}{2}$ matches up with $\frac{2}{4}$ because 2 parts of size $\frac{1}{4}$ is the same as having $\frac{1}{2}$, and also matches up with $\frac{3}{6}$ because that is 3 parts of size $\frac{1}{6}$. Similarly, they discussed how $\frac{1}{3}$ matches up with $\frac{2}{6}$ and how $\frac{4}{6}$ matches up with $\frac{2}{3}$. The teacher also used this as an opportunity to talk about how a specific amount can have many names and that these are called equivalent fractions. She then challenged her class to think about the fractions they were examining and what might be some other names for zero (e.g., $\frac{0}{4}$, $\frac{0}{6}$) and one whole ($\frac{4}{4}$, $\frac{6}{6}$). The class spent considerable time examining Marquise's work and comparing it to the other student representations, showing the value in surfacing and discussing student work with errors and faulty reasoning as it makes the mathematical ideas more obvious.

Next up was Sadie. Her work reinforced the discussion that was just held based on Marquise's work and showed how fractions that name the same amount might be shown in a number line diagram (Goal B). An observation and wondering raised by a student was whether it was okay to just make a dot, like Sadie to mark the fraction, or whether they should draw a line like Nathan. If this had not been observed, it was a topic the teacher intended to discuss. The students concluded that both ways worked for marking fractions on a number line.

Finally, the class looked briefly at Sakinah's work before the class period ended and discussed how the benchmark of $\frac{1}{2}$ can also be used to help them compare fractions (Goal D). In particular, the class examined how the fractions $\frac{3}{4}$ and $\frac{4}{6}$ were decomposed into $\frac{1}{2}$ then some more, that is, $\frac{3}{4} = \frac{2}{4} + \frac{1}{4}$ and $\frac{4}{6} = \frac{3}{6} + \frac{1}{6}$. They spent a few minutes noting which fractions from the task where more than $\frac{1}{2}$ and which were less than $\frac{1}{2}$. The teacher then asked students to think of other fractions that might be more or less than $\frac{1}{2}$ and to jot them down. Then Ms. Balistreri asked the students to talk with a partner and convince each other whether, indeed, their fractions were more or less than $\frac{1}{2}$.

Facilitating meaningful mathematics discourse rests on choosing a task with ample opportunities for discussion, selecting and sequencing the solution paths to support students, and asking questions that highlight and connect important mathematical ideas. The sequence described is but one of many possible ways to select and sequence a set of student work on a specific task in order to engage students in meaningful mathematics discourse. The selection and sequencing should connect back to the mathematical goals for the lesson, to students' prior mathematical experiences, and to the mathematical story line that a teacher wishes to build throughout the discussion.

What the Research Says: Meaningful Mathematical Discourse

A wide array of research over the past two decades has underscored the important connections between mathematics classroom discourse that focuses on reasoning and problem solving and positive student learning outcomes (e.g., Carpenter, Franke, and Levi 2003; Michaels, O'Connor, and Resnick 2008). In their research with students in an elementary school, O'Connor (2010) found that instruction characterized by opportunities for rich mathematics discourse was associated with increased learning gains for students. This was also coupled with cognitively challenging tasks (see chapter 3) and opportunities for students to engage in productive struggle (see chapter 9) as they made sense of and engaged in mathematics discourse.

In the past, classroom instruction was dominated by the use of low-level tasks which often lead to a pattern of talk in which the teacher initiates a question, students respond, and the teacher evaluates whether the response was correct or not, and then the cycle repeats. Mehan (1979) referred to this as the "Initiate-Respond-Evaluate" or "IRE" pattern of talk. This pattern does not afford students opportunities to engage in discussion. Usually one-word responses are exchanged between the teacher and students, and students have little opportunity to share mathematical thinking and reasoning. This response pattern also provides teachers with little information regarding what students actually know and understand.

Classroom instruction has gradually been shifting to include use of more high-level tasks. Inherent in these tasks are multiple ways in which students can solve the task, and thus offer the means for more classroom discourse on examining and comparing different solution paths. This shift to the use of more high-level tasks necessitates that teachers re-examine the pattern of talk in their classrooms. One such approach for moving to and managing whole-class discussions is the five practices model for orchestrating productive class discussions—anticipate, monitor, select, sequence, and connect (Stein et al. 2008; Smith and Stein 2011). Making regular use of research-based tools, such as the five practices model, can help teachers move beyond a discussion that is simply a show-and-tell reporting out of discrete strategies toward discussions that instead build mathematical ideas in systematic ways (Wood and Turner-Vorbeck 2001).

An important consideration when moving to more discourse-rich classrooms is the positioning of student thinking and strategies as central to class discussions (Engle and Conant 2002). However, just because we want students to talk more in mathematics classrooms does not mean that they know how to participate in a mathematics discourse or "math-talk" community (Hufferd-Ackles, Fuson, and Sherin 2004). Earlier in this chapter, we discussed the components and levels of a math-talk learning community (see fig. 7.3): (1) teacher role, (2) questioning, (3) explaining mathematical thinking, (4) mathematical representations, and (5) building student responsibility within the community. Hufferd-Ackles and colleagues conducted an intensive year-long case study of an urban third-grade mathematics classroom as the teacher and her students engaged in building a math-talk learning community. Through their research, they identified four levels in shifting from a teacher-centered to student-centered learning environments. At the lowest level, the teacher dominates the conversation, the teacher asks questions focusing on correct answers, very few if any representations are used beyond symbols, and the culture supports students' keeping their mathematical ideas and curiosities to themselves. At the highest level, students do most of the talking, students ask questions of each other to better understand the mathematics, students defend and justify their answers with little prompting from the teacher and often use math drawings, and students believe they have a responsibility in the classroom to support and learn from each other.

Another line of research on mathematics discourse has focused on the use of specific *talk moves* that teachers use to support students in learning productive ways of talking in mathematics classrooms. Increased use of talk moves, such as wait time and revoicing, not only increased the quantity and quality of student talk but it also led to significant gains on assessments of students' mathematical thinking and reasoning (Chapin and O'Connor 2007; Michaels, O'Connor, and Resnick 2008). Chapin and colleagues (2013) have identified four developmental steps to engaging students in academically productive talk in math class, that is, engaging students in talk that moves them toward the intended mathematics learning goals. Their steps include (1) helping individual students clarify and share their own thoughts, (2) helping students orient to the thinking of others, (3) helping students deepen their own reasoning, and (4) helping students engage with the reasoning of others. Within each of these steps they suggest talk moves or specific prompts that teachers can use to engage students, for example, wait time, turn and talk, stop and jot, restating, revoicing, adding on, press for justifications, agree or disagree, and compare and contrast. In essence, the purpose of using the talk moves is to support students in building a collaborative discourse community within the mathematics classroom.

Teachers can transform their classrooms from ones in which they are doing most of the talking and thinking to ones where the students are doing the "heavy lifting" of talking and thinking, and thus learning. As Reinhart (2000, p. 478) suggested, "Never say anything a kid can say" as he reflected on the transformation in his own teaching:

> Eventually, I concluded that if my students were to ever really learn mathematics, they would have to do the explaining, and I, the listening. My definition of a good teacher has since changed from "one who explains things so well that students understand" to "one who gets students to explain things so well that they can be understood."

Promoting Equity through Facilitating Meaningful Mathematical Discourse

The work of promoting meaningful mathematical discourse in the classroom has far-reaching implications for achieving equity in the classroom. In more traditional IRE patterns of classroom discourse, students who contribute correct answers, and do so quickly, are provided with immediate positive feedback. Students who provide no response or incorrect or incomplete responses are likely to be provided with negative or neutral feedback. The feedback is limited to the accuracy of their answer rather than the content of their mathematical thinking and reasoning. In a classroom that features meaningful mathematics discourse, students have opportunities to share their own mathematical thinking in addition to their answers, to receive feedback and critique from others, and evolve their thinking in a visible, public space. As such, a discourse-based mathematics classroom provides stronger access for each and every student —those who have immediate ideas on ways to approach solving problems, those who need more time to grapple with ideas and develop a reasoned approach, as well as those who have faulty reasoning or misconceptions. A discourse-based classroom also gives students access to their peers' thinking, providing them with more possible approaches to a task than just the one that the textbook shows or that the teacher chooses to demonstrate to the class.

However, if the discourse in the mathematics classroom privileges some students' voices over others, such as allowing only a few students to do most of the talking while other students are never or rarely heard, then we clearly have not achieved our goal of fostering equitable mathematics classrooms. Meaningful mathematics discourse has the potential to *challenge spaces of marginality* (Aguirre, Mayfield-Ingram, and Martin 2013) by systematically including more student voices and valuing the contributions of each student in discourse on important mathematical ideas. Aguirre and colleagues suggest that each of us as teachers reflect on the following question: "How do I make sure that all students have opportunities to demonstrate their mathematics knowledge during this lesson?" (p. 47). In equitable classrooms, each student is seen as having strengths and is positioned as capable of making valued contributions in solving high-level mathematics tasks whether working in small groups or engaged in whole-class discussions. No student idea is marginalized, but is rather seen as a developmental step toward mathematical understanding. In addition, equitable classrooms view mathematics authority as interconnected among students, teachers, and text materials, thus also acknowledging students as owners of solution paths and capable of making mathematical connections. In implementing lessons using tasks that promote reasoning and problem solving, we can glean several key suggestions from research on ways to intentionally foster each student's engagement in the mathematics discourse.

- Judicious use of *wait-time*, particularly after a student contribution gives each student time to process mathematical ideas (Herbel-Eisenmann, Steele, and Cirillo 2013; Mehan 1979).

- *Probing* student thinking through a teacher press publicly clarifies mathematical ideas in ways that are accessible to all students (Herbel-Eisenmann, Steele, and Cirillo 2013; Kazemi and Stipek 2001).

- *Inviting* student participation and *creating opportunities to engage with another's reasoning* in strategic ways help ensure that important mathematical ideas are raised, unpacked, and utilized by all students, not just the ones who first originated the idea publicly (Herbel-Eisenmann, Steele, and Cirillo 2013).

A discourse-based mathematics classroom also has profound implications for student positioning (Wagner and Herbel-Eisenmann 2009). Interactions between teachers and students in mathematics class constantly assign roles to one another, and these roles have implications for how students' learning dispositions and identities develop (Anderson 2009; Gresalfi 2009). These interactions in a discourse-focused mathematics classroom must help students see themselves as people who can know, do, and make sense of mathematics, challenging aspects of marginality that also lie within students' own identities. The language choices that teachers and students make, the norms and routines that are set in the classroom, and the types of mathematical interactions that are or are not encouraged can all support or inhibit the development of productive attitudes and practices towards mathematics. For example, careful monitoring of how students are selected to share their thinking might reveal inherent biases (such as calling on male students first or those students perceived as high-achieving, asking English-language learners to repeat others' ideas, always making a student's least-efficient method the first to be discussed) that indicate who gets access and that send students signals about their status. Messages about a fixed mind-set versus a learning mind-set can be conveyed to students. "Listen to what Marcus did because you know he understand this idea" versus "Compare and contrast the strategies used in your group, how are they similar, and how are they different." Teachers should attend to the ways in which students are positioned as capable or not capable of doing mathematics, and work to avoid or disrupt talk that may lead to unproductive conceptions of what it means to know and do mathematics.

Taking Action in Your Classroom

Throughout this chapter, you have examined the characteristics of meaningful classroom discourse and considered ways of facilitating it. Here we summarize some of the key messages for you to keep in mind as you take action in your own classroom.

- Mathematical discourse is the purposeful exchange of ideas through verbal, written, and visual communication.

- Goals of establishing a math-talk community in the classroom include building shared responsibility among students for learning mathematics and empowering them as learners and leaders with positive mathematical identities who believe they can contribute significantly to the mathematical work of the class.

- Classrooms should position students as owners and authors of mathematical ideas, representations, strategies, and reasoning who regularly ask questions to clarify their own understanding and to express their mathematical curiosities and reflections.

- Facilitation of whole-class discussions in the mathematics classroom does not just happen, but requires prior planning and preparation, which allows the discussions to be more manageable and intentional in moving students toward the mathematics learning goals of the lesson.

- Orchestrating productive whole-class discussions in the mathematics classroom is supported by the use of anticipating, monitoring, selecting, sequencing, and connecting student approaches and solution paths.

We now invite you to take action in your own professional setting. We suggest you select a high-level task for an upcoming lesson and intentionally plan to use the ideas suggested in this chapter for engaging your students in meaningful discourse of important mathematical ideas and relationships.

Taking Action in Your Classroom
Planning for Mathematical Discourse

1. Choose a task that has the potential to elicit multiple solution paths from your students. The task should engage students in "doing mathematics" (see chapter 3) and allow for use of multiple representations (see chapter 6). Clearly list the goals that detail the mathematics students will be learning in the lesson.

2. Anticipate the solution paths, both correct and incorrect, that students might use in working on the task, and prepare assessing and advancing questions to use while monitoring their work.

3. Decide on a possible sequence of solution paths that you might use during the whole-class discussion of the task, and make note of purposeful questions for connecting student approaches to the targeted mathematical ideas.

4. Teach the lesson and reflect on how your careful planning helped you manage and facilitate meaningful mathematical discourse that more purposefully moved students toward the intended learning goals.

CHAPTER 8

Elicit and Use Evidence of Student Thinking

Evidence of student thinking and understanding is critical in informing the decisions teachers make during instruction and to prepare for subsequent lessons. In this chapter, you will examine the effective teaching practice, *elicit and use evidence of student thinking.* According to *Principles to Actions: Ensuring Mathematical Success for All* (NCTM 2014, p. 53):

> Effective teaching of mathematics uses evidence of student thinking to assess progress toward mathematical understanding and to adjust instruction continually in ways that support and extend learning.

Listening to what students say, observing their actions, and analyzing their written work are all ways for a teacher to gather information on what students currently know and understand about key mathematical ideas. Doing so is also the means by which a teacher can support and advance student learning. A teacher only knows the extent to which students are meeting learning goals by the evidence seen on their paper or from what they say in math class. Effective teaching includes the skills of noticing students' mathematical thinking, interpreting student understandings, and then deciding how to respond on the basis of those understandings (Jacobs, Lamb, and Phillip 2010). According to Leahy and his colleagues (Leahy et al. 2005, p. 19), "Everything students do…is a potential source of information about how much they understand." This effective mathematics teaching practice on eliciting and using evidence of student thinking is an aspect of formative assessment. According to Wiliam (2007), "Formative assessment is an essentially interactive process in which the teacher can find out whether what has been taught has been learned, and if not, to do something about it" (p. 1054).

The chapter includes five Analyzing Teaching and Learning (ATL) activities.

- ATL 8.1: Examine a task and consider its potential for eliciting students' mathematical thinking.

- ATL 8.2: Analyze a set of student work from a first-grade classroom to determine what it reveals about student thinking.
- ATL 8.3: Watch a video from a third-grade classroom and notice how the teacher attends to and builds on student thinking.
- ATL 8.4: Study samples of student work related to the video lesson and consider how writing not only provides a window into students' thinking but also helps students consolidate their learning.
- ATL 8.5: Read a case from a fifth-grade lesson and examine how the teacher uses student thinking during the lesson as a basis for decisions that advance learning.

For each ATL, we encourage you to make note of your responses, and if possible, share and discuss your thoughts and ideas with colleagues. Once you share or write down your thoughts, continue reading the analysis of the ATL in which we relate the activity to the chapter's focal teaching practice. After the Analyzing Teaching and Learning activities, the chapter includes research findings on attending to student thinking to inform and adjust instruction and examines how the focal teaching practice promotes equity among students. We end the chapter by offering suggestions for applying the ideas on eliciting and using evidence of student thinking in your own classroom.

Surfacing Student Thinking through Tasks

A first step in eliciting student thinking is engaging students in tasks that have the potential to provide insights into their thinking about key mathematical ideas (Wiliam 2011). As we discussed in chapter 3, we can categorize tasks with potential to surface student understanding as high-level tasks (see fig. 3.1, page 41).

Engage in ATL 8.1: Examining the Potential of a Task

In ATL 8.1, we ask you to study the Make a Ten task and consider what potential it might hold for eliciting student thinking and understanding among a class of first-grade students. The task is classified as a "doing mathematics" task. Students must analyze the task and attend to its given constraints. It also engages students in complex and non-algorithmic thinking as the tasks suggests no specific pathway toward a solution. In fact, the task allows for many solutions.

Analyzing Teaching and Learning 8.1

Examining the Potential of a Task

Work through the Make a Ten task (shown below).

- What mathematical ideas might surface as first-grade students work on this task?

- How does the design of the task, particularly prompts 2 and 3, press students to engage more deeply with the mathematics of the task?

Make a Ten Task

1. Use two different colors of interlinking cubes to build a structure of ten. Draw a picture of your structure. Then write a number sentence that describes it.

2. Make a second structure of ten that looks different from your first structure of ten. Write a different number sentence for this structure of ten.

3. Explain how the first and second structures are similar to and different from each other.

Analysis of ATL 8.1: The Potential of a Task for Revealing Student Thinking

In the Make a Ten task, students are prompted to explore combinations of ten by using two colors of cubes to build structures. This task supports a key mathematics learning goal for first grade, that is, to understand, represent, and solve take-apart problem situations with unknown addends.

Due to the open-ended nature of this task, it also has the potential to surface students' emerging understanding of several important mathematical ideas. The ways in which students decide to select the number of cubes of each cube color and how they decide to arrange the cubes offers opportunities for informal discussions about the ways numbers work. For example, students can engage in exploration of and discussions about the ways in which quantities can be decomposed and recomposed to form a set of ten, as well as engage in informal use and discussion of the commutative and associate properties of addition. Some of the ideas that might surface include the following:

- Building relational thinking and understanding of equality by noticing that a change in colors does not change the total amount as being 10 (e.g., 4 red and 6 blue cubes is the same amount as 4 blue and 6 orange cubes).

- Exploring the writing of equivalent expressions with two or more addends as different ways to record their structures of 10, such as writing 6 + 4 for the first structure and then writing 4 + 2 + 4 + 2 for the new arrangement in the second structure.

- Informally applying the commutative property of addition by making a structure and then flipping the structure to show the opposite order of the two quantities (e.g., 6 green and 4 blue compared to 4 green and 6 blue).

- Informally applying the associative property of addition by noticing that three addends can be rearranged and combined in any order, for example, (2 + 5) + 3 = 2 + (5 + 3), while the total amount still remains the same (e.g., combining 2 blue and 5 green cubes then adding 3 red cubes is the same total amount of cubes as first combining 5 green and 3 red cubes and then adding 2 blue cubes).

The second prompt asks students to build a new structure while considering some of the constraints of the task, namely that the second structure must look different from their first and the number sentence must also be different. Students must distinguish what makes their structures different. Do they merely use different colors for the same combination, do they explore new combinations of ten cubes by using new quantities of each color, or do they rearrange the cubes from the first structure? As students write a new number sentence they must check to make sure it is different from the one used for the first structure while also describing the second structure.

A strategic aspect of the task is the third prompt to "explain how the first and second structures are similar to or different from each other." This requires students to think beyond just building combinations of ten and writing equations or expressions; it presses them to consider more profound underlying aspects of mathematical structure, that is, to explore how numbers and operations work.

Interpreting Student Thinking

Effective mathematics teaching uses evidence of student thinking as the basis for making instructional decisions. After eliciting student thinking, the next steps are to attend to the details in each student's mathematical work and interpret what those details reveal about his or her mathematical understanding. It is with this careful analysis of student thinking that we can then best decide how to respond to students on the basis of their understanding.

Engage in ATL 8.2: Examining the Details in Student Work

The Make a Ten task has the potential to surface students' thinking about a rich array of important mathematical ideas and support students in making progress toward the goal to understand and work with take-apart problem situations. Turn to ATL 8.2 and attend to the details in four pieces of student work from a first-grade class on the Make a Ten task.

Analyzing Teaching and Learning 8.2
Examining the Details in Student Work

A class of first-grade students engaged with the Make a Ten task (see ATL 8.1). Four student work samples are shown below. The students drew pictures of their structures and then wrote number sentences to describe each structure. Some students also drew lines to help show how their structures were similar and different.

- What do you notice in each student work sample? What is noteworthy to you?

- What did you learn about each student's mathematical thinking and understanding?

- Which mathematical ideas might you want to pursue further with each student and why?

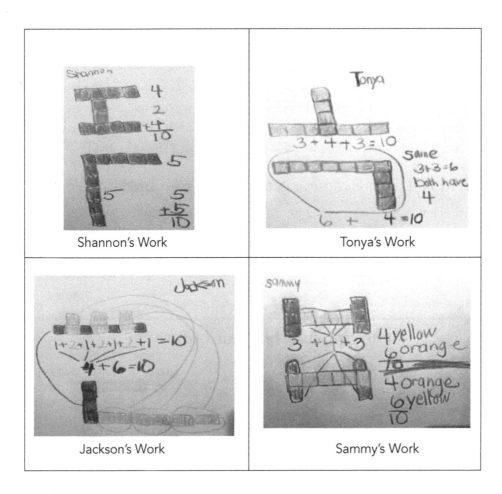

| Shannon's Work | Tonya's Work |
| Jackson's Work | Sammy's Work |

Analysis of ATL 8.2: Interpreting Student Understanding

Students enjoy this task because they get to build structures with cubes, while the constraints of the task, using two colors of cubes that total ten and building two different structures of ten, reveal their emerging mathematical ideas. All four responses to the Make a Ten task show that these first-grade students know how to make a visual record or representation of the structures that they constructed with cubes. These students also know how to write equations (i.e., make a symbolic representation) that describe each structure using two or more addends. Tonya and Jackson each rearranged their same set of cubes from the first structure to the second structure, whereas Shannon and Sammy changed the number of cubes of each color. Most interesting is how Tonya, Jackson, and Sammy each use lines to show connections between the two structures and equations, not leaving much doubt in our minds that they see a relationship between the two. While the drawn and written record of their work provides evidence of their thinking, asking each student to talk further about their structures would provide the teacher with even more evidence of their understanding and emerging mathematical observations and curiosities.

Shannon's first structure uses two colors and she writes 4 + 2 + 4, which clearly matches her structure and totals 10 cubes. She does not abide by the constraints of the problem for her second structure as she only uses one color, nor is it as clear how her equation, 5 + 5 = 10, matches her structure, but we can infer how she sees each group of five cubes. The struggle for Shannon was with the third prompt, describing a relationship between her two structures. She does not indicate that she recognizes the relationship between her two structures or her equations. The teacher might ask the student an assessing question, "How is 4 + 4 + 2 related to 5 + 5?" We mentioned in chapter 5 the use of assessing questions as the teacher's means of gaining greater clarification of student thinking. With this understanding, the teacher can then advance student learning. For Shannon, the teacher might advance her learning by asking her, "Write about ways the first structure can be changed to represent 5 + 5." The teacher will have to resist telling her how to write this explanation because, ultimately, the student's struggle with these ideas will lead to a deeper understanding of the mathematics. Rather, the teacher should use purposeful questions to discern what students know and then adapt the lesson to meet varied levels of understanding by students (NCTM 2014).

Tanya creates two structures, each with blocks of two different colors (pink and purple). She writes an equation that describes each structure. It is clear that she sees a relationship between the two structures and the equations. Tonya even labels the diagram, letting us know that 3 and 3 were combined from the first structure to create the 6 in her second structure. It is evident that she recognizes that 3 + 3 = 6 and that this is the only difference between her two equations as she also wrote "both have 4." Tanya knows she can decompose and recompose quantities and that the sum remains that same total amount, in this case, 10. She can also work successfully with addition equations that have two and three addends. The teacher might want to ask an assessing question, such as what does she mean by the word "same," to reinforce that the equal sign indicates how the structures might look different but have an equivalence in quantity. Then the teacher might use an advancing question, "How could you change your second structure so that you also decompose the 4?"

Jackson's work is very interesting. He has written 1 + 2 + 1 + 2 + 1 + 2 + 1 = 10 for his first structure. Then he clearly indicates that all of the green blocks (representing the twos) were combined and all of the brown blocks (representing the ones) were combined to make his second structure of 4 + 6. It is clear that he knows he can decompose and recompose amounts and that the structures represent the same amount of blocks. It would be informative to ask Jackson to talk about each of his structures. The arrows that he has drawn from the amounts in one equation to the amounts in another indicate that he might see how the two equations are related. An assessing question for Jackson might be "Tell me what all these lines mean?" to encourage him to talk about recomposing the 4 ones into a group of 4 and the 3 twos into a group of 6. An advancing question for Jackson might be, "Can you write 1 + 2 + 1 + 2 + 1 + 2 + 1 another way that shows how you rearranged the numbers for your second structure? This would prompt him to informally apply the commutative and associate properties showing another way to write another equivalent expression.

Sammy's work is noteworthy. He follows the constraints of the task by using two different colors, comparing structures, and writing equations. He writes 4 + 6 and 6 + 4. His structure indicates that he understands the order of the numbers does not matter, because he recognizes that 4 yellow and 6 orange blocks are the same total quantity as 4 orange and 6 yellow. Thus he is developing some informal understanding of the commutative property of addition. He indicates how the 4 is related in each structure, but not the 6. The teacher could ask an assessing question to probe his understanding of how 6 is seen in each structure. Sammy can be challenged to write a sentence about how the two structures and equations are related to each other. Writing is often difficult for students at first, so the teacher might ask Sammy to first describe this relationship and then encourage him to write what he has just described, or the teacher could write it as he dictates. Another option is to video record his explanation.

The students' written work reveals a great deal about what they know and understand regarding the mathematical learning goals for this lesson as well as what mathematical ideas they are exploring. By engaging the students in a discussion of what they did, the teacher can gain even greater clarification of what the students comprehend.

Attending to Student Thinking During Instruction

In our next Analyzing Teaching and Learning activity, we visit the third-grade classroom of Arthur Harris (not to be confused with the Robert Harris in chapter 1). The third-grade students are exploring number relationships, specifically odd and even numbers. The teacher challenges them to build the numbers with square tiles and to explore what makes a number odd and what makes a number even. Think for moment. What are the characteristics of odd and even numbers? How would you define an odd number? How would you define an even number?

Mathematical language and definitions play a key role in the study of mathematics. Students learn early on that sometimes the way a word is used in our everyday language differs from how we use that word in our study of mathematics. While we can look up mathematical definitions, we often find that they are rigorously and technically defined and cannot be directly used in our elementary classrooms. As Ball (2005) notes, "A definition of a mathematical object is useless, no matter how mathematically refined or elegant, if it includes terms that are beyond the prospective user's knowledge." An important aspect of the work of teaching mathematics is to develop mathematical definitions with our students that have mathematical integrity but are also comprehensible and usable as our students first encounter and explore specific mathematical ideas (Thames and Ball 2010).

Mathematicians often define even numbers as an integer that is divisible by 2. The word *divisible*, while similar to the words *division* or *divide*, has a different and very specific meaning. The word *divisible* means being capable of being divided by another number without a remainder. Even numbers are integers that when divided by 2 yield no remainder. Even numbers can be either positive or negative, and 0 is also considered an even number because 0 divided by 2 equals 0. An integer that is not divisible by 2 is an odd number, or in other words, an integer that cannot be divided exactly by 2 is an odd number. In Arthur Harris's classroom, he and his students are trying to define odd and even numbers with mathematical integrity in a manner that has meaning for his students. Through this work, they are learning to construct an argument and make conjectures, that is, they are learning to build a logical progression of statements to explore the truth of their conjectures.

Engage in ATL 8.3: Building on Students' Mathematical Ideas

In ATL 8.3, you will be watching a video of Arthur Harris and his third-grade students as they try to explain what determines whether a number is even or odd. Many of the students in this classroom are English language learners, several who have recently arrived to the United States. The school is a full English-language immersion school, so students immediately become part of English-speaking classrooms.

The lesson in the video is the first time students have discussed odd and even numbers. Mr. Harris wants his students to consider what it might take to justify whether their conjectures about odd and even numbers are likely to hold true for all odd and even numbers. Through their explorations and discussions, he wants his students to build their understanding that even numbers can be divided into two equal groups with no remainders and that odd numbers when divided by two always have one left over, that is, a remainder of one. With these goals for student learning, Mr. Harris can look for evidence that students are making progress toward the mathematics learning goals. Specifically, as students make claims, he wants to see students use several examples to support or refute each other's claims. He will also be looking to see that students can explain their reasoning as to why a claim is true or why it is false.

Mr. Harris explains to the class that they are working to make claims about odd and even numbers and are to support their claims with examples of their reasoning. He begins the lesson by asking students whether the numbers 3 and 6 are even or odd. The video shows the interactions that Mr. Harris has with the whole class and with two small groups. As you watch the video, consider how the teacher elicits and uses student thinking to continually inform and adjust his instruction in ways that support and extend student learning. A transcript is included in Appendix D to support your viewing of the video and its analysis.

Analysis of ATL 8.3: Responding to Student Thinking

As we observe the class discussion, the students are discussing whether 3 is an even or odd number. One student claims that it is odd because it does not have pairs. She states, "because 1, 3, and 5, they don't have pairs, but 2, 4, and 6, they do have pairs" (lines 5–6 in the video transcript). The teacher asks her to show and explain it to the class on the overhead projector. She shows how two square tiles can be put next to each other to make a pair and then tries to explain that the third tile does not have a partner, but struggles to find the words. The teacher does not state whether she is right or wrong, rather, he paraphrases her main ideas, "So it has something to do with this idea of pairs and this one left over."

The teacher then has the students work in small groups to examine the number 8 and discuss whether it is odd or even. As Mr. Harris monitors the small groups, the students seem to agree that 8 is even, however they are not sure how to explain or provide a justification for why it is an even number. Two lines of reasoning seem to emerge from the student discussions. Some students make pairs of tiles, that is, they make as many groups as they can that contain two tiles each (i.e., form 4 groups of 2 tiles each). The other line of reasoning is to try and split the tiles into two equal groups (i.e., form 2 groups of 4 tiles each).

When he visits group 2, he clearly hears both lines of reasoning and sees some confusion on the faces of the students, so he decides to make the two lines of reasoning explicit using the evidence he has gathered by listening to and observing their discussion. He states, "Let me ask you all this. What is the difference between doing it like this (*the teacher shows 2 groups of 4 tiles each*).… Or … doing it like this? (*The teacher shows 4 groups of 2 tiles each.*) How is this different or the same as this?" (lines 30–31). Mr. Harris learns that at least one of the students who has not yet spoken in the group recognizes that either way can be used, she says, "It's the same because it still has 4—it still has 2 groups of 4, and it has 4 groups of 2 (lines 32–33).

A class discussion then ensues regarding the number 8. Clearly the students are still struggling to find the language to explain why 8 is an even number. Acquiring the language to describe work is not always easy, so this student uses a counterexample to make his point. He says, "I know that 8 is even because 9 has a leftover. There's 1 left." (line 37). Even though the class discussion is about the number 8, the teacher recognizes that using counterexamples, such as the number 9, is an important skill used by mathematicians when formulating and refuting conjectures.

Mr. Harris builds on the students' thinking and engages the other students in the class in elaborating on the number 9 and the word *leftover* that was used by the student. He specifically asks, "What does that mean when he uses the word *leftover*? Can anybody clarify what that means?" (lines 43–44). The students lack clarity in their contributions, which is very common when students are learning to share their reasoning and to think about the reasoning of other students. One student replies, "It means it's not a pair because 8 has two … four groups of 8 is two pair, and then 9 is a leftover with. . . 9 is with the odd" (lines 45–46). Mr. Harris could have easily stepped into the conversation to add on and interpret her thinking but he resists, and instead he calls on other students in the class by saying, "Okay. Anybody else want to add to that?" (line 47)." This process of asking students to say back or to add on, slows down the pace of the lesson and provides the students with time to process what is being said, to consider what is or is not clear about the information, and how to shape their own responses. It also provides the teacher with time to think as he considers how to interpret the student thinking and make decisions on how he will continue to build on their thinking as the lesson progresses.

At this point in the lesson, Mr. Harris decides to move the discussion to the other line of student reasoning. Regarding the number 8, a student explains, "You can describe the even number because when you have it in pairs, you have 4 in each pair, and another pair you have 4, and there is no more left" (lines 55–56). Building from the student's contribution and thinking about 8 as comprised of 4 + 4, the teacher begins a discussion about adding doubles, which is a very familiar concept for third-grade students. The class examines 2 + 2 = 4, 4 + 4 = 8, 5 + 5 = 10, 6 + 6 = 12, and 7 + 7 = 14, which are written on chart paper, and determines whether the sum of each double is odd or even. While the students can readily see that the sum is even, they struggle to explain why. As the video clip ends, we see that Mr. Harris is providing time for his students to talk further in their small groups as he poses the challenge, "Why do you think this is happening? What I want you to do is we're going to talk in our groups, your small groups, and what I want you to discuss is how do doubles always make even numbers? Why is that always true?" (lines 87–90).

Throughout the lesson, Mr. Harris is very patient as he listens to the thinking of students, honors their contributions and perplexities, and asks students to think about and comment on each other's thinking and ideas. He uses the evidence he gathers to build on that thinking and move student learning toward the intended mathematical understanding of odd and even numbers, as well as engage this group of young mathematicians in developing the "habits of mind" of mathematical thinkers. For example, these students were engaged in looking for the underlying structure of odd and even numbers and were expected to construct viable arguments or justifications for what determines whether a number is odd or even and to consider, as well as critique, the reasoning of others (NGA and CCSSO 2010).

Eliciting Student Thinking through Writing

In our next Analyzing Teaching and Learning activity, we follow-up with Arthur Harris and his third-grade students as they continue their exploration of odd and even numbers into subsequent lessons. In the lesson you viewed in ATL 8.3, Mr. Harris held a short discussion with his students about the type of number that would result when adding doubles. This discussion was, in essence, a preview of the work for the next few school days. Take a few minutes and examine The Odd and Even task in figure 8.1. A few days after the lesson in the video, the students were posed with this task, which asked them to consider the outcome of adding any two even numbers or any two odd numbers as well as the outcome of adding an odd number and an even number. How would you respond to each of the questions posed to the students? How might you justify each of your responses? What types of responses might you expect to receive from students?

The Odd and Even Task

- Is the sum of two even numbers, even or odd, and how do you know?
- Is the sum of two odd numbers, even or odd, and how do you know?
- Is the sum of an odd number and an even number, even or odd, and how do you know?

Describe your observations and justify your claims with several examples.

Fig. 8.1. Task for third-grade students on exploring odd and even numbers

Engage in ATL 8.4: Writing as a Window into Students' Thinking

As a way to gather evidence of his students' thinking and to help his students start to consolidate their learning about odd and even numbers, Mr. Harris asked his students to put their ideas into writing. In doing so he hopes to determine whether his students now understand the following:

- Adding an even number and an even number will always result in a sum that is an even number, because when both even numbers are added, a larger even number is created, and an even number is always divisible by two.

- Adding an odd number and an odd number will always result in a sum that is an even number, because decomposing each odd number into two equal groups results with one "leftover" from each addend that can then be paired up.

- Adding an odd number and an even number will always result in a sum that is an odd number, because the even number is already even but the odd number will have one "leftover," which continues to be true when the numbers are combined.

With these mathematics goals for student learning, Mr. Harris can look for evidence that students are making progress toward reaching these goals. We ask you to engage in ATL 8.4 in which you will be studying the responses from two of the students on The Odd and Even task (fig. 8.3). Mr. Harris is looking for evidence in their writing that his students can make a claim about odd and even numbers, explain their reasoning, and use several examples to support or refute their claims.

Analyzing Teaching and Learning 8.4
Writing as a Window into Students' Thinking

Kristin and Seth are two students in Mr. Harris's third-grade classroom. The work shown on the next page was produced by these two students in response to the Odd and Even task (fig. 8.1). Study the student responses and consider how the writing provides a window into their thinking and understanding.

- What does each student seem to understand about adding odd and even numbers?

- What misconceptions or limited notions might still exist for these students?

- How might Mr. Harris use the evidence in their writing to further support or extend their ideas about odd and even numbers?

Kristin's discoveries on adding odd and even numbers

Kristin's examples of adding odd and even numbers using her choice of numbers

odd + odd   9+9=18= even

even + even   12+12=24=even

odd+even   10+9 = 19=odd

odd+odd	even+even	odd+even
11+11=22=even	14+14=28=even	20+3 = 23=odd
13+13=26=even	16+16=32=even	40+7 = 47=odd
19+19=38=even	24+24=48=even	100+7=107=odd

Is the sum of two even numbers, even or odd? How do you know?

I know even + even and even have to be
even because if you add two even numbers
together. And You'll get a even number, I know
because even all has partners and the
other even has partners so all them have partners

Is the sum of two odd numbers, even or odd? How do you know?

I know that odd and odd have
to be odd because if you add two
odd numbers together then you get
a odd number sometimes And sometimes if
you add odd and odd together you can get even
because the odd has one extra on each one and you
put it together.

Is the sum of an even and an odd number, even or odd? How do you know?

I know that odd + even sometimes = odd and
sometimes odd + even = even like 100+7=107=odd
and 40+6=46=even, odd + even will always = odd
because of the odd one in the odd number

Seth's discoveries on adding odd and even numbers

Seth's examples of adding odd and even numbers using his choice of numbers

1) 1+1=2 even ⟹ odd + odd = e
2) 9+9=18 even ⟹ odd + add
3) 10+10=20 even, even + even
4) 20+20=40 even, even + even
5) 20+30=50 odd, odd + even
6) 20+50=70 odd, odd + even
7) 18+18=36 even, even + even
8) 13+13=26 even, odd + odd
9) 14+14=28 even, even + even
10) 9+8=17 odd, odd + even

Is the sum of two even numbers, even or odd? How do you know?

I also discoverd that even + even = even because 20+20=40 and 40 is an even number because it end in a 0.

Is the sum of two odd numbers, even or odd? How do you know?

I know that odd to odd = even be caue 9+9=18 and 18 is an even number because it ends in a 8.

Is the sum of an even and an odd number, even or odd? How do you know?

I know even + odd = odd because 20+15=35

35 is odd because t doesn't have a partner. 20+15=35 20 has a partner but 15 has one left over so you put it with 20 and it still has one left over.

Analysis of ATL 8.4: Consolidating Student Understanding

Writing not only provides a window into students' thinking and reasoning but it also allows the teacher to assess what a student understands. Writing is also generative for students. As students engage in writing about their mathematical thoughts, they must generate a personal response to the question posed by drawing upon their current understanding. Through the writing process, students do much more than recall known information. The process of writing supports students in clarifying and organizing their mathematical ideas. It can also help students identify their own knowledge gaps as they try to put words and math drawings on paper. As they write, students are learning as they merge, connect, and consolidate their mathematical ideas.

Kristin's Thinking and Reasoning

Kirstin gives a sound justification for why adding an even number and an even number results in an even number. She says, "An even number has partners and the other even number has partners so they all have partners." She also provides three examples of adding even numbers.

Next, Kristin writes that adding two odd numbers results in an odd number. However, at the top of her paper she provided three examples that refute this claim. Kristin is clearly unsure about the result of adding two odd numbers, as reflected in her use of the word "sometimes." She wrote, "If you add two odd numbers together then you get a odd number sometimes." She then continued writing, "And sometimes if you add odd and odd together you can get even because the odd has one extra on each one and you put it together.".

When Kristin attempts to give a justification for why an even number plus an odd number results in a sum that is always odd, she again uses the word "sometimes." She provides three correct examples of an even number plus an odd number. Her reasoning is even correct. She justifies that "odd and even will always = odd because of the odd one in the odd number." This claim, however, is preceded by an incorrect example when she writes 40 + 6 = 46, thus adding two even numbers.

If Mr. Harris had asked students to only provide examples of each type of equation, he would have thought Kristin understood the mathematics because all of her initial examples at the top of her paper were correct. It is through her written justification that the teacher gains evidence of deeper understanding as well as the tenuousness of her claims. Mr. Harris can use the evidence of Kristin's thinking in her writing to further support and extend Kristin's learning. Kristin knows that examples can help her form conjectures or claims. She has written several equations for each claim and she makes use of her evidence to form generalizations. Because of the error in her claim about adding two odd numbers, Mr. Harris might want to have Kristin identify and represent some odd numbers and then explore these ideas a bit further. It would also be productive to have a conversation with Kristin, as well as the whole class, about whether the claims are "always true" or just "sometimes true." While third graders are not expected to write formal proofs to substantiate their claims, they can reason whether or not it seems likely that the claims should always be true (Flores 2002).

Seth's Thinking and Reasoning

Seth made three accurate claims about adding two odd numbers, two even numbers, and an even and an odd number. However, upon closer inspection of the evidence on his paper, some concerns emerge. His overall justifications seem to rely on what he appears to know about the "evenness" or "oddness" of the numbers from 0 to 9.

Seth provides several examples of the addition of two even numbers resulting in an even number. The reasoning that he provides for determining whether the sum is even is "because 20 + 20 = 40 and 40 is an even number because it end (sic) in a 0." In other words, he describes the equation without any discussion of the characteristics or underlying mathematical structure of even numbers that the class had explored and discussed. He focuses exclusively on the fact that the number 40 ends in a 0. Although he provides three other equations as examples of adding two even numbers, 10 + 10, 14 + 14, and 18 + 8, he does not realize that adding 20 + 30 and 20 + 50 are also examples of adding two even numbers.

When Seth justifies that the addition of two odd numbers is an even number, he again justifies by his example of an equation, in this case, 9 + 9 = 18. Rather than supporting his claim with evidence related to the one extra or "leftover" when dividing 9 into pairs or two equal groups, he justifies his answer as even "because it ends in an 8." The teacher might want to probe further into Seth's understanding of the number 18, such as whether or not he understands that both 8 and 10, which compose 18, are even and therefore 18 is even number.

Seth seems to give a sound justification for why 20 + 15 is an odd number. He claims that the number 20 is even because "20 has a partner" and then explains that "15 has one left over so you put it with 20 and it still has one left over." Once again Seth's explanation of his claim is based on one specific example. He provides several examples of what he thinks is an odd number plus an even number at the start of his work. He writes "20 + 30 = 50 odd, odd and even," and "20 + 50 = 70 odd, odd and even." His work seems to suggest that he believes that 30, 50 and 70 are odd numbers, because the first digit in each of these multiples of ten is an odd number (3, 5, and 7). Further evidence of this likely confusion is supported by the fact that Seth believes 20 and 40 are even numbers. Interestingly, he also seems to believe that 10 is even, which contradicts what appears to be his own faulty rule about what determines whether a number is even or odd.

The written work provides strong evidence for Mr. Harris that Seth holds several faulty ideas about odd and even numbers and that he does not yet understand their underlying structure. The teacher can use the information learned about Seth's thinking to give him additional opportunities to build two-digit numbers, particularly multiples of ten, with square tiles, and then determine whether they are odd or even numbers. This will help Seth discover that numbers that end in zero are in fact even. He will also discover that the number in the tens place does not determine if a number is even or odd.

Using Student Thinking to Advance Learning

The effective mathematics teaching practice on eliciting and using evidence of student thinking centers on using that evidence of student reasoning and understanding (or misunderstanding) to inform teacher actions *during instruction*, as well as to assess students' progress in learning mathematics. As students explore mathematical tasks and engage in mathematical discourse, teachers are constantly gathering information about their students and insights into how the students are using their current understanding in order to make sense of emerging and new mathematical ideas. In our next Analyzing Teaching and Learning activity, we go into the classroom of Ms. Fredrick where her fifth-grade students are working on the Pencil task (see fig. 8.2). The task involves understanding and using fractions within a problem-solving context about boxes of pencils. Take a moment and work through the task, making note of the mathematical ideas that are likely to emerge as students engage in making sense of the task and the mathematics.

The Pencil Task

1. Find the solution to the Pencil task, make a diagram, and write an equation.

    Mrs. Washington cleans her classroom on the last day of school and finds some pencils left over from the year. She knows there are 24 pencils in a full box. Mrs. Washington finds $3/4$ of a box in her desk. How many pencils does she find in her desk?

2. Now use what you know about the first box of pencils to help you think about and solve this problem.

    Mrs. Washington finds $1\frac{1}{8}$ boxes of pencils in the closet of her classroom. How many pencils does she find in the closet?

3. What patterns do you notice when solving the set of pencil problems?

Adapted from Institute for Learning (2015c). Lesson guides and student workbooks available at ifl.pitt.edu.

Fig. 8.2 Task for fifth-grade students on understanding operations with fractions

Engage in ATL 8.5: Structuring the Class Discussion

In ATL 8.5, you will read a case that takes you into the classroom of Ms. Loni Fredrick. She teaches fifth grade and decided to use the Pencil task (shown in fig. 8.2) to engage her students in exploring problem situations that involve multiplication with fractions.

Analyzing Teaching and Learning 8.5
Structuring the Class Discussion

Read the case of Ms. Fredrick and the Pencil task (see below). Consider how she elicited and used evidence of student thinking to inform her instructional decisions throughout the lesson.

- What can be learned about student thinking and understanding during the lesson?

- In what ways did the teacher use the student thinking to structure the class discussion?

- How might the teacher have prepared for this lesson that contributed to its success?

- How might the teacher build on what she learned in this lesson as she plans for the subsequent lesson that will be taught on the following day?

The Case of Ms. Loni Fredrick and the Pencil Task

1   Ms. Fredrick wanted her students to understand multiplication with fractions and mixed
2   numbers by making connections among contextual problem situations, visual diagrams,
3   and equations. More specifically, she wanted her students to apply their previous
4   understanding of multiplication and division to understand multiplication of a fraction
5   and a whole number (i.e., $^3/_4 \times 24$) and of a mixed number and a whole number (i.e.,
6    $1^1/_8 \times 24$). She selected the Pencil task (see fig. 8.2) for several reasons: (1) it aligned with
7   her mathematics goals for student learning; (2) it was challenging yet accessible because
8   students could make a drawing of the problem context and envision actions one might
9   make with concrete objects or boxes of pencils; (3) the two related problems made it
10   possible for students to engage in repeated reasoning by applying information from one
11   problem to the next.
12   Ms. Fredrick began the planning process by anticipating how students might
13   approach the task. This helps her be more attentive and aware of how students use
14   different approaches in solving the problems during the implementation of the lesson.

[handwritten annotation: Zone of Proximal Development]

---

15 It also prepares her to notice and then build on student thinking to help students make
16 important mathematical connections. For the first prompt, she anticipated that some
17 students might draw the 24 pencils and then partition them into 4 equal groups of 6
18 because the problem is about fourths. Once students determined the size of one-fourth
19 as 6 pencils, they could multiply the size of that part (one-fourth) by 3 because the
20 problem asks for three-fourths of the box. Other students might draw 4 pencils and
21 shade 3 of them, then draw 4 more pencils, shading 3 of them, and continue this process
22 6 times. Then they could count the number of shaded pencils in each of the 6 groups to
23 arrive at 18 pencils. Ms. Fredrick also knew that her students liked to use an area model
24 for multiplication situations, but she was concerned that this might result in a potential
25 error of more than 24 pencils, such as multiplying 4×24. Ms. Fredrick recorded the
26 anticipated solution paths on her monitoring chart. Then she generated questions related
27 to the strategies that she might ask during the lesson to assess what students understood
28 or to advance their understanding of the mathematics. She repeated this process for the
29 second prompt.
30   Ms. Fredrick launched the lesson with a brief discussion of the task and then had
31 students work in small groups on the Pencil task. The teacher monitored their work,
32 stopping at different groups to listen in on their conversations and making notes about
33 what students were doing and thinking. After checking in on each group, she circulated
34 a second time around the classroom, asking students assessing and advancing questions.
35 Some students were struggling to get started so she asked questions such as "What
36 information do you know?" "What are you trying to figure out?" "How can you show the
37 box of 24 pencils?"
38   Several student groups were making diagrams of 24 pencils, separating them into
39 4 groups with 6 pencils per group. Although these students were moving along in a
40 productive manner, she still asked them to explain their work because one of her goals
41 was to give students opportunities to construct arguments. For other groups, she asked
42 questions to move the students forward on some aspect of the mathematics. Consider,
43 for example, her exchange with group 4 (Ronaldo, Janelle, Morris, and Alexa) about the
44 incorrect area model they had produced for problem 1 (see fig. 8.3, group 4).

45 **Ms. F.:**   Explain your drawing and what it tells about the box of pencils?
46 **Janelle:**   We drew 24 pencils here *(points to the 24 columns in the drawing)*. Then
47   we made 4 parts and shaded 3 of the parts *(points to the 4 rows, 3 rows are*
48   *shaded)*.
49 **Ms. F.:**   Who can add on? You worked together right? Morris?
50 **Morris:**   We got 96 because we did 4×24 but we knew we only needed 3×24 because
51   we had $^3/_4$ of the box.
52 **Ms. F.:**   I'm confused. Can you talk about the box of pencils when describing what you
53   did? Alexa?

54	**Alexa:**	Well, see this is one box of pencils and there are 24 pencils in the box (*points*
55		*to the 24 columns*). We need to find out how many of the 24 pencils are left
56		because she doesn't have all of them. So I'm not sure now if 72 makes sense.
57		How can we have 72 left when she only started with 24? I think we did
58		something wrong.
59	**Ms. F.:**	What do others think about what Alexa is saying? Ronaldo?
60	**Ronaldo:**	We made 4 groups
61	**Janelle:**	We did but we cut each pencil into 4 parts (*chuckles*).
62	**Ronaldo:**	Oh, we did (*chuckles*).
63	**Ms. F.:**	So talking about the pencils really helped you to realize that 72 pencils does
64		not make sense. You only have 24 pencils to start with. Make a new drawing
65		showing the 24 pencils. Remember $\frac{3}{4}$ of the set of 24 pencils are left. Will this
66		be more or less than 24?
67	**Janelle:**	It is just a little bit less than 24.
68	**Ms. F.:**	I'm going to leave you to work and I'll come back and you can tell me about
69		the pencils. See if you can also write an equation that describes what you did.

70   After checking on all of the small groups, Ms. Fredrick quickly reviewed the
71 information she had collected on her monitoring chart. Group 1 produced a very simple
72 equal-group diagram that others in the class would easily understand (see fig. 8.3,
73 group 1). She decided to have this solution path shared first. Group 2 would go next.
74 They used a similar diagram; however, when writing their explanation, they referred
75 to the four groups as four boxes of pencils, rather than just one box of 24 pencils (see
76 fig. 8.3, group 3). Ms. Fredrick planned to have them present second as it would be
77 worthwhile for them to compare their work with group 1 and consider how to talk about
78 the sets correctly. Group 3 took a unique approach to solving the task (see fig. 8.3,
79 group 3). This group represented 24 pencils in a row, separated them into 6 groups of
80 4, took out 3 pencils from each set of 4 pencils, and then repeated this process 5 more
81 times. This would be the third group to present with comparisons to the previous two
82 solution paths. The lesson would end with group 4 sharing the error made with the area
83 model. To emphasize the value of keeping the context in mind when working on tasks,
84 Ms. Fredrick wanted the class to discuss what was wrong with group 4's diagram and
85 solution of 72 pencils.

86   Ms. Fredrick was using student thinking as the basis for her decisions in sequencing
87 the whole-class discussion of the task. As the presenters explained what their small
88 group did and why, the teacher invited other students to say back what they understood
89 to be true mathematically or to ask questions. She also asked questions that helped
90 students understand how multiplication is related to this problem situation. She knew
91 that because students were partitioning the set of 24 pencils into 4 equal groups and
92 taking 3 of those groups, they often wanted to write a division problem (e.g., 24 ÷ 3/4).

93 Some of the questions she planned to ask included "Why did you write $^3/_4 \times 24$?" "What
94 is the meaning of each factor in the multiplication problem?" "How does this match what
95 you know about multiplication when we worked with whole numbers?"

96 These questions lead to a discussion of the meaning of multiplication. One student
97 commented, "Well if she had found 5 full boxes of pencils, then it would be 5×24, but
98 she only found part of a box." Ms. Fredrick built on this idea and wrote the expression
99 on the board, labeling each factor: 5 complete groups × 24 pencils in each group. The
100 teacher next asked, "What if the teacher had found 1 full box. How would we write that
101 as an equation?" After some student suggestions, she wrote a new expression: 1 complete
102 group × 24 pencils in each group. Next she asked, "How does this help us think about
103 how to write the equation and how would we label each factor?" She had the students
104 do a quick turn and talk about how to write and label each factor in the equation. The
105 resulting class discussion lead to the equation, $^3/_4$ of a group × 24 pencils in each group.

106 Another idea that emerged in the discussion was instigated by a student comment,
107 "Well I know it has to be less than 24." Ms. Fredrick pursued this line of student thinking
108 with the class. Some of the questions she asked included "It has to be less than 24? How
109 do you know it has to be less?" and "What do you notice about the size of the product,
110 the 18 pencils from the set of 24 pencils?" Building from the student comment, these
111 questions gave her the opportunity to prompt students to reason about the size of a
112 product when finding a fraction of a whole set.

113 With fifteen minutes of class remaining, Ms. Fredrick asked the student groups to
114 take a look at the second problem, which describes a situation that uses the same size
115 box of pencils as the first problem. She suggested they reflect on their work from the
116 first problem to help represent and solve the new problem. She reminded them to make
117 sure they also wrote an equation that modeled the situation. She again visited the small
118 groups as they worked, asking questions and recording information on her monitoring
119 chart. This information helped her wrap up this portion of the lesson and plan for
120 continuing the work and discussion of the task in the subsequent lesson on the following
121 day.

$$\frac{24}{4}$$
$$96$$

$$\frac{24}{1} \div \frac{3}{4}$$

$$\frac{24}{1} \times \frac{3}{4} = \frac{72}{4} = 18$$

$$\frac{24}{1} \times \frac{4}{3} = \frac{96}{3} = 32$$

$$\frac{24}{3}$$
$$72$$

Group 1 – Equal Groups Diagram

Mrs. Washington cleans her classroom on the last day of school and finds <u>some</u> pencils left over from the year. She knows there are 24 pencils in a full box.

1. Mrs. Washington finds $\frac{3}{4}$ of a box in her desk. How many pencils does she find in her desk?

She found 18 pencils in her desk.

2. She finds $1\frac{1}{8}$ boxes in the closet. How many pencils does she find in the closet?

24 Pencils + ⦿⦿⦿ = 24+3=27

Group 2 - Division by Four

1. Mrs. Washington finds $\frac{3}{4}$ of a box in her desk. How many pencils does she find in her desk?

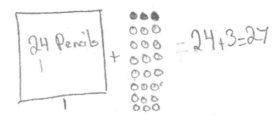

$24 \div 4 = 6$ 6 + 6 + 6 = 18

$\frac{1}{4}$ $\frac{1}{4}$ $\frac{1}{4}$ $\frac{1}{4}$

On my diagram I made 4 boxes that have 6 pencils in each. Then I colored in 3 to make 3 boxes $\frac{3}{4}$.

She found 18 pencils, because $6 + 6 + 6 = 18$.

2. She finds $1\frac{1}{8}$ boxes in the closet. How many pencils does she find in the closet?

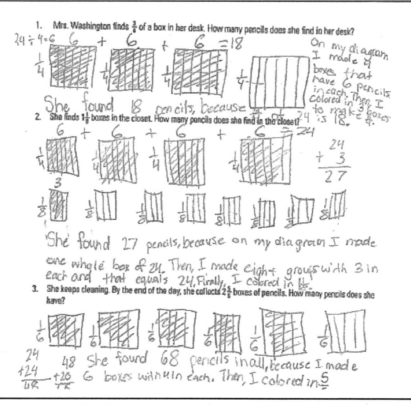

6 + 6 + 6 + 6 = 24

$\frac{1}{4}$ $\frac{1}{4}$ $\frac{1}{4}$ $\frac{1}{4}$

$\begin{array}{r} 24 \\ +3 \\ \hline 27 \end{array}$

3

$\frac{3}{8}$ $\frac{1}{8}$ $\frac{1}{8}$ $\frac{1}{8}$ $\frac{1}{8}$ $\frac{1}{8}$ $\frac{1}{8}$ $\frac{1}{8}$

She found 27 pencils, because on my diagram I made one whole box of 24. Then, I made eight groups with 3 in each and that equals 24. Finally, I colored in 4.

3. She keeps cleaning. By the end of the day, she collects $2\frac{5}{6}$ boxes of pencils. How many pencils does she have?

$\frac{1}{6}$ $\frac{1}{6}$ $\frac{1}{6}$ $\frac{1}{6}$ $\frac{1}{6}$ $\frac{1}{6}$

$\begin{array}{r} 24 \\ +24 \\ \hline 48 \end{array}$ $\begin{array}{r} 48 \\ +20 \\ \hline 68 \end{array}$ She found 68 pencils in all, because I made 6 boxes with 4 in each. Then, I colored in 5.

Group 3 – Makes Six Groups of Four

1. Mrs. Washington finds $\frac{3}{4}$ of a box in her desk. How many pencils does she find in her desk?

$\frac{3}{4} \times \frac{24}{1} = \frac{18}{1}$

In order to find out how many pencils Mrs. Washington has I multiplied $\frac{3}{4} \times 24$. The product of $\frac{3}{4} \times 24$ is 18. She found 18 pencils in her desk.

⑱

2. She finds $1\frac{1}{8}$ boxes in the closet. How many pencils does she find in the closet?

$1\frac{1}{8}$ 1 = ☐24 pencils $\frac{1}{8} \times \frac{24}{1} = \frac{24}{8} = $ ☐3 pencils

24+3= 27 pencils.

First I knew the 1 in $1\frac{1}{8}$ was 24 pencils. So then I mutiplied $\frac{1}{8} \times 24 = 3$. So I added 24 +3 = 27. That meant there were 27 pencils

Group 4 - Faulty Reasoning

They eventually got there, but why did that work???

1. Mrs. Washington finds $\frac{3}{4}$ of a box in her desk. How many pencils does she find in her desk?

24

$\frac{3}{4}$ –

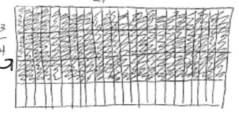

$\frac{3}{4} \times \frac{24}{1} = \frac{72}{4} =$

18 pencils

2. She finds $1\frac{1}{8}$ boxes in the closet. How many pencils does she find in the closet?

24 +

24

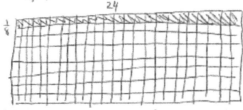

$\frac{24}{192} = \frac{1}{8}$

$24\frac{1}{8}$

Fig. 8.3. Student group work on the Pencil task

Analysis of ATL 8.5: Instructional Decisions Based on Student Thinking

Throughout the lesson, Ms. Fredrick attended to student thinking. She noticed what students were saying, the actions they were taking, and the information they were recording on paper. She then interpreted the evidence of student thinking and used it to inform her instructional decisions. Ms. Fredrick had anticipated specific student strategies as she planned the lesson, drawing from her previous years of teaching as well as from her knowledge of studying mathematical progressions and students' developmental learning trajectories for operations with fractions. Using this knowledge from the professional literature, from her previous experiences, and from her careful monitoring of student thinking during the lesson allowed her to make those in-the-moment decisions in ways that built on student thinking throughout the lesson.

Ms. Fredrick used what she learned from her interactions with the small groups and her quick analysis of their work to make decisions regarding which group, and sometimes even which student, would present their work during the whole-class discussion. She determined the order in which the solution paths would be presented and what connections would be made among the solution paths. Hence, the thinking of her students provided the foundation of the sequence of solution paths during the whole-class discussion.

Group 1 presented first. They drew 4 groups with 6 pencils in each group; then selected 3 of those groups for a total of 18 pencils as the portion of the box remaining. The students showed a diagram, but failed to talk about or write an equation. Their discussion, however, let her know that they understood the situation.

Group 2 presented second. Ms. Fredrick was worried about their understanding of the contextual situation. The students referred to the groups of 4 as boxes rather than understanding that the set of 24 pencils is 1 box of pencils. The students did seem to understand that they only have $3/4$ of the set of 24 pencils. The students wrote $24 \div 4 = 6$ on their paper showing that they separated the pencils into 4 groups, however, they referred to them as 4 boxes and needed to think further about the statement, "On my diagram I made $3/4$ boxes that have 6 pencils in each. Then I colored in 3 boxes to make $3/4$." The students did, though, conclude by stating, "She found 18 pencils because $3/4$ of 24 is 18." Ms. Fredrick wondered whether the students knew that they could write $3/4 \times 24$. The students' diagram and written work indicated that they understood the portion of the pencils that remained in the set of 24 pencils.

Group 3 presented third. They had a unique approach to solving the task. This group represented 24 pencils all in a row, separated them into groups of 4 pencils each, then identified $3/4$ of each group, thus marking 3 pencils from each group, and then repeated this process for all 6 groups. Next the students added the 3 pencils that were shaded in each of the 6 groups to arrive at 18 pencils. The students contrasted the work of this group with the previous groups.

Most students said they had not even thought about using such an approach, nor had they thought it would work, but they noted that the group did get the right answer. They wondered whether it would work for other problems. Ms. Fredrick encouraged students to keep this in mind and perhaps try it as they continued to examine similar situations. Another mathematical aspect of the work of this group that was highlighted was their writing of the equation, $3/4 \times 24$. Building from their sharing, the teacher launched into a discussion of the meaning of the factors in a multiplication equation, that is, the first factor indicates the number of groups and the second factor indicates the size of each group. She wanted students to understand that the meaning of the factors in a multiplication equation is the same whether the factors are whole numbers or fractions. In the Pencil task, $3/4$ indicates the number of groups (which happens to be less than one whole group) and 24 indicates the size of one complete group.

As Ms. Fredrick listened to the reasoning of group 4 she learned that they were not paying attention to the context of the situational problem. A student in the group said they needed to multiply $3/4 \times 24$ to get the answer, so the students applied an algorithm and got the correct answer. However, the group struggled with how to make a diagram that matched their equation. Since the equation was multiplication, the students tried to apply a previously studied area model for whole numbers to the fraction situation. As the students worked in their small group, the teacher asked students about their drawing and the context; as a result they were able to realize some of the confusion and decided to start over with a new diagram. This was the final group to present their work to the class. The class discussed group 4's faulty reasoning in drawing a diagram and their confusion in understanding how the algorithm relates to the context and the visual representations.

Over the course of the next few lessons, Ms. Fredrick and her students will continue to examine situations in which they need to find a fraction of a set of objects. For example, she intends to have them examine other contextual situations working with fractions less than 1, such as $2/6 \times 54$ and $5/8 \times 48$, as well as situations with mixed numbers, such as $1\frac{1}{4} \times 36$ and $2\frac{2}{6} \times 48$. She might also rearrange the groups now that she has a clearer sense of which students are struggling with various aspects of the mathematical work and which appear to be making solid progress so they can learn from the thinking and reasoning of each other. She has noticed that when she rearranges the groups after class discussions of tasks, students would often ask each other about the use of specific approaches and solution paths from previous lessons that they had been mulling over and wanting to better understand and perhaps try out. Thus, the students were drawing upon each other as resources in their mathematical work.

Ms. Fredrick carefully planned this lesson. She solved the task first. Then she anticipated ways in which the students might solve the task and determined specific questions that she could ask to gain clarification and assess what students knew, as well as questions to ask that would advance students toward the goal of the lesson. She developed a monitoring tool (discussed earlier in chapter 7) to use during the lesson to track student thinking and reasoning. Through this planning process, Ms. Fredrick prepared herself to notice and build on student thinking and support student learning by giving students ownership of the work. This careful planning also helped her manage the numerous decisions that teachers must make in the moment as they interact with students as well as support herself in not taking over the thinking and reasoning of her students, allowing her to encourage them in ways that fostered productive struggle with the mathematics. Ms. Fredrick's lesson is one example among others seen in this book of teachers who pay close attention to student thinking and reasoning and utilize the five practices for orchestrating a productive class discussion (Smith and Stein 2011) that we examined in chapter 7. Ms. Fredrick elicited evidence of student thinking through the lesson, and used that evidence to not only advance the learning of individual students but to also develop shared understanding as a mathematics learning community.

What the Research Says: Elicit and Use Evidence of Student Thinking

Eliciting and using evidence of students' mathematical thinking is an aspect of formative assessment. The focus of this teaching practice highlights the central role that student thinking needs to play in informing the daily, in-the-moment instructional decisions of teachers. As Wiliam (2007, pp. 1054, 1091) notes:

> Formative assessment is an essentially interactive process, in which the teacher can find out whether what has been taught has been learned, and if not, to do something about it...Day-to-day formative assessment is one of the most powerful ways of improving learning in the mathematics classroom.

A core task of teaching involves attending to and interpreting student thinking related to mathematical ideas (Lamb, Jacobs, and Phillip 2010; Sleep and Boerst 2012). This is the means by which teachers can determine what ideas appear to be clear to students and what ideas are muddled, and then determine next instructional actions. Attending to student thinking involves listening to what students say, observing their actions, and analyzing written records of their thinking (e.g., math drawings, diagrams, tables, graphs, equations, and sentences). Teachers who consistently elicit student thinking during a lesson are better able to meet their students' learning needs by using that evidence to adapt their instruction (Leahy et al. 2005).

Talk and writing go hand in hand and both provide a window into student learning. In fact, writing is most effective if talk precedes it (Rivard and Straw 2000). Rivard (2004) directly investigated the effect of writing following talk in eighth-grade science classrooms. They found that talk in conjunction with writing has a greater effect on students' achievement than talk alone or writing alone. This finding may be explained by the roles of talk and writing with talk taking a primary role in sharing knowledge while writing more aptly allows for deliberate organization and consolidation of knowledge (Gunel, Hand, and Prain 2007).

Similarly, Huinker and Laughlin (1996) utilized an approach in mathematics classrooms that they called "Think-Talk-Write." In this approach, they included a deliberate wait period for students to first "think" individually, then they "talk" with peers, and only then do they start to "write" in response to the given prompt or task. The writing of these students was much richer with more details and depth of discussion compared to students who immediately started writing. Writing plays an important role in teaching and learning as well as in development of students' mathematical identities. Student writing in the mathematics classroom documents emerging student understanding while also giving students ownership and authority over those mathematical ideas. When students write, they reflect on their thinking and come to a better understanding of what they know and what gaps remain in their knowledge (Rivard 1994), thus compelling students to take more ownership of their mathematical ideas as they "put their thinking on paper."

In a traditional paradigm of mathematics instruction, teachers often wait until the end of a unit of instruction (or the Friday quiz) to elicit evidence of student thinking and then try to determine what students know or do not know in order to assign a grade (Wiliam 2007). The effective mathematics teaching practice to *elicit and use evidence of student thinking* presents a much different vision for the use of evidence to inform daily teacher-student interactions in the mathematics classroom. The work begins during the planning process as teachers anticipate possible student strategies on a lesson task and link these solution paths to the mathematics learning goals of the lesson. The teacher then uses this planning information during the lesson as a gauge to determine what students know, what ideas are fuzzy, how best to respond to students as they work, and how best to structure the whole-class discussion that is centered on student thinking and builds toward the mathematics learning goals for the lesson (Smith and Stein 2011).

Eliciting and using evidence of student thinking both in planning for instruction and during the implementation of lessons relies on teachers having knowledge of research-based learning trajectories for particular mathematical ideas (Clements and Sarama 2004; Sztajn et al. 2012). In particular, the work of Clements and Sarama (2014) provide trajectories that show how students' mathematical thinking develops and builds naturally from preschool to about fourth grade. They have described trajectories for number and operations (e.g., subitizing, counting, composing and decomposing number, addition and subtraction), for geometry (e.g., spatial thinking, shapes, composition of 3D shapes), and for measurement (e.g., length, area, volume, angle measurement). Similarly, Confrey and colleagues have developed trajectories for equi-partitioning and work with fractions (Maloney, Confrey, and Nguyen 2014) and worked to blend mathematics progressions from standards documents with developmental learning trajectories (Confrey, Maloney, and Corley 2014). The trajectories provide teachers with tools to elicit specific aspects of mathematics knowledge, to categorize types of student thinking based on the evidence, and to make decisions about next developmental steps in student learning.

Promoting Equity by Eliciting and Using Evidence of Student Thinking

Whose work gets selected and discussed during a lesson sends important messages to students about the solution paths that are valued and valid in the mathematics classroom. Students' mathematical identities are shaped via this process. By carefully listening to and interpreting student thinking, teachers position students' contributions as mathematically valuable and contributing to a broader collective understanding of the mathematical ideas at hand (Davis 1997; Duckworth 1987; Harkness 2009). Teachers can use this everyday work of listening to student ideas and probing their thinking to highlight important mathematical ideas. This approach has the potential to strengthen students' identities as knowers and doers of mathematics as well as provide teachers a more nuanced view of their own students as learners (Crespo 2000). Until teachers elicit the ways in which students are thinking, they are blind to the ways in which students may be *drawing on multiple sources* of knowledge to think and reason mathematically, a feature of equity-based mathematics classrooms (Aguirre, Mayfield-Ingram, and Martin 2013).

Eliciting and using student thinking in ways that focus on the mathematics serves to recognize historically marginalized student populations or students who do not have a strong track record of success in mathematics. In particular, promoting a classroom culture in which mistakes or errors are viewed as important reasoning opportunities can encourage a wider range of students to engage in mathematical discussions with their peers and the teacher. By placing student thinking at the center of classroom activity, it is more likely that students who have felt evaluated or judged in their past mathematical experiences will make meaningful contributions to the classroom over time.

The essence of whole-class discussions is making student thinking visible and public for discussion and examination. While the selecting and sequencing of the student approaches should be guided by the mathematics learning goals, it also needs to occur in a manner that clearly demonstrates the value of each student and her or his ideas, whether they are correct or incorrect. Often it is the discussion of errors that leads most directly to deepening understanding, and as such each mistake can be an opportunity for learning if the discussion focuses on the source of the faulty reasoning. Engaging students in class discussions that analyze and compare students' thinking and reasoning across a variety of solution paths validates the contributions of each learner and supports the classroom as a mathematical learning community. How student work is shared has significant implications for whether or not students come to view themselves as competent in understanding and using mathematics. For example, a teacher might choose to identify and honor a student's idea as one worth sharing and discussing. The teacher can then invite other students in the class to evaluate their peer's ideas, removing herself or himself as the sole authority in the classroom. By doing this, students learn to listen and think critically about each other's mathematical ideas. Student participation in discussions also increases by explicitly encouraging other students to comment on their peer's work. Asking students to add on or paraphrase their peer's ideas opens doors for a diversity of views and strategies as being mathematically valuable, thus valuing the thinking and reasoning of each student. In the video lesson on the Odd and Even task (ATL 8.3), the teacher, Arthur Harris, demonstrated great patience and clear attention to valuing student thinking and building on their ideas during the lesson. Ms. Fredrick (ATL 8.5) also elicited and used students thinking during the lesson on the Pencil task. She made public the reasoning of the small groups during the whole-class discussion, both correct and incorrect approaches, and based the class discussion on student thinking in a manner that valued student approaches and ideas while also supporting the class in building shared understanding of the mathematics while moving the class toward the mathematical agenda of the lesson.

Taking Action in Your Classroom

Throughout this chapter you have examined and considered ways that teachers elicit and use student thinking during a lesson to give students ownership of their learning as well as to ensure that student learning builds on prior knowledge. Here we summarize some of the key messages for you to keep in mind as you take action in your own classroom.

- Gathering evidence of students' mathematical thinking entails listening to what students say, observing student actions, and analyzing student written work, including use of math drawings, words, and symbols.

- Mathematical tasks that promote reasoning and problem solving provide opportunities to surface students' mathematical curiosities, reveal current understandings, and discern emerging understandings of important mathematical ideas.

- Writing provides teachers with a window into students' thinking as well as helps students to clarify and organize their mathematical ideas, identify their own knowledge gaps, and consolidate their mathematical ideas.

- Anticipating possible student solution paths prior to a lesson makes it possible for teachers to better manage, recognize, attend to, and make use of student thinking and reasoning during the lesson.

- Noticing student thinking during instruction, using that evidence of student ideas as the basis for making in-the-moment instructional decisions, and building on student thinking to create shared understanding of mathematical ideas underlies effective teaching of mathematics.

We now invite you to take action as you consider what implications the ideas discussed in this chapter have for your own professional setting. We suggest you select an upcoming mathematics lesson, or series of lessons, and plan more intentionally to elicit and then use that evidence of student thinking to inform your instructional decisions. Then implement the lesson(s) and monitor your own observation and use of student thinking during your instruction.

Taking Action in Your Classroom
Eliciting and Using Evidence of Student Thinking

Select a lesson that you will soon be teaching centered on a task that promotes reasoning and problem solving and has the potential to elicit multiple solution paths among your students.

- Establish clear mathematics learning goals for the lesson and consider what students might say, do, or write as evidence of their thinking related to the goals.

- Anticipate the solution strategies, both correct and incorrect, that students might use in working on the task, and create a monitoring chart for tracking student thinking.

- Teach the lesson and reflect on the extent to which you elicited and made use of student thinking and the impact on student learning.

CHAPTER 9

Support Productive Struggle in Learning Mathematics

Learning with understanding requires one to wrestle with and reflect upon mathematical experiences to determine how new insights and information fit with existing ideas. In this chapter, you will examine the effective teaching practice, support productive struggle in learning mathematics. According to *Principles to Actions: Ensuring Mathematical Success for All* (NCTM 2014, p. 48):

> Effective teaching of mathematics consistently provides students, individually and collectively, with opportunities and support to engage in productive struggle as they grapple with mathematical ideas and relationships.

As students work to make sense of tasks and problem situations, they engage in productive struggle when they initially see no obvious or clear solution pathway. Hiebert and Grouws (2007) described mathematical tasks that lead to productive struggle as those that are "within reach but that present enough challenge, so there is something new to figure out" (p. 388). Classroom environments that support productive struggle give students time and space to grapple individually with mathematical tasks, to work in pairs and small groups, and to engage in whole-class discussions. It is often difficult for teachers to see students struggle, but it is through the struggle that learning occurs. Our role as teachers is to provide scaffolds, such as purposeful questioning, that honor and build on the thinking of students without removing the demands of the task or doing the thinking for them.

The chapter includes three Analyzing Teaching and Learning (ATL) activities.

- ATL 9.1: Watch a video clip of a third-grade classroom and investigate how a teacher helps her students make progress on a task exploring fraction concepts.

- ATL 9.2: Examine teacher-student dialogues and determine the types of interactions that help or hinder the perseverance of fifth-grade students on a task examining division with fractions.

- ATL 9.3: Read a transcript from a second-grade lesson and identify the teacher's strategies to support productive struggle among her students as they pose and justify quantitative statements about a set of orange and gray beads.

For each ATL, we encourage you to make note of your responses, and if possible, share and discuss your thoughts and ideas with colleagues. Once you have shared or written down your thoughts, continue reading the analysis of the ATL in which we relate the activity to the chapter's focal teaching practice. After the analyzing teaching activities, the chapter includes research findings on the role of productive struggle in learning mathematics and examines how the focal teaching practice promotes equity among students. We end the chapter by offering suggestions for applying the ideas on productive struggle in your own classroom.

Supporting Students in Grappling Productively with the Mathematics

In learning mathematics, it is only natural that students have to put forth effort to make sense of a problem and how to approach solving it when a strategy is not stated, implied, or immediately obvious. Struggle is an expected part of problem solving and learning. It is important, however, that the struggle for students is still within their reach and that it leads them to deeper understanding of the mathematics.

In our first Analyzing Teaching and Learning activity in this chapter, we investigate a third-grade classroom where students are working on the Half-of-a-Whole task, shown in figure 9.1. The task, although appearing fairly easy at first glance, contains just the right amount of challenge for students who are just beginning a unit of study on fractions. The task requires students to analyze a set of figures and determine those that show one-half shaded and those that do not. Take a moment to work through the task and note which figures are likely to be fairly easy for students to identify as halves and which figures are likely to create a bit of disequilibrium (Carter 2008) for students as they try to identify and justify whether one-half of a figure is shaded.

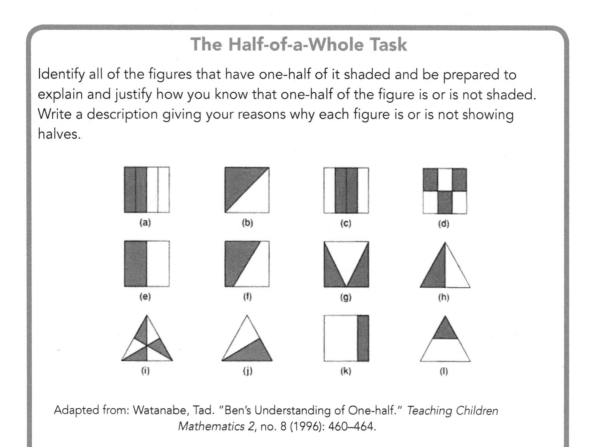

The Half-of-a-Whole Task

Identify all of the figures that have one-half of it shaded and be prepared to explain and justify how you know that one-half of the figure is or is not shaded. Write a description giving your reasons why each figure is or is not showing halves.

(a) (b) (c) (d)

(e) (f) (g) (h)

(i) (j) (k) (l)

Adapted from: Watanabe, Tad. "Ben's Understanding of One-half." *Teaching Children Mathematics 2*, no. 8 (1996): 460–464.

Fig. 9.1. A third-grade task on fraction concepts

Engage in ATL 9.1: Student Struggles and Teacher Supports

We now join Ms. Millie Brooks in her third-grade classroom. She wanted to surface students' initial understanding of fraction concepts as they began their new unit of study. She also wanted to engage students in a task that promotes reasoning and problem solving with multiple entry points and solution paths. The task meets both of these criteria for her students. It is a high-level task that, as we discussed in chapter 3, *all* students could enter and explore fraction concepts at some level while also having potential for engaging students in challenging mathematics. This is what we call a low threshold, high-ceiling task.

Ms. Brooks established two mathematics goals for the lesson, which she used as a target toward which she advanced student learning.

1. Students will understand that one-half of a figure can be represented in multiple ways as long as the areas of each half have equal size, regardless of the location of the pieces that comprise each half.

2. Students will notice and understand a numeric relationship between the numerator and the denominator for fractions that are equivalent to one-half, specifically, when the denominator is twice the value of the numerator, the fraction is equivalent to one-half.

Ms. Brooks set up the task by ensuring students understood its expectations. She then gave each student a set of enlarged figures, which they could fold or cut as needed to support their decision-making and justifications. The students first worked independently and then discussed their solutions as a small group. Her only stipulation was that when discussing a solution, the team members must make sure everyone in the group understood the strategies and reasoning related to that solution.

We ask you to turn to ATL 9.1. You will watch a video clip from Ms. Brooks' classroom and consider it through a lens of productive struggle. The teacher circulates around the classroom making brief visits to each group, listening to student explanations of their reasoning processes, and asking questions to assess their understanding. The video clip focuses on one small group of four students as they discuss their solutions to figure (d) in the task (see fig. 9.1). Ms. Brooks visits this group a total of three times, with approximately three to five minutes between visits. One student in the group has just claimed that figure (d) has one-half shaded and one-half not shaded. Ms. Brooks asks the other group members whether they agree or disagree with Zaria. A transcript is included in Appendix E to support your viewing of the video clip and its analysis.

Analyzing Teaching and Learning 9.1 more

Student Struggles and Teacher Supports

Watch the video clip of Ms. Brooks interacting with a small group of students.

- What are the students struggling with as they work on the task?

- What progress do students make in their understanding of the mathematics?

- How does the teacher support students in struggling productively in understanding the mathematics toward the intended learning goals?

You can access this video online by visiting NCTM's More4U website (nctm.org/more4u). The access code can be found on the title page of this book.

Analysis of ATL 9.1: How Student Learning Can Be Supported

We would consider this episode from Ms. Brooks' class an example of supporting productive struggle. By clearly identifying learning goals and selecting an aligned high-level task, Ms. Brooks was able to elicit students' thinking through her use of questioning and representations and, in so doing, helps students determine and justify why a figure shows halves. Key to supporting productive struggle is helping students make progress without telling them what to do and how to do it. According to NCTM (2000, p.19):

> Teachers must decide what aspects of a task to highlight, how to organize and orchestrate the work of the students, what questions to ask to challenge those with varied levels of expertise, and *how to support students without taking over the process of thinking for them and thus eliminating the challenge* [emphasis added].

Ms. Brooks engages her students in grappling productively with the mathematics in several ways. Here we discuss four ways in which she supports student struggle: (1) use of visual and physical representations, (2) use of probing questions, (3) use of teacher revoicing, and (4) the selection of a low threshold, high-ceiling task.

As students struggle to make sense of halves, Ms. Brooks provides visual and physical representations of the figures to help students grapple with the mathematical ideas and to formulate their justifications. Enlarged cut-out models allow students to manipulate the figures, cutting or folding them as needed. The students in the small group struggle to recognize that three-sixths as discrete pieces in figure (d) represents half of the figure. Mayah argues, "It doesn't show you halves because one is not shaded" (line 11 in the video transcript), referring to the top row that has two shaded parts and one part not shaded. Mayah is clearly struggling with prior knowledge, likely believing that half can only be represented with a contiguous area (e.g., adjacent parts) and halves must include two equal pieces. Ms. Brooks encourages the students to cut the figure apart and see how that might help with their reasoning. She suggests, "Don't be afraid to cut it up" (line 16). The students proceed to cut apart figure (d) and rearrange the parts. This helps Mayah make a comparison between her new arrangement of the sixths and that of the original figure, as shown below. Mayah states, "This is equal to half because like this is the same thing." Mayeh then explains that the rearranged figure (d) now looks just like figure (e) which clearly shows halves.

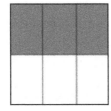

Fig. (d) rearranged

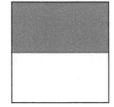

Fig. (e)

You can see Hensley is still grappling with and pondering Mayah's suggestion as he starts to rearrange the pieces back to show the original figure (d) (lines 51–52 in the transcript). Javier then joins in the conversation and shows his confidence in his solution as he excitedly presents his justification for the equivalence (lines 53–60). He proves that $^3/_6$ is equivalent to $^1/_2$ by placing the shaded portions on top of each other and indicating that they take up the same amount of area. Although only Zaria at first recognized that $^3/_6$ in figure (d) represented $^1/_2$, all four students were able to engage productively in the task because the teacher provided visual and physical representations and encouraged, even insisted, that students cut apart the figures and move around the pieces as justifications when sharing their reasoning with each other.

Another approach that Ms. Brooks uses to foster productive struggle with the mathematics is her continual probing of student thinking each time she returns to the group. She requires that students explain, elaborate, and clarify their thinking when working on the task. By asking probing questions, such as "Tell me whether or not this figure shows me halves" (line 2 in the transcript), "Prove it" (line 4), "Well, prove me wrong" (line 8). Students are challenged to give justifications as to why the figures show halves or why they do not show halves. One student demonstrates that the halves take up the same amount of area of the figure. Another student recognizes and explains how a numeric relationship exists between the numerator and the denominator for fractions that are equivalent to one-half. Ms. Brooks prompts the group to engage "collectively" as the mathematics teaching practice states, not just individually, so that as a group they are able to grapple with mathematical ideas and relationships. Her statements and questions convey to students that they are to work as a unit, listening to and building on each other's ideas. Throughout the video clip, Ms. Brooks not only probes individual student's thinking but also continuously encourages and prompts students to engage with the thinking and reasoning of others. Below are several examples:

- "So now I want you to get them to see what you saw, that this is half" (lines 15–16).
- "When I left here, you were held accountable for what you were saying. You had to prove to your group that that was a half" (lines 17–18).
- "Who can tell me what Zaria was talking about?" (lines 20–21).
- "Everyone write me a fraction" (line 37).
- "Hensley, do you agree that that's a half (line 43)?

Along with probing student thinking, a particularly important move that a teacher can make when facilitating discussion is revoicing of students' contributions. This move behaves very much like repeating or paraphrasing a student's contribution; however, it is often much more purposeful. Revoicing serves to organize a student's ideas and add pertinent mathematical details to a student's statements in order to prompt that student as well as other students to struggle a bit more with specific mathematical ideas. We can see one such example in line 34, as a student says "But I know that it is equal, because 3 are shaded and 3 are not shaded." Ms. Brooks revoices the student's contribution by saying, "Oh, so you know it's equal because 3 are shaded and 3 are not shaded? So we have an equal number that are shaded and an equal number that are not shaded" (lines 35–36). Revoicing the student's contribution and putting emphasis on the "equal number" is a means of helping students notice a numeric relationship between the numerator and the denominator for fractions that are equivalent to one-half. This revoicing supports student learning because it makes it possible to surface specific mathematical ideas and prompt students to grapple or think a bit more about the mathematics in a productive manner.

Finally, one more approach we would like to point out relates to the task selected by Ms. Brooks during her instructional planning. Ms. Brooks selected a task that is a low-threshold, high-ceiling task—a task in which all students can enter and explore the mathematics at some level while also having the potential for engaging students in more challenging mathematics. Take, for example, students who immediately recognize that figures (e) and (h) show halves, but have to draw upon spatial reasoning to consider figures (b) and (j). Other students might easily recognize these four figures but have to wrestle a bit with the figures that show more than two parts (e.g., figs. (a), (c), (d), and (i)). Finally, figures (f) and (g) provide still further challenges for many students. At first glance, this task is about the idea of halves; however, this task can lead to powerful generalizations and foundational ideas about fractions. Most important, perhaps, is the understanding that half the area of a figure can be shown in an infinite number of ways and that the parts do not need to be adjacent (i.e., the additive property of area). In addition, students can begin to also understand that the same amount of area of a figure (or the same point on the number line) can be identified with an infinite number of equivalent names, from a single number (e.g., $\frac{3}{6}$) to more complex expressions (e.g., $\frac{1}{6} + \frac{1}{6} + \frac{1}{6}$).

As you can see, several of the effective mathematics teaching practices serve to support student learning. In fact, it is the *interplay* among students' use of representations during mathematical discourse, the teacher's asking purposeful questions to elicit student reasoning, and the teacher's making use of student thinking that supports productive mathematical engagement in a high-level task. The teacher was careful to maintain the challenge of the task without taking over the process of thinking for the students. The struggle of these four students with the task was productive because the outcome was deeper understanding of the mathematics among the students.

Considering How Teachers Respond to Student Struggles

It is not easy for a teacher to resist "telling" students how to approach a task when a student seems to not know what to do or is very hesitant in getting started. To resist taking over the thinking of students, a teacher needs to have a tool kit of alternative approaches to call upon when students reach an impasse. In the next Analyzing Teaching and Learning activity, fifth-grade students are working on Seth's Birthday Cake task, shown in figure 9.2. The task requires students to make sense of a division situation involving fractions. Take a moment to work through the task, responding to both parts, and consider how students might approach the task.

Seth's Birthday Cake Task

After his birthday party, Seth had one-fifth of his cake leftover. Eight of his friends spent the night. His friends plan to eat the remaining cake as a snack later that night, and they each expect to receive an equal share of the remaining cake. They want to know what fractional part of the original cake will each friend get to eat for a snack. $\to \frac{1}{40}$

1. What fractional part of the cake did each friend eat for a snack? Draw and clearly label a diagram that shows how much of the cake is eaten by one person for the snack. Use words to explain your reasoning and decisions for how you drew the diagram.

2. Seth claims that to find the answer you can use the expression $8 \div 1/5$. His friend Frankie says that the expression would be $1/5 \div 8$. Who is correct? Why?

   Seth is correct

Adapted from Institute for Learning (2015a). Lesson guides and student workbooks available at ifl.pitt.edu

---

Fig. 9.2. A task on division contexts involving fractions

Engage in ATL 9.2: Student Impasse Scenarios

Ms. Tate gave the Seth's Birthday Cake task to her fifth-grade class. The students worked individually to solve the problem, and several of them got only so far in completing the task before they reached an impasse. As you engage in ATL 9.2, you will consider five scenarios presented as teacher-student dialogues and examine how the teacher intervened in an effort to support the students in making progress on the task.

Analyzing Teaching and Learning 9.2
Student Impasse Scenarios

Read the five scenarios shown below. As you read each scenario, respond to the following questions as you consider the effectiveness of the teacher-student interactions.

- What is the nature of the student's struggle? What impasse did he or she reach?

- How does the teacher help the student move beyond his or her impasse?

- To what extent did the teacher's response support productive struggle toward understanding the mathematics?

Scenario 1: Nhia

Nhia first drew a circle, and then crossed it out on her paper. She finally seemed to settle on the drawing of the rectangle shown below on the right for the birthday cake task.

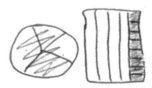

Teacher:	Tell me about your drawing.
Nhia:	I think this one might work. (*Points to* the *diagram on the right.*) This is the cake and I cut it into fifths. Then I cut one of those fifths into 8 pieces.
Teacher:	So, why did you cut it into 8 pieces?
Nhia:	Well, there were 8 friends and they shared that leftover piece so I cut it into eighths.
Teacher:	So now you have to describe the size of the piece that each friend got.
Nhia:	Yeah, but I don't get that. Is the answer $1/8$?
Teacher:	Remember when we did a problem like this the other day, and we had to make sure the whole was all cut into equal-size pieces? What is the whole in this problem?
Nhia:	The cake.
Teacher:	So right now you have some big pieces and some small pieces. How many small pieces would you have if you took all 5 of the big pieces and broke each one into 8 smaller pieces just like you did for that one part already?
Nhia:	40?
Teacher:	Yes. So now you can figure out how big the pieces are that each friend gets.

Scenario 2: Steven

Steven confidently drew a diagram of the birthday cake determining that each friend got $1/40$ of the cake to eat as a snack. However, he was not as sure which equation modeled the situation.

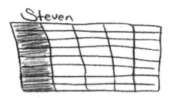

Teacher:	Tell me how you made your diagram.
Steven:	I drew a rectangle for the cake and then I cut it into fifths, and shaded $^1/_5$ because that's what was left of the cake. Then I cut each of those fifths into 8 pieces because there were 8 friends.
Teacher:	So do you know what the answer is yet?
Steven:	Yeah. Each friend got $^1/_{40}$ of the cake.
Teacher:	So, which expression do you think matches this situation? Do you agree with Seth or Frankie?
Steven:	I'm thinking Frankie ($^1/_5 \div 8$) because there was a fifth left and it had to be shared among the 8 friends.
Teacher:	So you think it is $^1/_5 \div 8$. What about the other expression, $8 \div ^1/_5$? <u>Is that different?</u>
Steven:	Well, we would have to say eight is 8 friends and divide each friend into fifths. That doesn't even make sense.
Teacher:	Interesting. So now write an explanation about which expression you think is right and try to explain why it can't be the other expression.

Scenario 3: Zhen

As the teacher approaches Zhen, he is reading and rereading the problem, but has not yet put anything on his paper.

Zhen:	I don't get it.
Teacher:	What are you suppose to figure out?
Zhen:	How to share the cake with 8 friends.
Teacher:	Okay, how might you start?
Zhen:	I don't know. They only got a fifth.
Teacher:	Okay, the first thing you need to do is draw a rectangle for the cake and then cut it into fifths because there was $^1/_5$ of the cake left. Then next you need to cut those pieces into 8 smaller pieces each for the 8 friends.
Zhen:	Make eighths?
Teacher:	No, cut the cake into fifths. Do that much first. Then I'll help you with what to do next.
Zhen:	Oh. *(The student draws a rectangle and partitions it into fifths.)*
Teacher:	Good, now shade $^1/_5$ to show how much cake was left.
Zhen:	*(The student shades $^1/_5$.)*
Teacher:	Good. Now cut the other way across the cake to get 8 pieces. How many small pieces are in the whole cake?

She just told him word for word what to do.

Teacher:	Good. Now cut the other way across the cake to get 8 pieces. How many small pieces are in the whole cake?
Zhen:	40.
Teacher:	Okay, so if each friend got one of those small pieces, what fraction of the whole cake did each friend get?
Zhen:	$\frac{1}{40}$?
Teacher:	Yes, each friend got $\frac{1}{40}$. Now go on the next part of the task.

Scenario 4: Diego

Diego determines that each friend gets 1/40 of the cake and then claims that both equations $8 \div \frac{1}{5}$ and $\frac{1}{5} \div 8$ work because the order does not matter with the commutative property.

Teacher:	Tell me about your thinking, why do you think both equations could be right?
Diego:	They're both right because you can just switch the numbers and you get the same answer.
Teacher:	Interesting, so tell me what you did here with your picture and why. (*Teacher points to the student's diagram.*)

$$\frac{1}{5} \div 8 = \frac{1}{40}$$
$$8 \div \frac{1}{5} = 40$$

Diego:	I made a rectangle for the cake and cut it into fifths 'cuz that's what they had left. Then I cut it into eighths 'cuz there were 8 friends sharing it. And each friend got $\frac{1}{40}$.
Teacher:	So, did what you just describe sound more like $8 \div \frac{1}{5}$ or more like $\frac{1}{5} \div 8$?
Diego:	Well…um… 8 friends shared that piece; I'm thinking it's more like $\frac{1}{5} \div 8$.
Teacher:	You said you thought you would get the same answer with either expression, so tell me about $8 \div \frac{1}{5}$ and how that would be the same.
Diego:	I could make 8 rectangles (*draws the picture below*) and cuts each into fifths (*subdivides each rectangle*). Each person gets one piece (*shades one part of each*

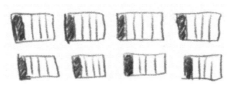

Teacher:	What do you think?
Diego:	I think this is different. This would be 8 cakes cut into fifths, and I got 40 fifths, not fortieths.
Teacher:	So are the expressions the same or different?
Diego:	No, they're different. I guess you can't just switch them. Frankie is right; it's $1/_5 \div 8$.

Scenario 5: Sophia

Sophia has not begun to solve the task. She is reading the problem as the teacher approaches her.

Teacher:	So, tell me about the story. What is happening?
Sophia:	There are 8 friends staying at Seth's house for his birthday.
Teacher:	That's part of it. Why don't you go back and read the problem again and see what else is happening.
Sophia:	Oh, okay.
Teacher:	Then start working on part 1 where it says to draw a picture of what is happening in the problem.

(handwritten margin notes: $5 \frac{1}{\cdot} \cdot 8$ $5 + \frac{1}{8}$ $\frac{1}{40}$ *each friend is getting $\frac{1}{40}$ of the entire cake. So Frankie is correct)*

Analysis of ATL 9.2: Productive and Unproductive Teacher Responses

Each of the students portrayed in the scenarios reached an impasse, that is, a point at which the student was no longer moving forward in his or her work on the task. In each scenario, the teacher intervenes to help the student move beyond the impasse, but does so in different ways. Some of the teacher's responses to the student struggles nudged them forward and allowed them to continue to engage productively with the task, while other responses were not as beneficial to student learning. How do we know when the struggle on a mathematics task is productive or unproductive? According to Warshauer (2015a, p. 390), struggle is productive if—

- the intended goals and the cognitive demand of the task are maintained;
- student's thinking is supported by acknowledging effort and mathematical understanding; and
- the student is able to move forward in the task through the student's actions.

A good way of recognizing if the struggle is productive is to ask yourself whether the student or the teacher is doing the thinking and the work. The student, when given support, should be able to use his or her own effort to move forward in solving the task and understanding the mathematics more deeply.

By studying teacher and student interactions in mathematics classrooms, Warshauer (2015a) identified four typical ways that teachers respond to student struggles. She placed the four teacher responses on a continuum from being least likely to most likely to support productive student engagement with a task. They are as follows:

- **Telling:** The teacher responds by suggesting an approach (e.g., use of a specific tool or representation), correcting an error, or supplying some piece of information. More often than not, telling responses diminish the cognitive demand of the task.
- **Directed Guidance:** The teacher redirects student thinking by breaking the problem into smaller parts or steps, directing a next step for the student in working on the task, or altering the task itself. Often the directed guidance funnels the student toward the teacher's way of thinking about the task rather than the student's way of reasoning.
- **Probing Guidance:** The teacher delves into the student thinking, asks for explanations and justifications, prompts student self-reflection, and surfaces errors and misconceptions. A probing response builds on student thinking and leads to new insights that allow the student to move forward with the task.
- **Affordance:** The teacher asks about the student thinking, encourages continued effort on the task, and provides time for the student to linger in his or her thinking. An affordance response reassures and motivates students to persist in building on their own ideas with little help or interference from the teacher.

In scenario 1, Nhia first drew a circle to represent the cake, but then crossed it out and drew a rectangle. She likely realized it would be hard to partition the circular diagram. In her second attempt she successfully partitioned the rectangle into fifths, shaded $\frac{1}{5}$ to represent the remaining part of the cake, and then further partitioned that $\frac{1}{5}$ into 8 pieces for the 8 friends. This is where she reached an impasse. Nhia did not know how to name one of those small pieces. Nor did she see a need to partition the other fifths, because the context says there is only a fifth of the cake remaining. The teacher tried several times to get Nhia to recognize that she must subdivide each of the fifths into 8 pieces. Then the whole cake would have same-size partitions and the student could name the size of each individual piece. The teacher became more directive when she asked Nhia to recall, "Remember when we did a problem like this the other day, and we had to make sure the whole was all cut into equal-size pieces." Then the teacher prompted, "So right now you have some big pieces and some small pieces. What can you do to get all the same-size pieces?" While the teacher offered the student a clear pathway to solve the task, and hence a way to move beyond the impasse, the pathway represented the teacher's thinking about how to solve the task rather than eliciting more of the student's thinking about the task. The teacher responded to the student impasse by using directed guidance. When students are led or funneled down a specific pathway, such as Nhia, the thinking demands of the task are diminished, and even though students are likely directed toward a correct solution, they may not make much progress in deepening their mathematical understanding.

Scenario 2 shows that Steven accurately constructed a diagram and named the portion of the whole that each student received as $\frac{1}{40}$. The student reached an impasse as he considered the second part of the task. While Steven could draw a clear diagram and find the answer to the problem, he was not sure which expression was a mathematical model of the problem context. The teacher engaged the student in talking about how he made the diagram. She then asked Steven, "So, which expression matches this situation? Do you agree with Seth or Frankie?" The student then thought out loud about why he thinks it might be $\frac{1}{5} \div 8$. The teacher followed up by asking "What about the other expression, $8 \div \frac{1}{5}$? How is that different?" The teacher provided limited guidance. She followed the student's thinking and asked questions that provided Steven with time to think about his work, to make connections between his diagram and the context, and thus, maintained a high-level of cognitive demand in working on the task. The teacher response is an example of affordance. These moves afford students the opportunity to linger in their thinking, often by asking students to verbalize their understanding of a task and to think out loud. In this way, students continue to utilize their own mathematical agency in making sense of problem situations while deepening mathematical understanding.

In scenario 3, Zhen was struggling to get started. He was reading and rereading the problem, but had not yet put anything on paper. He reached an impasse as he tried to make sense of the problem situation and all of its components. The teacher began by asking the student, "What are you suppose to figure out?" Zhen replied that he needed to figure out, "How to share the cake with 8 friends." His limited response to the teacher's question, along with his statements of "I don't get it" and "I don't know," likely prompted the teacher to simply respond by telling him what to do. While Zhen was able to follow the directions given by the teacher, and ended up with the correct answer, it is not clear what sense the student had made of this problem because the teacher stopped attempting to determine what the student understood about the task. Zhen was no longer struggling with the task, but the pathway he was following was based on the teacher's reasoning and Zhen was no longer concerned with understanding the task, but was just intent on following the teacher's directions. Caution needs to be taken when students state, "I don't know." Simply telling students what to do undermines their own confidence and agency in solving mathematics problems. Students may just need encouragement to trust in their own ideas, and some teacher probing to draw out their thoughts and get them to verbalize these ideas. These students may also be afraid of doing it wrong and don't want to make any mistakesal. Thus, the encouragement might be valuing mistakes as important steps toward understanding and letting students know that they can just cross out and try something else if their initial attempts seem not be working for them.

In scenario 4, Diego correctly drew a diagram and determined that each friend receives $\frac{1}{40}$ of Seth's birthday cake as a snack. However, he claimed that both expressions were correct because he thought the commutative property could be applied to the operation of division. The student has reached an incorrect solution, but did not yet realize it. The teacher did not respond directly to his statement, but rather asked questions to surface the misconception in his reasoning. She began by asking, "Interesting, so tell me what you did here with your picture and why." In this way, the teacher delved into the student thinking by asking for an explanation. To prompt Diego to engage in self-reflection on his understanding of the task and how to model it with a mathematical expression, the teachers asked, "So, did what you just describe sound more like $8 \div \frac{1}{5}$ or more like $\frac{1}{5} \div 8$?" To further prompt inquiry and self-reflection, the teacher went back to Diego's original assertion, "You said, you thought you would get the same answer with either expression, so tell me about $8 \div \frac{1}{5}$ and how that would be the same." Diego then decided to draw a picture to explore $8 \div \frac{1}{5}$ and realized that the equations do not result in the same solution, nor do they model the same contextual situation. The teacher used probing guidance to continually surface Diego's thinking and allow him to decide which actions to further pursue in working on the task. In this way, the high-level demands of the task were maintained and the student was moved to deeper understanding of the relationship of contexts involving division with fractions and the use of expressions as a mathematical model of those situations.

Scenario 5 began with Sophia rereading the problem as the teacher approached. She did not yet have anything drawn on her paper. It is not clear, but perhaps she had reached an impasse in making sense of the problem situation or maybe she was not sure how to draw a diagram to represent it, or perhaps she was not at an impasse at all. The teacher did ask, "So, tell me about the story. What is happening?" Unfortunately, the teacher did not delve further into what the student currently understood about the problem. Rather, the teacher suggested some general strategies of rereading the problem and to then start working by drawing a picture of what was happening in the problem. While the teacher was not directing the student to a particular pathway, it is unlikely that this type of support would help the student move forward in a productive manner. It might also have been the case that the student had already read the problem carefully several times and was already envisioning ways to draw the picture. The teacher did not probe her thinking, thus we do not know what the student might have been pondering. Perhaps the teacher interrupted her thinking. While the teacher response was intended to be supportive, it might actually negatively impact the student's beliefs about the nature of mathematical work, as it might send an implicit message that the student needs to work "faster" toward a solution rather than viewing mathematics as a reasoned discipline that requires time to ponder and make sense of mathematical situations. We see scenario 5 as being an example of a fifth type of teacher response, one that we have seen in classrooms in which we have worked, that we would categorize as unfocused or vague. In this type of response the teacher does not direct students to a particular strategy or build on students thinking, but instead provides a suggestion that is often too general to be helpful.

One thing to keep in mind is that the teachers' goal in intervening when a student or group is struggling is not to make sure that every student has a correct and complete response prior to a whole-group discussion of the task. Rather, the goal is to "support students' fledgling efforts to make sense of the task before them and to make sure their thinking is headed in a productive direction" (Cartier et al. 2013, p. 88). In the scenarios, Steven and Diego moved forward in their understanding of the mathematics of the task. Whereas Sophia and Zhen got the correct answer for the first part of the task, but it is not clear whether they developed any further understanding of the mathematics. Unfortunately, it is more likely that their dependency on the teacher for the "rules" to follow was strengthened. When students reach an impasse, the teacher's aim should be to maintain the cognitive demand of the task, acknowledge student effort to understand the mathematics, and build on students' thinking in helping them move forward through their own decisions and actions. Then during the whole-class discussion of the task and its mathematical connections, all students have the opportunity to "collect more pieces of information about the issue of the discussion and to understand the issue more deeply" (Hatano and Inagaki 1991, p. 346).

Identifying Strategies that Support Productive Struggle

Tasks that promote reasoning and problem solving and require students to justify their thinking are likely to be ones with which students struggle, therefore requiring perseverance. The Beads task, shown in figure 9.3, encourages students to investigate quantitative relationships, to make mathematical claims, and to provide informal justifications of those claims. The task provides a low threshold so that all students can enter into the task, and it also provides a high ceiling as students can challenge themselves to make more complex claims. Take a moment and list some mathematical claims you might anticipate from a class of first-grade students on the Beads task.

The Beads Task

What mathematical claims, or statements, can you make about this set of orange and gray beads? Make a list of claims, and then justify each claim by writing equations and drawing diagrams.

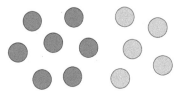

Adapted from Institute for Learning (2012b). Lesson guides and student workbooks available at ifl.pitt.edu

Fig. 9.3. A task on posing and justifying quantitative statements

Engage in ATL 9.3: Intentional Teacher Actions

Mr. Klein teaches first grade. His class is working on comparing different types of addition and subtraction word problems, including "add to/take from," "put together/take apart," and "compare" problem situations. He wants his students to work with the Beads task to explore quantitative relationships and to create their own problem situations, expecting them to use the different problem situations they were studying. He wants his students to demonstrate that they can describe how combining sets relates to the total amount, how a total amount can be decomposed into smaller sets, how sets can be compared to find a difference, and how one set can be increased to equal the same quantity as the other set. He also wonders, because the task is very open-ended, whether his students will create more complex claims that might have multiple steps and how they will justify those claims.

Mr. Klein has used this task in previous years with his students and he knows it encourages flexible thinking and creative problem solving. At the same time it allows him to find out what students understand about the parts and wholes in various situations, as well as their comprehension of the comparison of sets. He also knows that his students will struggle with the task. He has thought about ways he intends to support student struggle and to resist taking over the thinking of his students. He intentionally plans to use these four strategies (Warshauer 2015b):

- **Ask questions** that help students focus on the source of their struggle and that make students' thinking and ideas public so they can be collectively examined and discussed with others.

- **Provide encouragement** that causes students to reflect on the strategies they and others have used so far in working on the task and what other strategies might be helpful.

- **Give adequate time** that allows students to work individually and in small groups to work through their own emerging ideas and the ideas of their peers without the teacher helping too much and taking the intellectual work away from the students.

- **Acknowledge student contributions,** valuing student missteps and mistakes as well as accurate and appropriate suggestions and approaches, as an important and natural part of learning and understanding mathematics.

We now ask you to examine a discussion in Mr. Klein's classroom in ATL 9.3. The students are working in small groups to make claims about the beads and to decide how they would justify the validity of those claims. Each group of students was given a bag containing 7 orange beads and 5 gray beads. We listen in on the dialogue between the teacher and a group of students comparing the number of orange beads to the number of gray beads.

Analyzing Teaching and Learning 9.3
Intentional Teacher Actions

Read the excerpt from Mr. Klein and the Beads Task below in which Mr. Klein interacts with a small group of students working on the task.

- What are the students' struggling to understand about the mathematical demands of the task?
- How does the teacher support the students in struggling with the mathematical ideas and relationships without taking over the thinking and reasoning for them?
- In what ways does Mr. Klein support student task engagement by asking questions, providing encouragement, giving adequate time, and acknowledging student contributions?

Grade 1 Lesson Excerpt: Mr. Klein and the Beads Task

1	**Teacher:**	So what does this group know about the beads?
2	**Alejandro:**	There are 7 orange beads and 5 gray beads.
3	**Teacher:**	What else do you know about the beads?
4	**Kim:**	There are 12 beads.
5	**Teacher:**	So Kim made one claim. How did you figure that out?
6	**Kim:**	I just counted them all up and I got 12.
7	**Teacher:**	What else do you notice about the beads?
8	**Sebastián:**	I said that there are more orange beads than gray beads.
9	**Teacher:**	That's an interesting claim, Sebastián. How do you know that there are more
10		orange beads?
11	**Sebastián:**	I counted the orange beads and then the gray beads and I know 7 is more
12		than 5.
13	**Teacher:**	Is there any other way you could convince me that there are more orange
14		beads?
15	**Mateo:**	We could match them up.
16	**Teacher:**	Why don't you go ahead and do that. I also want you to make a picture and
17		write a number sentence that shows how you compared the beads. I'll be
18		back in a few minutes to see what you did. Remember everyone in the group
19		must understand and be able to talk about what you did because I might ask
20		anyone in your group to explain.
21		*(Mr. Klein leaves to interact with other student groups and returns about five*
22		*minutes later.)*
23	**Teacher:**	So who can explain the picture that your team drew?
24	**Sebastián:**	We drew 7 circles in one row and we drew 5 circles in the other row and
25		matched them up (shown below) and only 5 could be paired up, so 2 extra
		orange beads.

26

27	**Teacher:**	So I see how you are lining them up to compare the orange beads to the gray
28		beads so you can figure out how many are extra. What number sentence did
29		you write that tells you there are 2 extra orange beads if you match them up
30		to the gray beads?
31	**Mateo:**	$5 + 2 = 7$
32	**Sebastián:**	No we didn't do that, we did $7 - 5 = 2$

33	**Teacher:**	Okay so you don't agree with each other yet. Which of those number sen-
34		tences tell us about comparing the orange and gray beads? Talk about this
35		with each and I will be back.
36		*(Mr. Klein returns about three minutes later.)*
37	**Teacher:**	Which number sentence did you decide upon?
38	**Sebastián:**	We said 7 − 5 because we took 5 away and then there were 2 leftover.
39	**Teacher:**	Can you tell me more about how you see the 7 − 5 in your picture? I'm not
40		sure I understand yet.
41	**Alejandro:**	These are the 7 orange beads *(points to the top row of circles shown below)*. Then
42		we took away 5 beads that matched up *(points to the crossed off circles)*. Then
43		we had 2 left.

44

$$7 - 5 = 2$$

45	**Teacher:**	Does everyone agree with what Alejandro said? So what does the difference
46		of 2 tell us in 7 − 5 = 2?
47	**Students:**	That the answer is 2.
48	**Teacher:**	What would the 2 mean when looking at the orange and gray beads?
49	**Mateo:**	If we had 2 more gray beads we would have 7 gray beads like the orange
50		beads.
51	**Alejandro:**	No it's take away and the 2 tells what is left.
52	**Teacher:**	So, one way to think about this is that there are 2 left like Alejandro said.
53		It seems like Mateo has another way to think about it. Why don't you talk
54		about it and make a new picture and equation showing Mateo's thinking of
55		needing 2 more gray beads.
56		*(Mr. Klein leaves to work with another group and returns a few minutes later.)*
57	**Teacher:**	What did you write and draw this time?
58	**Alejandro:**	We made the same picture *(shown below)* but we wrote 5 + 2 = 7.

59

$$5 + 2 = 7$$

60

| 61 | **Teacher:** | I'm confused here. Can you talk about and label the numbers in your equa- |
| 62 | | tions so I know if you are talking about the gray beads or the orange beads? |

63	**Mateo:**	So if we had 2 more gray beads *(points to the spot for the two missing beads)*
64		then we would have the same as the orange beads
65	**Teacher:**	Do others agree or disagree?
66	**Students:**	We agree.
67	**Teacher:**	Kim, can you explain what Mateo said?
68	**Kim:**	Yeah. To match up to all the orange beads, we need 7 gray beads but we only
69		had 5, so we would need 2 more gray beads.
70	**Teacher:**	So with your other equation, $7 - 5 = 2$, who can explain what that means
71		again when you think about comparing the gray and orange beads?
72	**Sebastián:**	We matched up 5 gray and orange beads and crossed them off, which left 2
73		orange beads.
74	**Teacher:**	So, you had 2 extra orange beads, or you could say the difference between 7
75		orange beads and 5 gray beads was 2 beads.
76	**Sebastián:**	Yeah.
77	**Teacher::**	So when you are comparing things there are different ways to make claims
78		about it depending on how you see it. You might see it as needing 2 more or
79		having 2 extra, or maybe even as having 2 fewer or a difference of 2.

Analysis of ATL 9.3: Teacher Strategies that Promote Productive Struggle

The students featured in the dialogue with Mr. Klein generated several claims about the set of orange and gray beads. Mr. Klein knows his young learners are just beginning to make sense of comparison problem situations, so he focuses on the claims they make in comparing the orange beads and the gray beads. Specifically, he supports the students to justify and understand claims made by Sebastián and Mateo. With his gentle nudges, the students examine the claims more closely and make connections among their drawings, physical objects, equations, language, and thinking. The movement forward in understanding the mathematical ideas and relationships accomplished by the students provides evidence that the student effort was struggle that was productive.

Give Adequate Time

One feature of the discussion that stands out immediately is the amount of time students were given to work together and to explore the relationships between the two sets of beads. The teacher consistently checked in on the group and prompted their thinking without saying too much, and then left them to work through the ideas with each other (lines 15–21, 34–35, 53–56). In this way, the intellectual work remained within the purview of the students. Providing adequate time to grapple with the emerging mathematical ideas is an important strategy to use in supporting productive struggle.

Ask Questions

Another strategy to support productive struggle is to ask questions that focus students on the source of their struggles in making sense of the task or in moving to a solution. The intent of these questions is to make confusions or uncertainties more visible and accessible for discussion. Teachers can then ask further questions that might prompt students to consider prior knowledge or look at other ways to approach the problem. In the Beads task lesson, the students struggle with understanding each other's reasoning and do not agree on how to write the number sentence to match their claims. For example, the students disagree whether the equation should be $5 + 2 = 7$ or $7 - 5 = 2$ (lines 28–32). Mr. Klein acknowledged the disagreement and then asks, "Which of those number sentences tell us about comparing the orange and gray beads?" (lines 33–34). This question prompted students to return to what they knew about the beads and connect the equations back to the actual beads and to their drawing. Throughout the interactions, Mr. Klein asked questions to focus students on key mathematical ideas without taking over the thinking or reasoning of the students.

A bit later, when the teacher asks, "What would the 2 mean when looking at the orange and gray beads?" (line 48), it is clear that Sebastián and Mateo are still viewing the comparison of the beads differently. Sebastián sees it as having two extra orange beads. Mateo sees it as needing two more gray beads. Mr. Klein asks the group to draw a new picture that shows Mateo's way of thinking about adding two more beads (lines 53–55). This makes Mateo's thinking more visible and helps the group understand how the comparison of the beads can be viewed from multiple perspectives.

Acknowledge Student Contributions

Each time Mr. Klein revisits the group, he acknowledges what students are thinking and gives value to students' contributions (e.g., lines 5, 9, 52–55). While he does not say it explicitly, it is clear that he expects his young learners to wrestle with mathematical ideas as a natural part of learning mathematics. Prompting student actions and then leaving the group to work together without the teacher present, signals to the students that they are capable of solving the task and that they are responsible for helping each other understand the various solutions. Prompting and then leaving students to work together also signals that the teacher values the students' efforts and persistence in making sense of the task and finding solutions.

One way Mr. Klein acknowledges students' contributions is by marking the information as valuable for the group's learning. An example of marking is when Mr. Klein commented, "So I see how you are lining them up to compare the orange beads to the gray beads so you can figure out how many are extra" (lines 27–28). In doing so the teacher marks the idea as significant and increases the chance that other students will recognize the value of the idea. Another way to highlight a student's contribution is by asking other students to repeat or restate the idea, such as when Mr. Klein asked, "Kim, can you explain what Mateo said?" (line 67) and "Who can explain what that means again when you think about comparing the gray and orange beads?" (lines 70–71). Recapping students' contributions also serves to "pull together" multiple responses into a more coherent picture as Mr. Klein did at the end of the interaction. He states, "So when you are comparing objects there are different ways to make claims about it depending on how you see it. You might see it as needing 2 more or having 2 extra, or maybe even as having 2 fewer or a difference of 2" (lines 77–79). The recapping of students' ideas makes it possible to repeat very powerful big ideas of mathematics—that in comparison situations we are investigating the difference between two sets and that we can talk about how many more or how many fewer are in one set in relation to the other.

Provide Encouragement

Throughout the discussion, Mr. Klein encourages students to reflect on their own observations in order to explain their reasoning and ideas, such as when he states, "That's an interesting claim, Sebastián. How do you know that there are more orange beads?" (lines 9–10). Later on he asks students to reflect on the meaning of "two" in relation to the context when he asks, "Who can explain what that means again when you think about comparing the gray and orange beads?" (lines 70–71). In this way the teacher reinforces the mind-set that doing mathematics is more than just stating an answer. His recurrent interactions with the small group are also a form of encouragement, as well as of accountability. He specifically states that he intends to return to their group to ask them about their thinking, "Talk about this with each and I will be back" (lines 34–35). Each time he revisits the group he encourages students to make their ideas public, thereby, giving all students in the group more time to work, to think, and to learn from each other.

What the Research Says: Productive Struggle in Understanding Mathematics

Learning mathematics with understanding requires productive struggle, that is, wrestling with important mathematical ideas through tasks that promote reasoning and problem solving (Hiebert and Grouws 2007; VanLehn et al. 2003). It is through the struggle with mathematical ideas that students consider new insights in relation to prior learning. This supports the reorganization of existing knowledge structures in order to incorporate the new connections, thus resulting in new understanding (Festinger 1957; Piaget 1960). In essence, this is the natural process of sense making (Handa 2003), which results in deeper understanding of mathematics.

Teachers and students must both learn to accept struggle as a natural and important aspect of learning mathematics. International comparisons of classrooms provide insight into the opportunities students do and do not have to engage in productive struggle. In conjunction

Teachers and students must both learn to accept struggle as a natural and important aspect of learning mathematics. International comparisons of classrooms provide insight into the opportunities students do and do not have to engage in productive struggle. In conjunction with the Third International Mathematics and Science Study (TIMSS), researchers conducted a video study of nationally representative samples of eighth-grade mathematics lessons among high-performing countries (Hiebert and Stigler 2004; Stigler and Hiebert 1999, 2004). The countries included the United States, Australia, Czech Republic, Japan, and Netherlands, as well as Hong Kong, which was referred to as a country for the purpose of the study. The teachers were randomly selected, thus the videos captured typical teaching practices in each country. Some of the major findings relate to the focal teaching practice of this chapter on productive struggle.

- Japan used far more high-level tasks than the other countries; 54% compared to a range of 13% to 24% for the other nations, with the U.S. lessons using 17% high-level tasks. The remainder of the tasks focused on practicing skills.

- When U.S. teachers presented high-level tasks, they almost always lowered the cognitive demand by stepping in and doing the work for the students, or when discussing the task, they focused on how to solve the task and ignored the conceptual aspects of the problem.

- U.S. students rarely had opportunities to experience struggle with high-level tasks. Japan, Hong Kong, and Czech Republic teachers maintained high-levels of reasoning on such tasks approximately 50% of the time compared to less than 1% of the time in U.S. lessons.

The researchers concluded that U.S. students spend almost all of their class time practicing skills and rarely have opportunities to engage in high-level tasks. Teachers in the United States are just not comfortable with struggle, and are more likely than teachers in other countries to "rescue students" when they sense frustration or indecision by students.

Fortunately, classrooms are beginning to value the role of struggle in learning mathematics. Inagaki, Hatano, and Morita (1998) observed eleven fourth- and fifth-grade classrooms as students discussed alternative methods for adding fractions. The discussions exhibited key elements of productive struggle as students expressed their confusion and shared incorrect conjectures along with correct solution methods. The students demonstrated improved understanding in both their verbal statements and written work. Kapur (2010) found that seventh-grade students who persisted in solving complex problems (even when they were not successful) outperformed students who received only a lecture and practice intervention. Carter (2008) reported on how she changed the culture in her first-grade classroom by creating a climate that valued struggle. She explained the concept of disequilibrium as "the feeling of confusion associated with struggling with a mathematics concept" and that "confusion is something you go through, not a permanent state of being" (p. 136). Her intent was to normalize the feeling and discussion of disequilibrium in moving toward understanding. Their classroom motto became "If you are not struggling, you are not learning" (p. 136). In each of these cases, teachers and researchers are finding that students can learn to embrace struggle as a natural aspect of learning mathematics and that opportunities to engage in productive struggle lead to deeper and more robust mathematical understanding.

Promoting Equity by Supporting Productive Struggle in Learning Mathematics

Students' beliefs about the nature of learning mathematics and about their own abilities to learn mathematics begins in our elementary classrooms. Do students view mathematics as mostly memorizing facts and rules or do students see it as a coherent discipline focused on reasoning and sense making? Do students view mathematics as something they only do in school or do students see it as connected to their communities and cultures? How students view mathematics impacts how they see themselves as learners of mathematics and as members of mathematical communities and whether they believe that learning mathematics requires struggling with mathematical ideas and relationships. Central to equity-based practices is the belief that strengthening mathematics learning and cultivating positive mathematical identities requires engaging students in cognitively demanding tasks, encouraging students to see themselves as competent problem solvers, assuming that mistakes are sources of learning, and valuing students' knowledge and experiences (Aguirre, Mayfield-Ingram, and Martin 2014).

A critical shift that needs to occur is for students to view mathematics as a subject of learning and sense making rather than a subject of performance (Boaler, 2014). In order to set the stage for this, Boaler asserts that students "need tasks and questions in math class that have space to learn built in" (p. 2). This may involve tasks that have more than one answer, such as the Beads task (ATL 9.3) and the Make a Ten task (ATL 8.1). It includes tasks that are more complex or have multiple steps, such as the Caterpillar task (ATL 5.1), Walking Home from School task (ATL 7.3), and the Half-of-a-Whole task (ATL 9.1). It also includes tasks that have one correct solution (e.g., Band Concert task, ATL 1.1; Class Attendance task, 7.2) if they are presented in a manner that offers multiple entry points and values the multiple ways that students demonstrate their knowledge and solution pathways, thus leveraging multiple mathematical competencies, another equity-based practice (Aguirre, Mayfield-Ingram, and Martin 2014). In each of these task examples as discussed throughout this book, students were afforded opportunities to experience perplexities as well as to be curious about and grapple with mathematical ideas and relationships. Teachers can then carefully monitor and support students in ways that acknowledge and build on their ideas to ensure the struggle with the task is productive in moving students toward the intended learning goals while maintaining the cognitive demand and student ownership of actions (Warshauer 2015a).

How teachers handle mistakes in the mathematics classroom also influences students' beliefs about the nature of learning mathematics and whether or not one should struggle in that learning, as well as their beliefs or mind-sets about themselves as learners. Often mistakes are viewed negatively and are seen as something to be avoided, even though they are a regular and everyday occurrence in mathematics classrooms. Aguirre, Mayfield-Ingram, and Martin (2014) warn that we must avoid actions that connect "mathematical identity solely with correct answers and quickness" and that "explicitly discourages mistakes and immediately corrects them" (p. 46). How people view mistakes has been linked to their mind-set, that is, their view of learning and intelligence (Dweck 2006). Moser and colleagues (2011) examined neural networks in the brain when people made mistakes. Individuals with a fixed mind-set (i.e., a belief that intelligence is a stable characteristic and cannot be changed) had a weak brain reaction to mistakes. Whereas, individuals with a growth mind-set (i.e., a belief that intelligence develops through effort in using appropriate strategies) had a stronger brain reaction, which occurs when the individual is aware of the error and seeking to learn from it. Making mistakes and missteps are a natural part of the struggle in learning mathematics and do not determine one's mathematical identity. We need to help students see mistakes as opportunities for learning and as a natural part of the struggle in learning mathematics. As teachers, we need to create learning environments in which mistakes are openings for discussions and viewed as steps toward deeper understanding.

Allen and Schnell (2016) suggest four pillars of practices for supporting the development of students' positive and powerful mathematical identities. They include (1) knowing and believing in your students, (2) redefining mathematical success, (3) prioritizing student voice, and (4) monitoring identity formation. We do not know what students think and believe about mathematics unless we ask them. Ms. Painter, a fourth-grade teacher, recently asked her students, "What do you think it means to be smart in math?" The results were revealing. While she strove to support growth mind-sets among her students, she found that a few of her students still believed that being smart in math meant you were fast, "You answer problems quickly and you do good on tests," or that the answers came easily, "I think it means that all the math problem answers just come to your mind no matter how the problem is, even 50 × 50 = 2500." However, most of her students revealed that struggling to learn mathematics and making mistakes did not define their mathematical identity. Some of their responses are below:

- "It's not about how fast you work. It means to know a lot of strategies and things that help you."
- "It means you know most of the problems but not all of them and you know how to defend your answers."
- "It means you can solve math problems and have strategies to solve harder problems. And you always check your work before handing it in."

- "It means to be able to answer problems correctly and you do not have to do it fast or slow but you can make mistakes because everyone makes mistakes."

One other student in the class when asked what it meant to be smart in math replied, "I wish I knew." Ms. Painter used the information from her students to engage them in further discussions on defining success in mathematics, the role of mistakes in learning, and the importance of struggling and persistence in trying to use the strategies they were learning. Ms. Painter has continued to monitor the mathematical identities of her students and to implement intentional actions to foster the development of positive mathematics identities.

Allen and Schnell (2016) remind us of the need to continuously monitor our own assumptions about our students because "our students become the words we use" and a "budding mathematician resides in everyone of them" (p. 405). Our students develop false notions about the learning of mathematics—that it should come easily and one should be able to get answers quickly and if not, then you are not smart or capable in mathematics. The mathematics teaching practice on productive struggle reminds us that we must help students realize that to learn mathematics well, one must wrestle with mathematical ideas. The teaching practice also reminds us as teachers to provide students time to struggle, to not take over the thinking for them, and to provide supports, such as questioning and use of representations, so that the struggle is productive in moving students toward deeper mathematical understanding.

Taking Action in Your Classroom

Throughout this chapter, you examined and considered ways that teachers can support productive struggle among their students in learning mathematics. Here we summarize some of the key messages for you to keep in mind as you take action in your own classroom.

- Engaging students in productive struggle is essential to developing deep conceptual understanding in mathematics.

- Tasks that have a "low threshold and high ceiling" have greater potential for engaging students in productive struggle because all students can enter and explore the mathematics at some level and push themselves toward more challenging mathematics.

- Teachers support productive struggle by providing students with probing guidance and affordance without taking over the thinking for students by telling or providing too much direction.

- High-quality mathematics classrooms establish a culture in which productive struggle, including openness to mistakes, is seen as a normal and accepted part of learning mathematics.

We now invite you to take action as you consider what implications the ideas discussed in this chapter have for your own professional setting. We suggest you select a specific task for an upcoming lesson, anticipate student engagement with the task, and brainstorm ways to support students in productive struggle toward understanding the intended mathematics.

Taking Action in Your Classroom
Supporting Student Struggle on a Challenging Mathematical Task

Choose a task that promotes reasoning and problem solving that you plan to implement in your classroom. (See chapter 3 for a discussion of these types of tasks.)

- What will you see students doing or hear students saying that would serve as evidence of productive struggle with the task?

- What would you see or hear as evidence of unproductive struggle with the task?

- Describe ways you might use any of the four strategies discussed in ATL 9.3—questioning, providing encouragement, giving adequate time, and acknowledging student contributions—to support student engagement in productive struggle so that they can make progress toward the mathematics learning goals of the lesson.

CHAPTER 10

Pulling It All Together

Teaching mathematics is complex. It requires teachers to deeply understand the mathematics being taught, to know how student learning of that mathematics develops and progresses across grades, and to "be skilled at teaching in ways that are effective in developing mathematics learning for all students" (NCTM 2014, p. 7). As you worked through chapters 2 through 9, you have had the opportunity to explore each of the eight effective mathematics teaching practices and to develop a deeper understanding of what each practice entails and how it supports ambitious teaching. In other words, you were learning ways to become more skilled in your instructional work. Ball and Forzani (2010, p. 45) argued that

> [i]dentifying a set of practices that aims at complex outcomes for all students is a first step toward strengthening the teaching profession. These practices could provide a common foundation for teacher education, a common professional language, and a framework for appraising and improving teaching.

In this chapter, we discuss the eight teaching practices as a set of connected teaching behaviors aimed at achieving complex outcomes for the mathematics learning of each and every student. Specifically, throughout this concluding chapter we refer back to activities that you explored in earlier chapters, work through one new Analyzing Teaching and Learning (ATL) activity, and reexamine those activities to emphasize four key points that were threaded throughout the book.

1. The eight effective mathematics teaching practices are a coherent and connected set of instructional pedagogies that when implemented together create a classroom learning environment that supports the vision of mathematics teaching and learning advocated by NCTM, and provide opportunities for each and every student to achieve the world-class standards put into place by states and provinces.

2. Ambitious teaching requires thoughtful and thorough lesson planning that is driven by clear mathematics goals for student learning and demands considerable thought in anticipating what students are likely to do in response to a task and what teachers can do and provide as supports to ensure students wrestle productively with the challenging mathematical aspects of a task.

3. Improving teaching takes time and requires deliberate reflection on whether what was taught was learned and on what the teacher did that may have supported or inhibited student learning, and then making judicious adjustments to instruction on the basis of what the teacher learned through the reflection process.

4. Instruction must be equitable by ensuring each and every student learns mathematics with deep understanding. Toward this end, the five equity-based practices for mathematics classrooms must be considered hand in hand with the eight effective mathematics teaching practices.

Building a Teaching Framework for Mathematics

The "Case of Robert Harris and the Band Concert Task," which we revisited throughout the book, served as a touchstone in considering how the set of teaching practices are weaved together to support learning. Hence the case was intended to make salient the synergy of the effective mathematics teaching practices showing that the success of Mr. Harris's band concert lesson was the result of integrating the teaching practices in a coherent manner rather than by attending to individual teaching practices. In figure 10.1 we present a framework for mathematics teaching that shows the relationships between and among the teaching practices and how they work together to support ambitious instruction as they did in Robert Harris's classroom.

As we discussed in chapter 2, mathematics learning goals serve to focus and frame the teaching and learning that occurs throughout a lesson and over the course of a unit. Hence *establish mathematics learning goals to focus learning* sits at the top of the framework, signifying that setting goals is the starting point for all instructional decision making. The clarity and specificity of goals, and how such clarity and specificity support subsequent instruction, is clear in nearly every narrative and video case we examined (with the exception of the "Case of Mr. Stevenson" in chapter 3 and Ms. Chong's lesson in chapter 5 where the absence of clear and specific learning goals may have contributed to students not getting opportunities to think and reason afforded by the task). Take, for example, Ms. Brooks' lesson (introduced in chapter 9) featuring the Half-of-a-Whole task. Ms. Brooks wanted her students to understand that (1) one-half of a figure can be represented in multiple ways as long as the areas of each half have equal size, regardless of the location of the pieces that comprise each half, and (2) that a numeric relationship exists between the numerator and the denominator for fractions that are equivalent to one-half, specifically, when the value of the denominator is twice the value of the numerator, the fraction is equivalent to one-half. Ms. Brooks' goals served as a guide in both planning and implementing the lesson, from the task selected for students, the materials made available to support students as they worked, and the questions asked to probe students' thinking to the way in which she analyzed and synthesized student contributions. The goals were not just statements to be posted on the board and forgotten— they served as a beacon to guide the lesson from beginning to end.

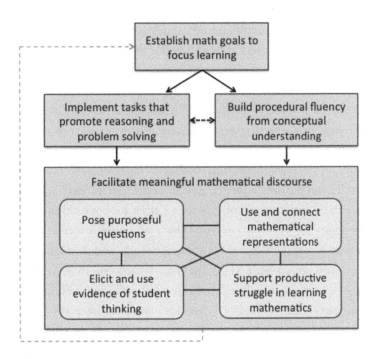

Fig. 10.1. A teaching framework for mathematics that highlights the relationships between and among the eight effective teaching practices

If goals represent the destination for students' mathematical learning in a given lesson, then tasks are the vehicles that move students from their current understanding toward those goals. This is the second level of the framework shown in figure 10.1. Depending on the goals of a lesson (or sequence of lessons), teachers might select tasks that promote reasoning and problem solving or engage students in building procedural fluency from conceptual understanding (as denoted by the dashed arrows between these two teaching practices). As discussed in chapter 4, tasks that promote reasoning and problem solving provide the conceptual base on which fluency can be developed. In turn, students use and apply those procedures in subsequent problem solving situations. Thus these two teaching practices support each other.

In each narrative and video case that we examined throughout the book, the teacher selected a task that promoted reasoning and problem solving as the basis for instruction, and in all but two cases, the cases of Mr. Stevenson and Ms. Chong, the task was consistent with the goals for the lesson. For example, the Caterpillar task used by Ms. Bouchard is a "doing mathematics" task, based on the criteria presented in the Task Analysis Guide (see fig. 3.1, pages 41–42). Her first-grade students were not given a prescribed pathway for solving the task, but rather they were allowed to draw upon their prior experiences and select from a variety of available materials in order to make sense of combining five quantities, which will build toward strategies for combining multiple addends. As a result, students discovered that they could combine the quantities in various ways and the total remains the same. Through their work on the Caterpillar task, some of Ms. Bouchard's students also constructed equations, providing an opportunity for these very young learners to discuss the equivalent equations that emerged from their problem solving. Ms. Bouchard's lesson did not focus explicitly on developing procedural fluency, but they were developing foundational understanding of quantities and ways of working flexibly with them, which will serve as the basis for moving toward procedural fluency in subsequent lessons.

The heart of any lesson is mathematical discourse (represented by the large rectangle in fig. 10.1). As students are provided with opportunities to communicate their emerging understandings to others, either orally or in writing, they are engaged in discourse. Discourse provides the opportunity for students to share ideas and clarify understanding, develop convincing arguments regarding why and how things work, and develop a language for expressing mathematical ideas (NCTM 2000). Oral discussions that occur as a whole class, in small groups, or with partners provide a particularly powerful opportunity for teachers to elicit and listen in on student thinking. Teachers can then use those insights to move both individual students and the entire class toward the mathematical goals that are the target of the lesson. Written discourse, including the use of pictures, words, and symbols, provides opportunities for students to clarify, organize, and consolidate their mathematical ideas to present or communicate them to others.

Discourse is mediated by use of the four mathematics teaching practices situated within the discourse rectangle in figure 10.1, that is, pose purposeful questions, use and connect mathematical representations, elicit and use evidence of students' thinking, and support productive struggle. Together, these teaching practices interact (in service of the goals and reliant upon the tasks) to engage students in meaningful discourse. As students work individually or collaboratively in small groups, teachers use purposeful questions to elicit and gather evidence of students' mathematical thinking. Teachers then use those insights into student thinking to encourage connections among representations and support continued engagement and productive struggle with important mathematical ideas. Teachers also use the evidence to inform their decisions in preparation for whole-class discussions, such as determining what strategies, ideas, or representations to select for presentation and discussion.

During the class discussion, teachers ask questions for the purpose of building shared understanding of specific mathematical ideas toward the goals of the lesson. Having goals in mind also informs assessment of student learning by knowing what to look for and listen for as evidence of students' progress toward the goals. Hence, facilitating meaningful discourse makes students' thinking public and accessible to the teacher, serving as formative assessment that feeds back into teachers' instructional decisions for the next lesson. This reflective feedback loop is represented in figure 10.1 by the dashed line connecting the bottom of the mathematics teaching framework model back to goals as the teaching cycle continually repeats.

To examine how these four teaching practices (i.e., questions, representations, evidence, and struggle) play out during a whole-class discussion, we return to the classroom example of Ms. Brooks and the discourse on the Half-of-a-Whole task (ATL 9.1, page 214). The teacher posed *purposeful questions* to move students' thinking toward the learning goal of recognizing the reasons why a fraction represented halves (e.g., "Tell me whether or not this figure shows me halves"). Her questions served to *elicit evidence of student thinking* as well as to continuously prompt students to engage with the reasoning of other students (e.g., "Who can tell me what Zaria was talking about?"). Ms. Brooks was then able to use students' current thinking as the basis for subsequent questions and instructional decisions. The *use of mathematical representations* was essential to the discourse and student sense making as the teacher prompted them to cut apart the diagrams and use them in support of their explanations and justifications. Although students were at times ambiguous or incorrect (e.g., Mayah grapples with whether a figure is or is not showing halves), Ms. Brooks allows the mathematical justifications to unfold organically rather than correcting or clarifying the ideas herself. By soliciting input from different students, she is *supporting productive struggle* by making a wide range of ideas available for students to consider as they clarify their own understanding. Hence, through these four teaching practices (i.e., pose purposeful questions, elicit and use evidence of student thinking, use and connect mathematical representations, support productive struggle in learning mathematics), Ms. Brooks facilitated the mathematical discourse of her students in making sense of the meaning of equivalent fractions. We can also see how these four teaching practices were weaved together (in partner, small-group, and whole-group discussions) in the narrative cases of Robert Harris (chapter 1) and Ms. Fredrick (chapter 8) to support students in working on tasks that promote reasoning and problem solving and to ultimately move them toward the established learning goals for the lesson.

Enacting the effective mathematics teaching practices requires purposeful actions and decisions on the part of the teacher, such as selecting goals and tasks for a lesson, identifying essential questions to elicit specific aspects of students' mathematical thinking (e.g., strategies, ideas, struggles, and misconceptions), and determining mathematical connections to surface throughout the discourse. Making these decisions in the moment as a lesson unfolds and reacting in ways aligned with the effective teaching practices, place a high demand on teachers' processing ability during a lesson. Fortunately, teachers can engage in "thinking through" many of these actions and decisions in the lesson planning process. In so doing, teachers can purposefully plan to embed the effective mathematics teaching practices into their instruction for individual lessons and sequences of lessons.

Thoughtful and Thorough Lesson Planning

Intentional advance planning is the key to effective teaching. Intentional planning shoulders much of the burden of teaching by replacing on-the-fly decision making during a lesson with careful investigation into the *what* and *how* of instruction *before* the lesson is taught (Stigler and Hiebert 1999, p.156). According to Fennema and Franke (1992, p. 156):

> During the planning phase, teachers make decisions that affect instruction dramatically. They decide what to teach, how they are going to teach, how to organize the classroom, what routines to use, and how to adapt instruction for individuals.

The teachers featured in our examples throughout the book gave careful consideration to what they were going to teach and how they were going to support student engagement and learning prior to the actual implementation of their lessons. The lesson plan for the Half-of-a-Whole task (see Appendix F) provides an example of the type of thoughtful and thorough lesson planning that is needed in order to support ambitious teaching focused on the engagement and learning of each and every student. The components of the lesson plan are shown in figure 10.2. This approach to lesson planning embodies many of the ideas we have discussed throughout this book. The planning process supports implementation of the effective mathematics teaching practices and the enactment of equity-based practices for mathematics classrooms.

Lesson Planning Template: Ambitious Teaching of Mathematics	
Mathematics Learning Goals What understandings will students take away from this lesson?	**Evidence of Student Thinking** What will students say, do, and produce that will provide evidence of their understandings?
Task What is the main activity that students will be working on in this lesson?	**Instructional Support—Tools, Resources, Materials** What tools or resources will be made available to give students entry to, and help them reason through, the task?
Prior Knowledge What prior knowledge and experiences will students draw upon in their work on this task?	**Task Launch** How will you introduce and set up the task to ensure that students understand the task and can begin productive work, without diminishing the cognitive demand of the task?
Anticipated Solution Paths What are the various ways that students might approach and solve the task, including correct, incorrect, and incomplete solutions?	**Instructional Support—Purposeful Teacher Questions** What assessing questions will you ask students to support their exploration of the task? What advancing questions will you ask to bridge from what they did to the mathematical ideas you want them to learn?
Class Discussion—Selecting and Sequencing Which anticipated approaches and solution paths do you want students to share and compare? In what order? Why?	**Class Discussion—Connecting Responses** What specific questions will you ask so that students make connections among the presented solution paths and make sense of the mathematical ideas you want them to learn?

Fig. 10.2. Components of a lesson plan for ambitious teaching

The plan begins with identifying clear and specific mathematics learning goals, as well as evidence of what students will be doing or saying to indicate that they have meet these goals. The plan then focuses on the task—identifying what task will be used, what instructional supports will be provided to students for working on the task, ways to tap into students' prior knowledge needed to enter and work on the task, and how the task will be launched. Another instructional support is the purposeful questions that teachers ask to elicit student thinking so responses can be used to advance mathematical understanding and encourage productive struggle. The class discussion sections provide a roadmap for facilitating the mathematical discourse of the task. It provides a plan for selecting and sequencing student approaches and making explicit connections to the mathematical ideas that were targeted in the lesson. The lesson-planning template also provides a useful framework to draw upon during instruction in response to unanticipated student responses. With a clear sense of the goals of the lesson and its mathematical storyline created through careful planning, a teacher is liberated to make sense of unexpected responses and to make principled decisions about how best to handle them.

As you can see, the lesson plan is driven by a series of questions. The goal is to prompt teachers to think deeply about a specific lesson and how to advance students' mathematical understanding during the lesson. The emphasis in the plan is on what students will do and how to support them rather than on teacher actions. According to Smith, Bill, and Hughes (2008), "By shifting the emphasis from what the teacher is doing to what students are thinking, the teacher will be better positioned to help students make sense of mathematics" (p. 137).

The teachers with whom we have worked consistently comment that planning lessons in this way helps them to enact lessons that maintain students' opportunities for reasoning and problem solving while allowing teachers to pose purposeful questions and facilitate meaningful discourse. As one teacher commented:

> Sometimes it's very time-consuming, trying to write these lesson plans, but it's very helpful. It really helps the lesson go a lot smoother and even not having it in front of me, I think it really helps me focus my thinking, which then [it] kind of helps me focus my students' thinking, which helps us get to an objective and leads to a better lesson. (Smith, Bill, and Hughes 2008, p. 137)

Teachers, including the one quoted above, find that this type of lesson planning is time-consuming but worthwhile. Working with colleagues might allow you to divide and conquer the planning of multiple lessons. Over time, you and your colleagues will begin to accumulate a library of lesson plans. To help you get started, we have included a lesson-planning template in Appendix G. As you consider the components for ambitious teaching, you will likely find that planning lessons in this manner not only strengthens your enactment of the effective mathematics teaching practices but also further deepens and advances your students' learning of mathematics.

Finally, we also note the importance of moving beyond the planning of individual lessons to planning sets of related lessons and ongoing classroom routines that build student understanding over time. As stated by Hiebert and colleagues (1997, p. 31):

> Students' understanding is built up gradually, over time, and through a variety of experiences. Understanding usually does not appear full-blown, after one experience or after completing one task. This means that the selection of appropriate tasks includes thinking about how tasks are related, how they can be chained together to increase the opportunity for students to gradually construct their understandings.

Some examples of related lessons throughout this book include the examination of tasks on relating addition and subtraction (chapter 3), the extension of Robert Harris's band concert lesson into the next lesson to explore the distributive property (chapter 4), and a sequence of tasks that Ms. Cutter uses to build toward fluency with multiplication (chapter 4). In addition, we examined two classroom routines in which teachers can chain ideas together, providing students with related learning experiences, in order to gradually deepen and extend student learning over time. For example, Ms. DiBrienza's use of addition strings for building procedural fluency (chapter 4) is an ongoing routine in her classroom, as is Ms. Chavez's use of the class attendance data (chapter 7).

Deliberate Reflection

Like most worthwhile and complex endeavors, enacting the effective teaching practices will improve with time, experience, and *deliberate reflection*. Improvement requires identifying what is working or not working and then being willing to make the necessary changes. Reflecting on classroom experiences makes teachers aware of what they and their students are doing and how their actions and interactions are affecting students' opportunities to learn. As we first stated in chapter 1, cultivating a habit of systematic and deliberate reflection may hold the key to improving one's teaching as well as sustaining lifelong professional learning. Such reflection, however, is only the starting point for transforming teaching. According to Artzt and Armour-Thomas (2002, p. 7):

> Teachers must also be willing and able to acknowledge problems that may be revealed as a result of the reflective process. Moreover, they must explore the reasons for the acknowledged problems, consider more plausible alternatives, and eventually change their thinking and subsequent action in the classroom.

To frame the reflection process, Hiebert and colleagues (2007) suggest four areas for analyzing the teaching within a specific instructional episode, such as a lesson. They suggest the reflection process include (1) specifying the learning goal or goals; (2) examining evidence of teaching actions and student learning, such as a video recording and student artifacts; (3) forming hypotheses about the effect of the teaching actions on students' learning; and (4) identifying ways to improve specific teaching actions. They provide the following reflective questions related, respectively, to the four areas:

- What are students supposed to learn?
- What did students learn?
- How did the teaching help (or not help) students learn?
- How could teaching more effectively help students learn?

Often the first two questions receive most of our attention and time—what were students suppose to learn (the goals) and did they learn it (the evidence). Throughout this book, you engaged in activities focused on the latter two questions—in what ways did the teaching help or not help students learn and how could the teaching be more effective in advancing student learning. We would argue that it is these two latter questions that demand more attention as each individual works toward more skilled professional teaching practice. As you take the ideas from this book and apply them in your own professional settings, we encourage you to use the four reflection questions and the teaching framework (see fig. 10.1) as tools for deliberate analysis and reflection toward improving your use of the eight effective teaching practices for mathematics.

Engage in ATL 10.1. Reflecting On and Improving Teaching

We conclude the book with one final Analyzing Teaching and Learning activity and ask you to apply the four reflective questions from Hiebert and colleagues (2007), discussed above, to a narrative teaching case by determining whether students learned what was intended, identifying how teaching might have supported or inhibited student learning, and envisioning how the teaching might be improved. In ATL 10.1, we ask you to consider how Ms. Chiprean, a fourth-grade teacher, might use these four questions to engage in deliberate reflection in order to improve her teaching. In the lesson, Ms. Chiprean engages her students in solving the Brownie task that you first encountered in chapter 5.

The Case of Ms. Chiprean and the Brownie Task

1   Fourth-grade teacher Ms. Chiprean wants her students to understand fair-sharing
2   situations that result in fractional shares. This will not only deepen her students'
3   understanding of fractions but also help her students develop the ability to fair-share
4   remainders in their work with multi-digit division, as well as build foundational
5   understanding for interpreting a fraction as division of the numerator by the
6   denominator, an expectation for her students next year in fifth grade. Like her colleague
7   Ms. Palmer in chapter 5, she selected the Brownie task (shown next page) for the lesson
8   because it was aligned with her goals, was cognitively challenging, and had multiple entry
9   points and solution paths.

10	**The Brownie Task**
11	There are 7 brownies. Four friends are sharing the brownies so that
12	everyone gets exactly the same amount. How much of the brownies will
13	each friend get? What do you call that amount?

14   Ms. Chiprean decided to launch the task by holding up a plate of 7 brownies (all the
15   same size) and asking 4 students to stand up in front of the room. "If these 4 students
16   were going to share this plate of 7 brownies with no leftovers, I wonder how much
17   each person would get?" She thought showing students 7 real brownies might motivate
18   interest in the task, and having 4 students stand up might help students see that there
19   would be more than 1 brownie per student. Before sending the students off to work in
20   small groups on the task, she asked a few questions to check on their understanding of
21   the task (e.g., What are you trying to figure out? How much do you think each person
22   might get?). She emphasized that the brownies were to be shared fairly so that each
23   person received the exact same amount and that all of the brownies had to be used up.
24   She reminded the groups to work together and be prepared to report to the whole class.
25   As students began working on the task in their groups, Ms. Chiprean walked around
26   the room monitoring their work and conversations. Her first impression was that
27   students were not using strategies that would help them in finding and explaining the
28   solution. For example, group 2 wrote $7 \div 4 = 1$ r3. Group 5 wrote $4 \times 2 = 8$ and said they
29   can't give each person 2 because they would need 8 brownies. They were stuck. Group 3
30   was drawing pictures of the brownies; they appeared to be showing both halves and some
31   fourths, but when asked what they were doing, they started to erase their work, saying
32   they heard someone say it was 1 brownie per person. In addition, group 6, who had
33   been trying to get her attention for several minutes, claimed to have no idea how to get
34   started.
35   With nearly half the class off to a rocky start, she decided to bring the class back
36   together so that the whole group could figure out how to make sense of the given
37   information. Toward that end, Ms. Chiprean emphasized the importance of giving each
38   person a fair share or the same amount of the 7 brownies. She reemphasized that all 7
39   brownies must be shared. She was sure this was now clear to the students. The teacher
40   then offered the students three ways of starting the task, and recorded the approaches
41   as shown in figure 10.3. The first strategy was to think of it as a division problem. The
42   students should imagine giving each person 1 whole brownie, which would then leave
43   them the challenge of figuring out how to share the remaining 3 brownies among the 4

44 students. The second strategy she suggested was to begin by cutting all the brownies into
45 halves, share the halves among the 4 students, and then figure out what to do with any
46 halves that could not be shared. The third approach suggested was to begin by cutting all
47 the brownies into fourths and then share the fourths among the 4 students.

48

	First Friend	Second Friend	Third Friend	Fourth Friend
Division Approach 7 ÷ 4 = 1 r 3 Show how to share the 3 brownies among 4 students.				
Sharing Halves Approach Cut all the brownies into halves and share the halves.				
Sharing Fourths Approach Cut each brownie into fourths and share the fourths.				

49 **Fig. 10.3.** Three strategies for the Brownie task

50 Most of the groups that had previously struggled were now using one of the three
51 identified strategies. Group 6, who previously could not get started, used the sharing
52 fourths approach. They partitioned each brownie into fourths, shared those fourths,
53 and found out that each person got 7 of those smaller one-fourth-size pieces. Groups 3
54 and 5 used the division approach. They gave each person 1 brownie, and then after a bit
55 of discussion, they realized they could cut each of the 3 leftover brownies into fourths
56 and then share those fourths; each person getting 1 whole brownie and $^3/_4$ of another
57 brownie. Group 2 continued to insist that students should not be forced to take more
58 of the brownies than they desired. Ms. Chiprean asked them to pretend that all 4 of the
59 students had to have an equal share because they all loved brownies; then she suggested
60 that they try using the sharing-fourths approach, being very fair and giving each person
61 $^1/_4$ of each brownie until all of the brownie pieces were shared. The teacher stopped back
62 to check in on group 2 after a few minutes, and found that they had partitioned the
63 brownies into fourths and gave each person $^7/_4$.
64 Ms. Chiprean brought the whole class together and asked the students, "So now that
65 you had more time to work on the problem, how much of the brownies will each person
66 get? What would be their fair share?" She asked students from group 6 to report first.
67 Shantel, a member of the group, said, "We decided that each person will get $^7/_4$." Jamal,

68   a member of group 3, jumped in, "We didn't get that. We gave each person 1 whole
69   brownie and ³/₄ of a brownie." Ms. Chiprean asked everyone if both answers were right.
70   Some students nodded their heads and a few students did a thumbs-up, indicating
71   consensus.
72   With a few minutes left in the class, Ms. Chiprean told students that for homework
73   they needed to complete a similar problem in which they would share 9 brownies among
74   4 students. She explained that they would find the details on their homework site.

Analysis of ATL 10.1: Relating Teaching Actions to Student Learning

In order to deliberately reflect on one's teaching, it is necessary to collect lesson artifacts in order to support reflection. These artifacts can include an audio or video recording of the lesson, samples of student work (collected or photographed), charts or photographs of work produced by the teacher or students during the lesson, and lesson plans developed in preparation for the lesson. The detailed notes of a classroom observer, such as an instructional coach, principal, mathematics specialist, or colleague, can also provide evidence of what occurred during instruction and aid in reflecting on the lesson. For our purposes, we will assume that Ms. Chiprean had three artifacts on which to draw upon in her reflection on the lesson: a lesson plan prepared prior to the lesson, an audio recording of the lesson, and copies of the group work created during the lesson.

What are students supposed to learn?

Ms. Chiprean might begin her analysis of the lesson by considering her goals for the lesson, and then reflect on what students appeared to learn related to those goals. She wanted her students to understand that fair shares of a group of discrete objects (the 7 brownies) may require partitioning one or more objects into smaller parts, that each person gets the same-size share, and that all of the sharing material (7 brownies) is exhausted or used up. She knew that students had prior knowledge of and experiences with partitioning an individual rectangle, similar to a brownie, so she assumed students could draw upon those experiences in the Brownie task. In addition she wanted her students to begin using fraction language and symbols meaningfully.

What did students learn?

In listening to the audio recording of the lesson and looking at the group work, she concluded that students were able to partition the brownies to arrive at one of the two expected solutions of ⁷/₄ (lines 52–53, 61–63) or 1 whole and ³/₄ (lines 54–57). Given that the students had arrived at the two correct solutions to the problem and the fact that the class seemed to agree that both solutions were correct, Ms. Chiprean might reach the conclusion the both solutions were understood by all students.

How did the teaching help (or not help) students learn?

Although students had arrived at the two correct solutions to the problem using the partitioning strategies that Ms. Chiprean had targeted, this provides evidence of what students could do (a performance goal outcome), not what they understood or even what they had learned (a mathematics learning goal outcome). A further analysis of the lesson might lead Ms. Chiprean to see that these strategies emerged only after she presented three ways to work on the task and strongly suggested that the students try one of the strategies she presented (lines 39–47). Once the suggestion was made to use these ways of partitioning the brownies, the students had little more to do than follow the steps presented and perform a rule for sharing the brownies. Ms. Chiprean might also recognize that little to no discussion occurred regarding the meaning of the resulting fractions in context, 7 parts (brownie pieces) of size $1/4$ of a brownie ($7/4 = 1/4 + 1/4 + 1/4 + 1/4 + 1/4 + 1/4 + 1/4$;) and 1 whole brownie and 3 parts (brownie pieces) of size $1/4$ of a brownie ($1 3/4 = 1 + 1/4 + 1/4 + 1/4$). Nor did the class discuss what it means to partition the 7 brownies in different ways and why the different ways are equivalent, that is, that 1 whole brownie received by each student in groups 3 and 5 could also be partitioned into fourths, or groups 2 and 6 could compose 1 whole brownie from 4 of their fourths.

Ms. Chiprean may have then become aware that she directed too much of what went on during the lesson and that she did too much of the thinking for students. In particular, if she thought about the factors of maintenance and decline of high-level tasks (fig. 3.2, pages 49–50), she might have realized that she helped her students too much, removing the problematic aspects of the task when she presented students with three ways of partitioning and sharing the brownies. She might also recognize that she was focused on ensuring that each group found a correct solution rather than providing students with sufficient time to wrestle with the demanding aspects of the task in order to make sense of the situation.

How could teaching more effectively help students learn?

In considering how the lesson could be improved, Ms. Chiprean might first realize that while she anticipated the correct approaches that students might use to solve the task, she had not considered the difficulties they would encounter. By focusing on both correct and incorrect approaches during the planning process, she may have been better prepared to deal with her struggling students.

She might then reflect on how she could use the effective mathematics teaching practices to improve her instruction and student learning. This might help her recognize that when students struggled with the task (lines 26–34), she needed to foster their productive struggle without taking over the thinking for them, such as using those supports suggested in chapter 9. This could involve asking questions to elicit students' thinking regarding what they understood about the brownie context and the need to partition individual brownies to create fair shares of the whole set of brownies. She could provide probing guidance by encouraging students to self-reflect and offer their own ideas for potential next steps in working on the task. Group 2 wrote 7 ÷ 4 = 1 r3; she could have asked, "What does 1 r3 tell you about the brownies? What more could you do with those remaining 3 brownies?" Group 5 wrote 4 × 2 = 8 and said they could not give each person 2 brownies because they would then need 8 brownies. Ms. Chiprean could have said, "You are correct, you can't give each person 2 brownies but what can you give each person?" Group 3 was drawing pictures of the brownies that appeared to be showing both halves and some fourths but when asked what they were doing, they started to erase their work, saying they heard someone say it was 1 brownie per person. Ms. Chiprean could have said, "Trust yourself. You cut some into halves. How many halves could you pass out to each person?"

Perhaps the most important takeaway from her reflection would be the realization that her actions during the lesson need to be guided by the mathematics learning goals of the lesson. That she needs to consider, every step of the way, how she is going to help students reach the learning goals without taking over the thinking for them. The bulk of the work that students did do focused on trying to immediately apply a procedure for division or multiplication rather than engaging in the problem context and drawing from their own informal experiences with sharing. The final discussion with the whole class did not bring out the thinking of students and it did not explicitly address the goals Ms. Chiprean had set. The student work produced during the class (both what students did and what students said) provided Ms. Chiprean with virtually no evidence that students met her learning goals. With this realization, Ms. Chiprean would now be positioned to prepare her next lesson and to provide more support for her students so that they walk away from the lesson not only learning what was intended but feeling a sense of ownership of the ideas.

How does reflecting inform teaching?

Reflecting on a lesson should inform the planning of the next lesson, which in turn informs the implementation of the lesson and enactment of the teaching practices, which then provides further evidence of students' learning upon which to reflect. This process is represented by the *teaching cycle* in figure 10.4.

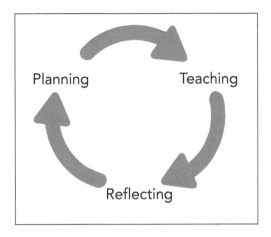

Fig. 10.4. The Teaching Cycle

As with planning, we note the importance of reflecting on sequences of lessons, as well as individual lessons, to assess the teaching and learning that occurs over time. We encourage you to take advantage of opportunities for reflection individually, collaboratively with colleagues, or with the support of an instructional coach. As suggested by Hiebert and colleagues (2007), basing reflections on evidence of teaching actions and student learning helps the teacher form hypotheses about the effects of particular teaching actions on students' learning and to identify ways to improve specific teaching moves.

Instruction Must Be Equitable

In chapters 2 through 9, we considered the specific ways in which the effective mathematics teaching practices can individually support equitable learning opportunities for students. Throughout those chapters, we discussed the ways in which the teaching practices support the development of students' identities as mathematical knowers and doers, including students who may have been historically marginalized. We also examined the role of the teaching practices in creating publicly accessible thinking and reasoning spaces for each and every student. When the eight teaching practices are used together in combination, powerful opportunities are created over time to ensure meaningful mathematical learning for all students, regardless of their history and prior experiences.

Just as it is important to carefully analyze students' mathematical learning and development over the course of a year, it is equally important to document and reflect on students' identity formation in the elementary grades (Allen and Schnell 2016). The effective mathematics teaching practices can be used as a backdrop for reflecting on students' participation and contributions in mathematics classrooms. For example, as you engage students with tasks that vary across the cognitive demand categories discussed in chapter 3, you can note the ways in which students might engage with different types of tasks and how that engagement might shift within a lesson or over a series of lessons. Is the student eager to tackle a high-level task or does the student become quiet and withdraw from discussions? A teacher might note, for example, that a student has strong mathematical reasoning skills when he works on his own, but is hesitant to share that thinking in small-group or whole-group discussions. Providing that student with feedback that reinforces the validity of his thinking, encouraging him to engage with other students, and creating opportunities for the student to pose and answer questions about mathematics can potentially change that student's perspective of what it means to do mathematics and what is valued in the mathematics classroom. The development of students' mathematical identities has powerful implications for their future as members of mathematics communities of practice, and as such, students' mathematical identities should be evaluated periodically, including an analysis for evidence of change, and then efforts should be implemented to challenge or affirm students' views of themselves, as well as how others perceive them in the mathematics classroom.

In addition to classroom-based equity concerns, systemic equity considerations in the elementary grades are also important to challenge. For example, grouping practices, such as ability grouping, separates students with previous track records of mathematical success from students who have not yet exhibited strong mathematics achievement. This separation is detrimental to student learning opportunities because groups that aggregate previously unsuccessful students almost always study less mathematics content in less depth than more successful students. As such, it is critical for teachers to consider how they can use goals, tasks, discourse, and questioning to design instruction that has the potential to reach each and every student by providing access to high-level tasks and support to struggle productively. Established assessment practices, such as the use of timed tests, also have implications for equity. Such practices send the message to students that success in mathematics requires being able to get correct answers quickly. Time tests devalue reasoned mathematical thinking based on understanding, problem solving, and sense making, and reinforce fixed mathematical mind-sets in which students think they are either born with or without mathematical ability and that it is something they essentially cannot change (Boaler 2015). Teachers must become advocates for dismantling systemic conditions that lead to inequitable mathematics learning opportunities and outcomes for students. According to *Principles to Actions* (NCTM 2014, p. 60):

> Access and equity in mathematics at the school and classroom levels rest on beliefs and practices that empower *all* students to participate meaningfully in learning mathematics and to achieve outcomes in mathematics that are not predicted by or correlated with student characteristics…Support for access and equity requires, but is not limited to, high expectations, access to high-quality mathematics curriculum and instruction, adequate time for students to learn, appropriate emphasis on differentiated processes that broaden students' productive engagement with mathematics, and human and material resources.

As you engage in the cycle of planning, teaching, and reflecting, it is critical to consider how your instruction will or did support the mathematics learning of each and every student. If each of your students is not engaging in reasoning and problem solving and making reasonable progress towards your lesson goals, then you need to reflect on the factors that may be impacting students' lack of success and take corrective action. Unless all students are experiencing success in your mathematics classroom in terms of their developing mathematical knowledge, as well as their positive mathematical identities, more work needs to be done.

Next Steps: Ongoing Work in Improving Mathematics Teaching

Though you are at the end of this book, hopefully your journey in exploring the effective mathematics teaching practices in your own classroom is just beginning. If you have worked through the book alone, consider revisiting the activities with a colleague. If you have worked through the book with colleagues, consider how to continue to encourage each other to plan, teach, and reflect on your teaching in ways that highlight the effective teaching practices and support each and every student's mathematics learning. You might analyze additional teaching cases (e.g., videos of classroom lessons) or other artifacts of mathematics teaching (e.g., tasks or sets of student work) and discuss the extent to which the eight mathematics teaching practices are apparent or lacking and what impact this appeared to have on student learning. Another opportunity for continued growth might include forming a book club where a group of teachers read about an effective teaching practice, and then meet (face-to-face or virtually) to engage in a professional development module highlighting that teaching practice (e.g., a chapter or activity in this book or resources available online though the *Principles to Actions* Toolkit, www.nctm.org/PtaToolkit).

You might also consider co-planning mathematics lessons with colleagues using the eight effective teaching practices as a framework. Invite your mathematics coach (if you have one), administrator, or other instructional leader to participate. As suggested earlier in this chapter, teams of teachers could collaborate to plan sequences of lessons and begin to develop a library of lessons that promote reasoning and problem solving and/or develop procedural fluency from conceptual understanding. When you have an opportunity to teach the co-planned lessons (or other similar lessons), observe each other with particular attention to what effective mathematics teaching practices are being used in the lesson and how the teaching practices did or did not support students' learning of mathematics toward the intended learning goals. Several tools for analyzing tasks, implementation of tasks, questions, and whole-group discussion identified throughout this book could serve as a basis for collecting and examining evidence of teaching actions and student learning that inform instructional improvements on the effective teaching practices.

Furthermore, rather than attending to all eight effective mathematics teaching practices at once, you and colleagues might select a focal teaching practice (or practices) to be at the forefront of your teaching and reflecting, with connections to other teaching practices acknowledged as playing "supporting roles." When sharing your work with administrators or instructional leaders, you might engage them in considering how the effective mathematics teaching practices could become part of the school or districts' formal observation, feedback, and evaluation structures, and why it would be beneficial to do so (e.g., the positive impact on students' learning and engagement).

Final Thoughts

Changing one's teaching is hard work that takes sustained and meaningful effort over time. Enacting the effective mathematics teaching practices will improve with experience, thorough and thoughtful lesson planning, and deliberate reflection. Simply being introduced to the mathematics teaching practices does not mean that they become immediately adopted by teachers and used in ways that reflect ambitious mathematics instruction. In fact, these teaching practices often bring to the surface important unproductive beliefs for teachers. Do I truly believe that students can develop conceptual understanding before being introduced to procedures? Do I believe that I can support meaningful student learning for a diverse group of students that may have had very different mathematical experiences in previous grades? What prompts me to intervene with a small group of students rather than leave them to work, and are my interventions supporting productive struggle or taking it away? Teachers need time to reflect on their beliefs and current teaching practices and to make changes in one's teaching actions that better support students' mathematics learning (Goldsmith and Schifter 1997). This is a gradual process and purposeful journey for each of us to take individually, as well as collectively, as a teaching professional.

As a reader of this book you have already taken an important step toward thinking more deeply about teaching and learning in your classroom. Persistence and commitment will help you continue the journey to instructional improvement. We close with a quote from *The Teaching Gap* (Stigler and Hiebert 1999, p. 179):

> The star teachers of the twenty-first century will be those who work together to infuse the best ideas into standard practice. They will be teachers who collaborate to build a system that has the goal of improving students' learning in the "average" classroom, [and] who work to gradually improve standard classroom practices…The star teachers of the twenty-first century will be teachers who work every day to improve teaching—not only their own but that of the whole profession.

ATL 2.2 and 2.4 Video Transcript: Amanda Smith and the Donuts Task

This transcript accompanies the video clip in ATL 2.2 and ATL 2.4. It features a lesson taught by Amanda Smith with kindergarten students working on the Donuts task.

[Screen] If you have three chocolate and four vanilla donuts, then how many donuts do you have?

1	**Student:**	This, this is it. (*Student shows 3 counters and 4 counters.*)
2	**Teacher:**	Do you agree with Jay Clayton? (*Teacher puts up 3 fingers and 4 fingers and*
3		*engages students in counting all.*)
4	**Students:**	Yes…7…
5	**Teacher:**	So what should we do? What should we do down here?
6	**Student:**	What we have up here that's what we write down here.
7	**Teacher:**	Oh. Can you show us?
8	**Student:**	Uh-huh.
9	**Teacher:**	How many did Cooper say? He had 3 and 4 more.
10	**Student:**	7.
11	**Teacher:**	How do you know?
12	**Student:**	Because 3 + 4 = 7. (*Student points to 3 counters and 4 counters.*)
13	**Teacher:**	3 + 4 = 7. Do you agree with that?
14	**Students:**	Yeah.
15	**Teacher:**	Yeah, alright. Good job, Alex. Thank you.

[Screen] Are three chocolate donuts and four vanilla donuts more or less than four vanilla and three chocolate donuts?

16	Teacher:	If I can think about my problem as 4 vanilla and 3 chocolate—can I think like
17		that? (*Teacher moves set of 4 counters from the right to the left side and 3*
18		*counters to the left to the right.*)
19	Student:	Yes because you can…'cause it still makes 7.
20	Teacher:	Claire says that still makes 7. Do you agree with her?
21	Student:	Yes.
22	Teacher:	Oh, Claire, can you go show us?
23	Student:	If 4 vanilla were over here and 3 chocolate were over here and we switched
24		them, it would still make 7 but it just got switched around. (*Student points to the*
25		*counters.*)
26	Teacher:	She said, Yetzaira, she said it got what?
27	Student:	3 plus—
28	Teacher:	Who heard what Claire said? It got—Will?
29	Student:	Switched around.
30	Teacher:	How would we write that?
31	Student:	I know.
32	Teacher:	Let's see. How would we—
33	Student:	If we wrote 4 and then we wrote a plus sign and then we put 3 then we would
34		put…we would put equal and then we would put 7 again. (*Clair points to the*
35		*display on the overhead.*)
36	Teacher:	Oh. So Claire says that we would do it like this. 4 + 3 = 7. Evan, what are
37		different? What do you notice? (*Teacher records 4 + 3 = 7.*)
38	Student:	This 3 is to the right and this one is to the left.
39	Teacher:	Alright. So you're telling me that it should look like this. It should look like that 3.
40		So is that what you're thinking? So here we have how many? (*Teacher writes 3*
41		*correctly.*)
42	Student:	4.
43	Teacher:	How many? 4, 5, 6, 7. So can we count on and get 7? (*Teacher counts on from 4,*
44		*touching counters one by one and counting on three more touching her chin.*)
45	Student:	Yeah.
46	Teacher:	Awesome. Great job, boys and girls. Ok now, Cooper. Let's look back down here.
47		at what you drew for us. Do you notice anything, Cooper, about what you drew
48		on this side and what you drew on this side in relation to our equations? Hmmm.
49		Can you tell us? (*Teacher points to Cooper's drawing of circles showing 3 + 4 and*
50		*4 + 3.*)

51	**Student:**	There is more over there.
52	**Teacher:**	You can just tell us, Renee.
53	**Student:**	I had 3 down; that's for the chocolate. And 4 down; that's for the vanilla. Then…
54	**Teacher:**	Then what did you draw here?
55	**Student:**	The vanilla on the top and the chocolate on the bottom.
56	**Teacher:**	Is that the same as our equations?
57	**Student:**	Yes, ma'am.
58	**Teacher:**	So, Cooper, were you already thinking that 3 and 4 and…
59	**[End of audio]**	

ATL 2.3 Video Transcript: Kristen Walker and the Polygon Investigation

This transcript accompanies the video clip in ATL 2.3. It features a lesson taught by Kristen Walker with fifth-grade students working on the Polygons Investigation task.

1 2	Teacher 2:	The second thing I want you to do is I want you to write why you say yes, and why you say no. Adrian, could you summarize the directions for the class?
3 4	Student 1:	You write yes if you think it is a polygon, and you write no if it, you don't think it is a polygon. And you write why.
	Group 1	
5 6	Student 2:	Some of those are all straight lines, but they're not polygons. *(Student points to the figures on the board.)*
7	Teacher 2:	Okay.
8	Student 3:	Well, that circle, um, well…*(Student points to the figures on the board.)*
9 10	Student 2:	No, but like, that, the square, with the triangle…*(Student points to the figures on the board.)*
11	Student 3:	Well this, uh, well that's 'cause they're connected.
12	Student 2:	Oh yeah.
	Group 2	
13	Student 5:	Because, the shape of the… *(The students discuss figure 11.)*

Fig. 11

14	Student 1:	Well, you said it wasn't…
15	Student 5:	Yeah…
16	Student 1:	…so what do you think it is?
17	Student 5:	Because, it doesn't make sense, the little picture, how it's shown. See, it's just like a
18		little straight line, with another parallel line to it. *(The student is referring to figure 11.)*

Group 3

19	Student 6:	Uh, this one. There's something like that up on the overhead.
20	Student 7:	Yeah but see, it's got something…it's not exactly the same kind, 'cause it's slanted…
21	Student 6:	Yeah.
22	Student 7:	So I think this would be a polygon. Put a question mark by it. *(Puts a question mark by*
23		*figure 5.)*

Fig. 5

24	Visitor:	Why are you questioning that one? Tell me your thinking.
25	Student 7:	Because…because I'm not sure if, um…
26	Student 6:	We're not sure…
27	Student 7:	…if it's a polygon.
28	Student 6:	Yeah.
29	Visitor:	What part of it makes you question it? *(Points to figure 5.)*
30	Student 6:	Well, there's something up there in 'Not Polygons' that looks like it.
31	Visitor:	Oh.
32	Student 6:	We're not sure.
33	Visitor:	Do you agree with her? Does this one look like one that's not a polygon?
34	Student 7:	*[Nods yes.]*

Group 4

36	Principal:	So it matches the first two, what else?
37	Student 8:	And then this one is no because, um, even though it's straight lines, it's not closed in.
38		*(Student points to figure 2.)*

Fig. 2

39	Student 9:	The lines are crossing each other. *(Student points to figure 5.)*
40	Principal:	Uh-hmmm.
41	Student 10:	And then over here it'd be a no because, um, this is um, these are straight, or kind of
42		straight, and this one is completely straight and that one is going up this way and the
43		other one's going that way. *(Points to figure 7.)*

Fig. 7

44	Student 9:	Well, uh…yeah, and if you…
45	Student 10:	And it's not completely closed.
46	Principal:	Not completely closed.
47	Student 10:	'Cause there's another line going out. *(Points to the line that extends beyond the figure in*
48		*figure 7.)*
49	Principal:	Huh. Okay. So, going back to number 12? *(Points to figure 12.)*

Fig. 12

50	Student 10:	Um, no extra lines.
51	Principal:	Does it fit with your definition so far?
52	Student 10:	Yes, because straight lines.
53	Student 9:	Then it may be…
54	Principal:	Well if something is holding you back from saying, "Yeah, we know that's a polygon,"
55		what might that be?
56	Student 9:	The sides aren't exactly the same, so we got kind of confused.
57	Principal:	Mmm-kay.

Institute for Learning Classroom Video (2016). *Polygon Investigation* (Kristen Walker, Teacher) [Video transcript]. Copyright ©2016 by The University of Pittsburgh. Used/Reproduced with permission from The Institute for Learning, University of Pittsburgh.

ATL 4.2 Video Transcript: Jennifer DiBrienza and the Additions String Task

This transcript accompanies the video clip in ATL 4.2. It features a lesson taught by Jennifer DiBrienza with first-grade students working on the Addition Strings task.

1	**Teacher:**	7 plus 3. So many thumbs went up right away. Let's see, Mathew.
2	**Student:**	10.
3	**Teacher:**	How'd you know, Mathew?
4	**Student:**	I just knew it.
5	**Teacher:**	You just knew it? How many kids just knew 7 plus 3? Great. Keeping that
6		in mind, the next one, you ready? *(Teacher records 17 + 3 on the board.)*
7		17 plus 3. Give a minute of think time. Tasmine.
8	**Student:**	20.
9	**Teacher:**	20, how'd you get that answer?
10	**Student:**	I put 17 in my head and put 3 on there.
11		*(Teacher draws an open number line and writes 17 at the start of the number line.*
12		*Makes three jumps on the number line and writes 18, 19, 20 respectively.*
13	**Teacher:**	Okay, you said you put 17 in your head and then what?
14	**Student:**	I counted 3 more.
15	**Teacher:**	So you counted on from 17, you counted 1, 2, 3 more?
16		So what's that? 18?
17	**Student:**	19.

18	**Teacher:**	19.
19	**Student:**	20.
20	**Teacher:**	20. Okay, great. Who did it Tasmine's way? Okay, who tried a different way?
21		Destiny?
22	**Student:**	I know, like, it's on the top 7 plus 3 equals 10 plus—and then I knew just 17 plus
23		3 was 20.
24	**Teacher:**	So you—this helped you figure this one out? Okay, how did it help you figure it
25		out.
26	**Student:**	'Cause it was like 10 plus 10 equals 20.
27	**Teacher:**	It was like 10 plus 10 equals 20. So you already knew you had ten and you just
28		knew you had to add 10 more on? Anybody else want to try and explain that?
29		Danelle?
30	**Student:**	She broke up the 17 into the 10 plus a 7 and she gave the 3 to the 7 so that equal
31		10 so 10 plus 10 equal 20.
32	**Teacher:**	Okay, I'm going to put a new one up. Keep Destiny's strategy in mind. What's 27
33		plus 3? *(Writes 27 + 3 = __ on the board.)* Aneesa.
34	**Student:**	I have 27 in my head and 27, 20…27, 28, 29, 30.
35	**Teacher:**	Okay, so you counted on from 27, you started at 27 and you went 28, 29, 30.
36		*(Draws an open number line and writes 27 at the start of the line. Marks three*
37		*jumps, writing 28, 29, 30 at each of the respective marks. Records 27 + 3 = 30.)*
38		Okay. What did you notice?
39	**Student:**	It's going by all zeros.
40	**Teacher:**	Oh, they all end in a zero?
41	**Student:**	Up to the one thing.
42	**Teacher:**	So you notice they all end in zeros. What else did you notice?
43	**Student:**	And threes, 1, 2, 3, and 7.
44	**Teacher:**	Whoa, 10, 20, 30?
45	**Student:**	And tens and threes.
46	**Teacher:**	And threes.
47	**Student:**	And sevens.
48	**Teacher:**	And sevens.
49	**Student:**	*[inaudible comment]*
50	**Teacher:**	Raphael? So people notice that there's sevens in every column here, there's
51		threes going down here and it's going 10, 20, 30. Why do you think that's
52		happening? Let's look over here on our hundreds board. We started out with 7,
53		right?
54	**Student:**	Yeah.

55	**Teacher:**	Jamie.
56	**Student:**	Yes.
57	**Teacher:**	We start out with 7 and we added 3 right? 1, 2, 3. And then
58		when we did 17 you said we added 10 more on, right? *(Teacher points to the*
59		*numbers on the hundreds chart.)* Let's see, 1, 2, 3, 4, 5, 6, 7, 8, 9, 10. Look, we just
60		moved down one right?
61	**Student:**	And 27.
62	**Teacher:**	27 is right below it. How many more do you think if I start at 17, how
63		many more do you think I have to add to get to 27? *(Points to 17 on the hundreds*
64		*chart and then moves down to 27.)* I'm going to move on to the next one.
65		If 37 plus 3 more is 40, what's 37 plus 5? *(Records 37 + 5 = __.)* I want to see
66		lots of hands up, 37 plus 5. I'm going to give everyone a chance to think about it.
67	**Student:**	I had 37 in my head.
68	**Teacher:**	You had 37 in your head. *(Records an open number line on the board and writes*
69		*37 at the start of the number line.)*
70	**Student:**	Then I counted 5 more.
71	**Teacher:**	You counted 5 more, 38, 39, 40, 41, 42 like that? *(Starts at 37, marks a jump,*
72		*records 38, marks a jump and records 39, marks a jump and records 40, and*
73		*continues until 42 is reached.)* Okay, did anybody do it differently? I want to know
74		what you noticed. Did anyone do it differently?
75	**Student:**	I ah…broke up the 5 into 3 plus 2.
76	**Student:**	I think 3, the 37.
77	**Teacher:**	Okay to the 37.
78	**Student:**	Yes.
79	**Teacher:**	Okay.
80	**Student:**	And that equals 40.
81	**Teacher:**	You just knew that one, right?
82	**Student:**	Yeah.
83	**Teacher:**	Okay, and what did you have left?
84	**Student:**	And I had left the 2.
85	**Teacher:**	And that left 2. So, instead of just making jumps of one you started at 37 and
86		you knew the 3 more made 40 so you knew you had to add 2 more and that
87		would give you 42. *(Draws an open number line and records 37. Marks a jump of*
88		*3 and records a sum of 40. Then makes a jump of 2 and records a sum of 42.)*
89		Yeah? Is that how you were thinking about it?
90		**[End of audio]**

ATL 8.2 Video Transcript: Arthur Harris and the Odd and Even Task

This transcript accompanies the video clip in ATL 8.2. I It features a lesson taught by Arthur Harris with third-grade students working on the Odd and Even task.

1	Teacher:	Do you have a reason why you think 3 is even or odd? Yes? Which one do you think
2		it is, even or odd?
3	Student:	Odd.
4	Teacher:	Okay. And why?
5	Student:	Because if you – because 1, 3, and 5, they don't have pairs, but 2, 4, and 6, they do
6		have pairs.
7	Teacher:	Come to the overhead and show me what you mean by they don't have pairs, please.
8	Student:	These two, they don't have pairs because if you put these—one is—there's one more,
9		but you don't have another one to put together with this one. (*Student shows three*
10		*square tiles, moves two tiles together, and then notes the remaining tile.*)
11	Teacher:	Okay. Good. So it has something to do with this idea of pairs and this one leftover.
12		Let's look at another number. (*The small groups examine the number 8.*)
13		
14	**Group 1 Discussion**	
15	Student:	Yeah, because each one should have like, it's even number, each one of us should have
16		two. And if each one of us has two, that would be a pair. That would be a pair number
17		because two is an even number, and two has to go with the pair.
18	Teacher:	Okay.
19		

Group 2 Discussion

20

21   Student: 8 plus 4 equals 8, and [*inaudible*].

22   Teacher: Do you agree or disagree?

23   Student: Agree.

24   Teacher: Why?

25   Student: Well, because when you have like these, or you put them like that, you have four

26   groups and two in each group. And then when you put it like that, you have two in

27   each group, but you have four groups [*inaudible*].

28   Teacher: Okay. Let me ask you all this. What is the difference between doing it like this (*the*

29   *teacher shows 2 groups of 4 tiles each*). Okay. Or, let me use yours, doing it like this? (*The*

30   *teacher shows 4 groups of 2 tiles each.*) How is this different or the same as this?

31   Yes, ma'am?

32   Student: It's the same because it's still has 4—it still has 2 groups of 4, and it has 42 groups

33   of 2.

34   Teacher: Okay.

35

Whole-Group Discussion

36

37   Student: I know that 8 is even because 9 has a leftover. There's one left. (*Student shows 4 groups*

38   *of 2 tiles on the overhead.*)

39   Teacher: Okay. We'll, pull another one out, and you show us 9. Explain to us why you think 8

40   is even again?

41   Student: Because I know that 8 is even because 9 is a leftover. (*Student adds 1 more square tile to*

42   *the set of 4 groups of 2 tiles displayed on the overhead.*)

43   Teacher: Okay. What does that mean when he uses the word "leftover"? Can anybody clarify

44   what that means? Yes, ma'am?

45   Student: It means it's not a pair because 8 has two…four groups of 8 is two pair, and then 9 is

46   a leftover with…9 is with the odd.

47   Teacher: Okay. Anybody else want to add to that?

48   Student: I think it's an even number, and it'll…the reason why the 9 is left over is because

49   everyone has a pair except the 9. And if the 9 had a pair, it would be with the evens.

50   But it's an odd number.

51   Teacher: Okay.

52   Student: The 9 is an odd number.

53   Teacher: We looked at…and other groups, too, looked at another way to describe an even

54   number.

55   Student: You can describe the even number because when you have it in pairs, you have 4 in

56   each pair, and another pair you have 4, and there is no more left.

57   Teacher: What do you call that when you have, for example, 4 and 4? (*The teacher records*

58   *4 + 4.*)

59   Student: Double.

60   Teacher: Okay. Can somebody give me another double fact? Yes, ma'am?

61   Student: 5 plus 5.

62	Teacher:	Okay. 5 plus 5. (*The teacher records 5 + 5.*)
63	Student:	6 plus 6.
64	Teacher:	Okay. (*The teacher records 6 + 6.*) One more.
65	Student:	7 plus 7.
66	Teacher:	Okay. 7 plus 7. (*The teacher records 7 + 7.*) Would each one of these answers be even
67		or odd?
68	Student:	Yes.
69	Students:	Even.
70	Teacher:	Why?
71	Student:	Because 2 plus 2 is 4, and 4 is even. 5 plus 5 is 10, and 10 is even. 6 plus 6 is 12, and
72		12 is even. And 7 plus 7 is 14, and 14 is even.
73	Teacher:	So let's look over here at these even number patterns that we looked at. (*Teacher
74		points to chart paper with doubles facts 4 + 4 = 8, 5 + 5 = 10, 6 + 6 = 12,*
75		*7 + 7 = 14.*) And we've talked about how doubles added together will make an even
76		number. When we had 2 plus 2 (*the teacher adds 2 + 2 to the chart*), what are the
77		addends, even or odd?
78	Student:	Even.
79	Teacher:	Even. Let's look at 5 plus 5. Are the addends even or odd?
80	Student:	Odd.
81	Teacher:	Hold on, Otis. Yes, ma'am?
82	Student:	Even.
83	Teacher:	The addends, 5 and 5?
84	Student:	Odd.
85	Teacher:	Odd. Let's look at the next one. 6 plus 6. Even or odd? Back there. Yes, ma'am?
86	Student:	Even.
87	Teacher:	You think they're even? 6 and 6 is even. Why do you think that this is happening?
88		What I want you to do is we're going to talk in our groups, your small groups, and
89		what I want you to discuss is how do doubles always make even numbers? Why is
90		that always true?
91	[End of audio]	

ATL 9.1 Video Transcript: Millie Brooks and the Half-of-a-Whole Task

This transcript accompanies the video clip in ATL 9.1. It features a lesson taught by Millie Brooks with third-grade students working on the Half-of-a-Whole task.

1   Javier: He said it was like five times bigger than the…

2   Teacher: Tell me whether or not this (*points to figure d*) shows me halves.

Fig. d

3   Mayah: It doesn't show you halves.

4   Teacher: Prove it.

5   Mayah: It doesn't show you halves…

6   Teacher: I say it does. Prove it to me.

7   Mayah: Because…

8   Teacher: Well, prove me wrong.

9   Mayah: Two. It shows you 2. It's 2.

10   *[Crosstalk]*

11	Zaria:	It doesn't show you halves because one is—because one is not shaded. Three are
12		shaded in this, but then there are three that are not shaded. (*Student points to 3*
13		*white parts and 3 shaded parts.*)

Fig. d

14	Teacher:	Oh, so you're telling me that 3 are shaded. I want you to convince them now,
15		because you saw it. So now I want you to get them to see what you saw, that this is
16		half. Okay? If you need to cut it up, cut it up. Don't be afraid to cut it up. Okay?

Teacher leaves to monitor other small groups and returns in two minutes.

17	Teacher:	When I left here, you were held accountable for what you were saying. You had to
18		prove to your group that that was a half. Okay?
19	Zaria:	I only proved it to them two. I didn't prove it to him because he didn't...
20	Teacher:	Okay. Mayah, show me why that's a half. All right. Who can tell me what Zaria
21		was talking about before I left? Yes?
22	Hensley:	She was talking about how it was half, but...
23	Teacher:	Show me the shape. Show me the shape. Okay?
24	Hensley:	But this one was half. (*Student holds up figure d showing* $^3/_6$.)

Fig. d

25	Teacher:	Okay.
26	Hensley:	But we didn't think so, so she said, do you think it's more than 3 or less than 3?
27		It's half. And then we said less than 3. So she was trying to tell us how it was half,
28		but we didn't believe what she said.
29	Teacher:	You still don't believe her? Mayah, why don't you believe her?

30	Mayah:	I kind of don't believe her, because how—let me see this. Because of how there are 3
31		shaded, but there's not one only shaded, like this one. (*Student points to the 3 shaded*
32		*parts on figure d and compares it to the one shaded part on figure e.*)

Fig. d   **Fig. e**

33	Teacher:	Okay.
34	Mayah:	But I know that it is equal, because 3 are shaded and 3 are not.
35	Teacher:	Oh, so you know it's equal because 3 are shaded and 3 are not shaded? So we
36		have an equal number that are shaded and an equal number that are not shaded?
37		Okay. Can you write me a fraction for that? Everyone, write me a fraction for this.
38	Mayah:	(*Writes on the paper.*)

Teacher leaves to monitor other small groups and returns in three minutes.

39	Mayah:	(*Cuts apart figure d and rearranges the pieces to look like figure e.*)
40		This is—this is equal to half because like this is the same thing. This is
41		the same exact same thing, because we have three that are shaded that look just like
42		this, and three on the bottom that are not shaded that look just like this.

Fig. d. Rearranged   **Fig. e**

43	Teacher:	Okay. Hensley, where's your shape like that? Hensley, do you agree that that's a half?
44	Hensley:	Yes. That's a half.
45	Teacher:	Okay. Mayah, now prove to him that this is the same as this. (*Teacher points to*
46		½.)
47	Mayah:	Hensley, look, this is the same as this, but it's just into pieces. And this one's not
48		into pieces. See, there's...what...there's 3 ones on the bottom, but this one
49		doesn't have 3 right at the bottom. It has 3 shaded at the top. This one doesn't
50		have 3 shaded at the top. It just has some straight big pieces, which is all into one.

| 51 | Hensley: | But still, but we cut it up diff…like, processes, because like, because this one was |
| 52 | | here before, so… (*Student moves the sixths around to show the original figure d.*) |

Fig. d

53	Javier:	Yeah, but then we cut it up, and then this…and then this was equivalent to this
54		one, because this is how I know it fits, because if you go like this with them…
55		(*Student puts the 3 sixths on top of the shaded 1 half of figure e.*)

Fig. d. Rearranged   **Fig. e**

56	Teacher:	Why don't you do the same? (*Hensley cuts apart his figure d.*)
57	Javier:	First, the three shaded, on the part that's shaded, at the top.
58	Teacher:	Okay. Don't move so fast for him. Hensley? Tell him again.
59	Javier:	You put…so this is…this here is one half, but then if you put the three pieces here,
60		then it'll fit in the shaded part, the shaded part.
61	Mayah:	But Hensley was saying that you could put two of these in here like that. That's what
62		Hensley said at first. But I told him we have to use all of our shapes.
63	Teacher:	What makes it half?
64	Hens-ley:	Because like these pieces, like if you put this together, if you put these together, it
65		will be half when you put the shaded parts on the other one. And then if you put
66		these on this one.
67	Teacher:	Okay.
68	[End of audio]	

APPENDIX F
Lesson Plan for the Half-of-a-Whole Task

Mathematics Learning Goals *What understandings will students take away from this lesson?*	**Evidence of Student Thinking** *What will students say, do, and/or produce that will provide evidence of their understandings?*
• Students will understand that one-half of a figure can be represented in multiple ways as long as the areas of each half have equal size, regardless of the location of the pieces that comprise each half. • Students will notice and understand a numeric relationship between the numerator and the denominator for fractions that are equivalent to one-half, specifically, when the denominator is twice the value of the numerator, the fraction is equivalent to one-half.	• Students identify all figures that show one-half shaded (a, b, c, d, e, f, g, h, i, j). • Students provide a written justification for each figure indicating understanding that the amount of area for the shaded and unshaded regions is equal in size. • Students explain that the numerator is the number of parts shaded and that the denominator is the total number of equal parts in the whole, and in the case of one-half, the denominator is twice the value of the numerator. • Students show equivalent fractions and justify their equivalence ($1/_2 = 2/_4 = 3/_6$) by indicating that the shaded area takes up the same amount of space in each square (or triangle), which are all equal in size, thus have a valid comparison with equal-size wholes.
Task *What is the main activity that students will be working on in this lesson?*	**Instructional Support—Tools, Resources, Materials** *What tools or resources will be made available to give students entry to—and help them reason through—the activity?*
Students will be working on identifying figures that show halves and explaining how they know the figure shows halves. *Identify all of the figures that have one-half of it shaded and be prepared to explain and justify how you know that one-half of the figure is or is not shaded. Provide a written description giving your reasons why each figure is or is not showing halves.* 	Provide each student with one set of enlarged figures. Provide students with scissors so they may cut apart the figures in order to decompose and recompose the figures as needed to support their reasoning and justifications. Provide students with paper and crayons for recording their written descriptions and justifications on paper using words and diagrams.

Prior Knowledge	Task Launch
What prior knowledge and experiences will students draw upon in their work on this task?	*How will you introduce and set up the task to ensure that students understand the task and can begin productive work, without diminishing the cognitive demand of the task?*
Most students have experience involving work with halves from previous grade levels, as well as from their everyday experiences, some of which have likely lead to faulty ideas about fractions. It is likely that some students will think that to show halves an object must be partitioned into only two pieces, but they may or may not have a solid understanding that the two parts in the whole must have equal areas. It is also likely that students have limited experience with shaded partitions that are not adjacent and limited experience in naming equivalent fractions.	Display the task, showing all of the figures. Hold up the enlarged fraction pieces. You might say: "Some of the figures have one-half shaded and some figures do not. It is your job to determine which ones show halves and explain your reasoning to your group members. Everyone in your group should agree on the figures that have one-half shaded. Feel free to cut or fold the shapes if that helps you. List the figures or circle the figures that show halves. Then write about how you know a figure does or does not show halves."

Monitoring Tool

Anticipated Solution Paths	Instructional Supports—Teacher Questions	Who/What	Order
Identifies halves as comprised of two pieces. Student can identify figures showing one of two equal pieces shaded, such as (b) and (e), and also recognizes the figures that do not show two equal pieces (k) and (l).	• How do you know figure (e) shows one-half? • How do you know figure (k) does not show one-half? • Each one has two pieces, why are you claiming that only (e) shows halves?		
Recognizes two-fourths shows halves because it looks like halves. Student can identify 2 shaded parts of size ¼ (two-fourths) as equivalent to one-half, regardless of the placement of the fourths within the whole for figures (a) and (c). Explains that it still looks like one-half shaded or shows that it can be matched up to figure (e).	• Tell me about figure (a). Some students claim it shows halves and some say it does not. Defend your claims. • You claim that both figure (a) and figure (c) show halves. Show us what you mean? • Can you use your scissors and figure out a way of comparing the pieces?		
Recognizes three-sixths shows halves because the amount of area is the same. Student can identify 3 shaded parts of size ⅙ (three-sixths) as equivalent to one-half, regardless of the placement of the sixths within the whole. Explains that 3 shaded sixths take up the same amount of area as the three-sixths that are not shaded, as in figures (d) and (i).	• Imagine that we have a figure showing four-eighths of it shaded. Does this figure also show one-half shaded? Why or why not? • What if we have a figure with five-tenths shaded? Is that equivalent to one-half being shaded? • Can you name a fraction of your own that is equivalent to one-half?		
Equivalency is determined by having equal areas. Student recognizes that figures may not look alike and that the pieces may be different sizes, but if the area shaded comprises half of the total area of the figure, then it is equivalent to one-half shaded.	• You think figures (d) and (i) show halves. Cut apart the figures and convince me that they are equivalent to one-half being shaded. • Suppose I told you that someone said figure (f) shows one-half shaded. Could this be true? Figure out a way to convince me that it does or does not show one-half being shaded.		
Not all halves are equal, the size of the whole matters. Student recognizes that half of a triangle is not equivalent to half of a square in the given figures. Explains that they are different because the wholes are not the same size.	• You said figures (e) and (j) both show halves. Is the shaded half of figure (e) equal to the shaded half of figure (j)? Why or why not? • Write an explanation for how these two figures show halves, yet they are not equivalent to each other.		

Solution Paths with Errors and Misconceptions		Questions to Address Errors and Misconceptions				
Thinks shaded parts must be adjacent. Student assumes that figure (c) and figure (d) do not show halves because the unshaded or shaded pieces are not side-by-side.		• Someone claims that (c) and (d) show halves. What do you think? • Use your scissors to cut apart figures (c) and (d) and experiment with rearranging the pieces and see what you can discover.				
Orientation Confusion. Cannot rotate the shaded regions mentally to determine if both parts take up the same amount of area as in figures (f) and (g).		• Work with a partner to examine figures (f) and (g). How can you move and turn them to compare the sizes of the shaded parts? • Someone claimed she compared the parts by cutting them apart and put parts on top of each other. What do you think about this idea?				
Unanticipated Solution Paths						

Class Discussion: Sharing, Comparing, and Connecting

Selecting and Sequencing *Which anticipated approaches and solution paths do you want students to share and compare? In what order? Why?*	Connecting Responses *What specific questions will you ask so that students make connections among the presented solution paths and make sense of the mathematical ideas you want them to learn?*
Identifies halves as comprised of two pieces.	• Which figures have one-half of it shaded? How do you know that one-half is shaded? Who agrees? Who disagrees? • She claims that halves can be put on top of each other and they are the same size. Is there another way of knowing if a figure shows halves? • What about figure (k)? It has two pieces; does it show halves? Why or why not? • What does it mean for a figure to show halves? Explain how you know a figure shows halves.
Recognizes two-fourths shows halves because it looks like halves.	• Tell me about figure (a). How many people think it shows halves? How many people do NOT think it shows halves? How is figure (a) like figure (e) that we just talked about? How are the two figures different? • Let's look at figures (a) and (c). Someone said figure (a) shows halves but (c) does not show halves. What do you think? • What fraction can we write to describe how much of figure (a) is shaded? What fraction can we write for figure (c)? • So the fraction that names the shaded portion for both of these figures is ²⁄₄, so it doesn't matter where the pieces are in the figure as long as what needs to be true for us to write the same fraction? • You said the fraction was ²⁄₄ but you also said that the shaded portion was the same as one-half. I'm confused? • What else can you tell me about what it means for a figure to show halves?
Recognizes three-sixths shows halves because the amount of area is the same. and Equivalency is determined by having equal areas.	• So you think figure (d) shows halves, but someone else said it shows sixths. Tell us again why you think it shows halves. • What do others think? Who has another way to explain why you think figure (d) has one-half shaded? • Can a figure with more than two equal pieces show halves? If so describe how the figures can show halves. • You said they have to cover the same amount of space or area. Can someone show us an example of that? • What fraction could we write for the shaded portion of figure (d)? What fraction names the unshaded portion? • Let's write down the fractions we've talked about so far, ¹⁄₂, ²⁄₄, and ³⁄₆. What are some things you notice about these numbers? • What does the denominator tell us? What does the numerator tell us? How do I know just by looking at the fraction ³⁄₆ that it is equivalent to one-half? What about ⁴⁄₈, is that equivalent to ¹⁄₂? What about ¹⁰⁄₂₀? Name some other fractions that are equivalent to one-half. • What does it mean for a fraction to be equivalent to one-half? How does that relate to the figures we've talked about so far?

286   Taking Action   *Grades K-5*

Class Discussion: Sharing, Comparing, and Connecting
(continued)

Not all halves are equal, the size of the whole matters.	• Let's look at figure (h). Someone said that it shows halves. How could you convince me that it shows halves?
	• We also talked about how figure (e) shows halves. How can both of these figures show halves? They don't look the same?
	• What is different and what is the same about figures (e) and figure (h)?
	• Could we say that $\frac{1}{2}$ of figure (d) is equivalent or the same as $\frac{1}{2}$ of figure (h)? Why or why not?

Homework/Assessment

Using same-size squares, ask students to create two new figures that show one-half of its area shaded and two figures that do not show one-half of the area shaded. They should provide a written explanation and justification for how they know the figures do or do not show one-half shaded.

Lesson Plan Template for Ambitious Teaching of Mathematics

Mathematics Learning Goals *What understandings will students take away from this lesson?*	**Evidence of Student Thinking** *What will students say, do, or produce that will provide evidence of their understandings?*
Task *What is the main activity that students will be working on in this lesson?*	**Instructional Support—Tools, Resources, Materials** *What tools or resources will be made available to give students entry to—and help them reason through—the activity?*
Prior Knowledge *What prior knowledge and experiences will students draw upon in their work on this task?*	**Task Launch** *How will you introduce and set up the task to ensure that students understand the task and can begin productive work, without diminishing the cognitive demand of the task?*
Anticipated Solution Paths *What are the various ways that students might approach and solve the task, including correct, incorrect, and incomplete solutions?*	**Instructional Support—Teacher Questions** *What assessing questions will you ask students to support their exploration of the task?* *What advancing questions will you ask to bridge between what they did and those mathematical ideas you want them to learn?* Be sure to consider questions you might ask students who cannot get started, as well as questions for students who finish quickly so that you are to ready to probe for deeper reflection or to extend their learning.

Use the monitoring tool on the next page to provide the details on Anticipated Solution Paths and Instructional Support—Teacher Questions. Prior to teaching the lesson, complete the white cells. During implementation of the lesson, add unanticipated solution paths, identify which students use specific paths in the "Who" column, and indicate the order in which you intend to have students present in the "Order" column.

Monitoring Tool				
Anticipated Solution Paths	Instructional Support		Who/What	Order
	Assessing Questions	Advancing Questions		
Unanticipated Solution Paths				

Implementing High-Level Tasks." *Mathematics Teaching in the Middle School 14*, no. 3 (2008): 132-138.

Class Discussion: Sharing, Comparing, and Connecting	
Selecting and Sequencing *Which anticipated approaches and solution paths do you want students to share and compare? In what order? Why?*	**Connecting Responses** *What specific questions will you ask so that students make connections among the presented solution paths and make sense of the mathematical ideas you want them to learn?*

Homework/Assessment

Based on: Smith, Margaret S., Victoria Bill, and Elizabeth K. Hughes. "Thinking through a Lesson: Successfully Implementing High-Level Tasks." *Mathematics Teaching in the Middle School* 14, no. 3 (2008): 132–38.

REFERENCES

Aguirre, Julia, Karen Mayfield-Ingram, and Danny Bernard Martin. *The Impact of Identity in K–8 Mathematics*. Reston, Va.: National Council of Teachers of Mathematics, 2013.

Alber, Rebecca. "Defining Differentiated Instruction," Edutopia (blog), April 13, 2014, http://www.edutopia.org/blog/differentiated-instruction-definition-strategies-alber

Allen, Kasi and Kemble Schnell. "Developing Mathematics Identify." *Mathematics Teaching in the Middle School* 21, no. 7 (2016): 398–405.

Ames, Carole, and Jennifer Archer. "Achievement goals in the classroom: Students' learning strategies and motivation processes." *Journal of Educational Psychology* 80, no. 3 (1988): 260–267.

Anthony, Glenda, Roberta Hunter, Jodie Hunter, and Shelley Duncan. "How Ambitious is 'Ambitious Mathematics Teaching'" *SET: Research Information for Teachers*, no. 2 (2015): 45–52.

Artzt, Alice F., and Eleanor Armour-Thomas. *Becoming a reflective mathematics teacher*. Mahwah, N.J.: Erlbaum, 2002.

Ashcraft, Mark H. "Math Anxiety: Personal, Educational, and Cognitive Consequences." *Current Directions in Psychological Science* 11, no. 5 (2002): 181–185.

Ball, Deborah Loewenberg. "What Mathematical Knowledge is Needed for Teaching Mathematics?" Paper presented at the U.S. Department of Education Secretary's Mathematics Summit, Washington, D.C., February 2003.

Ball, Deborah Loewenberg, and Francesca M. Forzani. "Teaching Skillful Teaching." *Educational Leadership* 68, no. 4 (2010): 40–45.

Ball, Deborah Loewenberg. "With an Eye on the Mathematical Horizon: Dilemmas of Teaching Elementary School Mathematics." *The Elementary School Journal* 93, no. 4 (1993): 373–397.

Balu, Rekha, Pei Zhu, Fred Doolittle, Ellen Schiller, Joseph Jenkins, and Russell Gersten (2015). *Evaluation of Response to Intervention Practices for Elementary School Reading* (NCEE 2016–4000). Washington, D.C.: Institute of Education Sciences, U.S. Department of Education.

Baroody, Arthur J., Meng-lung Lai, and Kelly S. Mix. "The Development of Young Children's Early Number and Operation Sense and its Implications for Early Childhood Education." In *Handbook of Research on the Education of Young Children* edited by Bernard Spodek and Olivia N. Saracho, pp. 187–221. Mahwah, N.J.: Lawrence Erlbaum, 2006.

Bill, Victoria. "Odd and Even Task." Pittsburgh, Pa.: University of Pittsburgh Institute for Learning, 2008.

Bill, Victoria, and Margaret S. Smith. "Characteristics of Assessing and Advancing Questions." University of Pittsburgh: Institute for Learning, 2008.

Bishop, Alan. "The Social Construction of Meaning: A Significant Development for Mathematics Education." *For the Learning of Mathematics* 5, no. 1 (1985): 24–28.

Boaler, Jo, and Megan Staples. "Creating Mathematical Futures through an Equitable Teaching Approach: The Case of Railside School." *Teachers College Record* 110, no. 3 (2008): 608–645.

Boaler, Jo, and Karin Brodie. "The Importance, Nature, and Impact of Teacher Questions." In *Proceedings of the 26th Annual Meeting of the North American Chapter of the International Group for the Psychology of Mathematics Education*, vol. 2, pp. 773–81. Toronto: Ontario Institute for Studies in Education of the University of Toronto, 2004.

Boaler, Jo. "Open and Closed Mathematics: Student Experiences and Understandings." *Journal for Research in Mathematics Education* 29, no. 1 (1998): 41–62.

Boaler, Jo. "Research Suggests that Timed Tests Cause Math Anxiety." *Teaching Children Mathematics* 20, no. 8 (2014): 469–473.

Boaler, Jo. *Mathematical Mindsets: Unleashing Students' Potential Through Creative Math, Inspiring Messages, and Innovative Teaching*. San Francisco: Jossey-Bass, 2015.

Boaler, Jo. *The Mathematics of Hope: Moving from Performance to Learning in Mathematics Classrooms.* (September 13, 2014). Retrieved from http://youcubed.org/

Boerst, Timothy A., Laurie Sleep, Deborah Loewenberg Ball, and Hyman Bass. "Preparing Teachers to Lead Mathematics Discussions." *Teachers College Record* 113, no. 12 (2011): 2844–2877.

Boston, Melissa and Anne Garrison Wilhelm. "Middle School Mathematics Instruction in Instructionally Focused Urban Districts." *Urban Education*, (2015): 1–33.

Brenner, M. E., S. Herman, H. Z. Ho, and J. M. Zimmer. Cross-National Comparison of Representational Competence. *Journal for Research in Mathematics Education* 30, (1999): 541–557.

Brown, Ann L., and Mary Jo Kane. "Preschool Children can Learn to Transfer: Learning to Learn and Learning from Example." *Cognitive Psychology* 20, no. 4 (1988): 493–523.

Bruner, Jerome S. *Toward a Theory of Instruction*. Cambridge, Mass.: Belkapp Press, 1966.

Cai, Jinfa, Ning Wang, John C. Moyer, Chuang Wang, and Bikai Nie. "Longitudinal Investigation of the Curricular Effect: An Analysis of Student Learning Outcomes from the LieCal Project in the United States." *International Journal of Educational Research* 50 (2011): 117–136.

Carle, Eric. *The Very Hungry Caterpillar*. New York: Philomel Books, 1969.

Carpenter, Thomas P., and James M. Moser. "The Acquisition of Addition and Subtraction Concepts in Grades One through Three." *Journal for Research in Mathematics Education* (1984): 179–202.

Carpenter, Thomas P., and Richard Lehrer. "Teaching and Learning Mathematics with Understanding." In *Mathematics Classrooms that Promote Understanding* edited by Elizabeth Fennema and Thomas A. Romberg, pp. 19–32. Mahwah, N.J.: Lawrence Erlbaum Associates, 1999.

Carpenter, Thomas P., Elizabeth Fennema, and Megan L. Franke. "*Cognitively Guided Instruction: A Knowledge Base for Reform in Primary Mathematics Instruction*." The Elementary School Journal (1996): 3–20.

Carpenter, Thomas P., Megan Loef Franke, and Linda Levi. *Thinking Mathematically: Integrating Arithmetic and Algebra in Elementary School.* Portsmouth, N.H.: Heinemann, 2003.

Carter, Susan. "Disequilibrium and Questioning in the Primary Classroom: Establishing Routines That Help Students Learn." *Teaching Children Mathematics* 15, no. 3 (2008): 134–137.

Cartier, Jennifer L., Margaret S. Smith, Mary Kay Stein, and Danielle K. Ross. *5 Practices for Orchestrating Productive Task-Based Discussions in Science.* Reston, Va.: National Council of Teachers of Mathematics, 2013.

Chapin, Suzanne H., and Catherine O'Connor. "Academically Productive Talk: Supporting Students' Learning in Mathematics." In *The Learning of Mathematics*, edited by W Gary Martin, Marilyn Strutchens, and Portia Elliott, pp. 113–128. Reston, Va.: National Council of Teachers of Mathematics, 2007.

Chapin, Suzanne H., Catherine O'Connor, and Nancy Canavan Anderson. *Talk Moves: A Teacher's Guide for Using Classroom Discussions in Math (3rd ed.)* Sausalito, Calif.: Math Solutions, 2013.

Charles, Randall I. "Big Ideas and Understandings as the Foundation for Elementary and Middle School Mathematics." *Journal of Mathematics Education Leadership* 7, no. 1 (2005): 9–24.

Civil, Marta, and Núria Planas. "Participation in the Mathematics Classroom: Does Every Student Have a Voice?" *For the Learning of Mathematics* 24, no. 1 (2004): 7–12.

Civil, Marta. "Building on Community Knowledge: An Avenue to Equity in Mathematics Education." In *Improving Access to Mathematics: Diversity and Equity in the Classroom*, edited by Na'ilah Suad Nassir and Paul Cobb, pp. 105–117. New York: Teachers College Press, 2007.

Clements, Douglas H., and Julie Sarama. *Learning and Teaching Early Math: The Learning Trajectories Approach* (2nd ed.). New York: Routledge, 2014.

Clements, Douglas H., and Julie Sarama. "Learning Trajectories in Mathematics Education." *Mathematical Thinking and Learning* 6, no. 2 (2004): 81–89.

Cobb, Paul, and Lynn Liao Hodge. "A Relational Perspective on Issues of Cultural Diversity and Equity as They Play Out in the Mathematics Classroom." *Mathematical Thinking and Learning* 4, no. 2–3 (2002): 249–284.

Collins, A. "Representational Competence: A Commentary on the Greeno Analysis." In *Theories of Learning and Research into Instructional Practice*, edited by Timothy Koschmann, pp. 105–112. New York: Springer, 2011.

Common Core State Standards Writing Team. *Progressions for the Common Core State Standards for Mathematics: Operations and Algebraic Thinking (draft).* Tucson, Ariz.: Institute for Mathematics and Education, University of Arizona, 2013.

Common Core State Standards Writing Team. *Progressions for the Common Core State Standards for Mathematics: Number and Operations in Base Ten (draft).* Tucson, Ariz.: Institute for Mathematics and Education, University of Arizona, 2015.

Confrey, Jere, Alan P. Maloney, and Andrew K. Corley. "Learning Trajectories: A Framework for Connecting Standards with Curriculum." *ZDM* 46, no. 5 (2014): 719–733.

Crespo, Sandra. "Seeing More Than Right and Wrong Answers: Prospective teachers' Interpretations of Students' Mathematical Work." *Journal of Mathematics Teacher Education* 3, no. 2 (2000): 155–181.

Daro, Phil, Frederic A. Mosher, and Tom Corcoran. *Learning Trajectories in Mathematics: A Foundation for Standards, Curriculum, Assessment, and Instruction.* Philadelphia.: Consortium for Policy Research in Education, 2011.

Davis, Brent. "Listening for Differences: An Evolving Conception of Mathematics Teaching." *Journal for Research in Mathematics Education* (1997): 355–376.

Delpit, Lisa. *Multiplication is for White People: Raising Expectations for Other People's Children.* New York: The New Press, 2012.

DiSessa, Andrea A., and Paul Cobb. "Ontological Innovation and the Role of Theory in Design Experiments." *The Journal of the Learning Sciences* 13, no. 1 (2004): 77–103.

Doyle, Walter. "Work in Mathematics Classes: The Context of Students' Thinking during Instruction." *Educational Psychologist* 23, no. 2 (1988): 167–80.

Dreyfus, T. and T. Eisenberg. "On Different Facets of Mathematical Thinking. In *The Nature of Mathematical Thinking,* edited by R. J. Sternberg and T. Ben-Zeev, pp. 253–284. Mahwah, N.J.: Lawrence Erlbaum Associates, 1996.

Driscoll, Mark, Johannah Nikula, Jill Neumayer DePiper. *Mathematical Thinking and Communication: Access for English Learners.* Portsmouth, N.H.: Heinemann, 2016.

Duckworth, Eleanor. *The Having of Wonderful Ideas and Other Essays on Teaching and Learning.* New York: Teachers College Press, 1987.

Dweck, Carol S. "The Perils and Promises of Praise." *Educational Leadership* 65 no. 2 (2007): 34–39.

Dweck, Carol S. *Mindset: The New Psychology of Success.* New York: Random House, 2006.

Dweck, Carol. S. *Mindsets and Math/Science Achievement.* New York: Carnegie Corporation of New York Institute for Advanced Study, 2008.

Elliott, Elaine S., and Carol S. Dweck. "Goals: An Approach to Motivation and Achievement." *Journal of Personality and Social Psychology* 54, no. 1 (1988): 5–12.

Engle, Randall W. "Working Memory Capacity as Executive Attention." *Current Directions in Psychological Science 11* (February 2002): 19–23.

Engle, Randi A., and Faith R. Conant. "Guiding Principles for Fostering Productive Disciplinary Engagement: Explaining an Emergent Argument in a Community of Learners Classroom." *Cognition and Instruction* 20, no. 4 (2002): 399–483.

Fennema, Elizabeth, and Meghan Franke. "Teachers' Knowledge and Its Impact." In *Handbook of Research on Mathematics Teaching and Learning,* edited by Douglas Grouws, pp. 147– 164. Indianapolis, Ind.: Macmillan, 1992.

Festinger, Leon. *A Theory of Cognitive Dissonance.* Evanston, Ill.: Row, Peterson, 1957.

Flores, Alfinio. "How Do Children Know that What They Learn in Mathematics is True?" *Teaching Children Mathematics* 8, no. 5 (2002): 269.

Fosnot, Catherine Twomey, and Maarten Ludovicus Antonius Marie Dolk. *Young Mathematicians at Work: Constructing Number Sense, Addition, and Subtraction.* Portsmouth, N.H.: Heinemann, 2001.

Franke, Megan L., Elham Kazemi, and Daniel Battey. "Mathematics Teaching and Classroom Practice." In *Second Handbook of Research on Mathematics Teaching and Learning,* edited by Frank K. Lester Jr., pp. 225–256. Greenwich, Conn.: Information Age Publishing, 2007.

Fuchs, Lynn S., Robin F. Schumacher, Jessica Long, Jessica Namkung, Carol L. Hamlett, Paul T. Cirino, Nancy C. Jordan, Robert Siegler, Russell Gersten, and Paul Changas. "Improving At-risk Learners' Understanding of Fractions." *Journal of Educational Psychology* 105, no. 3 (2013): 683–700.

Fuson, Karen C., and Aki Murata. "Integrating NRC Principles and the NCTM Process Standards to form a Class Learning Path Model that individualizes within Whole-Class Activities." *National Council of Supervisors of Mathematics Journal of Mathematics Education Leadership* 10, no. 1 (2007): 72–91.

Fuson, Karen C., and Sybilla Beckmann. "Standard Algorithms in the Common Core State Standards." *NCSM Journal of Mathematics Education Leadership* 14, no. 2 (2012): 14–30.

Fuson, Karen C., Mindy Kalchman, and John D. Bransford. "Mathematical Understanding: An Introduction." In *How Students Learn: History, Mathematics, and Science in the Classroom,* by the National Research Council, Committee on *How People Learn: A Targeted Report for Teachers,* edited by M. Suzanne Donovan and John D. Bransford, pp. 217–256. Washington, D.C.: National Academies Press, 2005.

Gersten, Russell, Sybilla Beckmann, Benjamin Clarke, Anne Foegen, Laurel Marsh, Jon R. Star, and Bradley Witzel. *Assisting Students Struggling with Mathematics: Response to Intervention (RtI) for Elementary and Middle Schools* (NCEE 2009–4060). Washington, D.C.: Institute of Education Sciences, U.S. Department of Education, 2009.

Goldenberg, E. Paul, Nina Shteingold, and Nannette Feurzeig. "Mathematical Habits of Mind for Young Children." In *Teaching Mathematics through Problem Solving: Prekindergarten– Grade 6,* edited by Frank K. Lester Jr., pp. 15–30. Reston, Va.: National Council of Teachers of Mathematics, 2003.

Goldin, Gerald, and Nina Shteingold. "Systems of Representations and the Development of Mathematical Concepts. In *The Roles of Representation in School Mathematics,* edited by Albert A. Cuoco and Frances R. Curcio, pp. 1–24. Reston, Va: National Council of Teachers of Mathematics, 2001.

Goldsmith, Lynn T., and Deborah Schifter. "Understanding Teachers in Transition: Characteristics of a Model for the Development of Mathematics Teaching." In *Mathematics Teaching in Transition,* edited by Elizabeth Fennema and Barbara Scott Nelson, pp. 19–54. Mahwah, N.J.: Lawrence Erlbaum Associates, 1997.

Grant, Heidi, and Carol S. Dweck. "Clarifying Achievement Goals and Their Impact." *Journal of Personality and Social Psychology* 85, no. 3 (2003): 541–533.

Greeno, James G. "Instructional Representations Based on Research about Understanding." In *Cognitive Science and Mathematics Education*, edited by A. H. Schoenfeld, pp. 61–88. Hillsdale, N.J.: Lawrence Erlbaum Associates, 1987.

Greeno, James G., and Rogers P. Hall. "Practicing Representation." *Phi Delta Kappan* 78, no. 5 (1997): 361–67.

Greer, Brian. "Representational Flexibility and Mathematical Expertise." ZDM 41, no. 5 (2009): 697–702.

Gresalfi, Melissa S. "Taking Up Opportunities to Learn: Construction Dispositions in Mathematics Classrooms." *Journal of the Learning Sciences*, 18 (2009): 327–369.

Gresalfi, Melissa Sommerfeld, and Paul Cobb. "Cultivating Students' Discipline-specific Dispositions as a Critical Goal for Pedagogy and Equity." *Pedagogies* 1, no. 1 (2006): 49–57.

Gresalfi, Melissa Sommerfeld. "Taking Up Opportunities to Learn: Constructing Dispositions in Mathematics Classrooms." *The Journal of the Learning Sciences,* 18, no. 3 (2009): 327–369.

Griffin, Sharon. "Laying the Foundation for Computational Fluency in Early Childhood." *Teaching Children Mathematics* 9, no. 6 (2003): 306–09.

Gunnel's, Murat, Brian Hand, and Vaughan Prain. "Writing for Learning in Science: A Secondary Analysis of Six Studies." *International Journal of Science and Mathematics Education* 5, no. 4 (2007): 615–637.

Gutierrez, Rochelle. "Why (Urban) Mathematics Teachers Need Political Knowledge." *Journal of Urban Mathematics Education* 6, no. 2 (2013): 7–19.

Handa, Yuichi. "A Phenomenological Exploration of Mathematical Engagement: Approaching an Old Metaphor Anew." *For the Learning of Mathematics* 23, no. 1 (2003): 22–29.

Harkness, Shelly S. "Social Constructivism and the Believing Game: A Mathematics Teacher's Practice and Its Implications." *Educational Studies in Mathematics* 70, no. 3 (2009): 243–258.

Hatano, Giyoo, and Kayoko Inagaki. "Sharing Cognition through Collaborative Comprehension Activity." In *Perspectives on Socially Shared Cognition*, edited by Lauren B. Resnick, John M. Levine, and Stephanie D. Teasley, pp. 331–480. Washington, D.C.: American Psychological Association, 1991.

Hattie, John A. C. *Visible Learning: A Synthesis of over 800 Meta-Analyses Relating to Achievement.* New York: Routledge, 2009.

Hattie, John, and Helen Timperley. "The Power of Feedback." *Review of Educational Research* 77, no. 1 (2007): 81–112.

Haystead, Mark W., and Robert J. Marzano. *Meta-Analytic Synthesis of Studies Conducted at Marzano Research Laboratory on Instructional Strategies.* Englewood, Colo.: Marzano Research Laboratory, 2009.

Heinz, Karen. "Shifting Mathematical Authority from Teacher to Community." *Mathematics Teacher* 104, no. 4 (2010): 315–318.

Henningsen, Marjorie A., and Mary Kay Stein. "Mathematical Tasks and Student Cognition: Classroom-Based Factors That Support and Inhibit High-Level Mathematical Thinking and Reasoning." *Journal for Research in Mathematics Education* 28, no. 5 (1997): 524–549.

Herbal-Eisenmann, Beth A., and M. Lynn Breyfogle. "Questioning Our Patterns of Questioning." *Mathematics Teaching in the Middle School* 10, no. 9 (2005): 484–489.

Herbel–Eisenmann, Beth A., Michael D. Steele, and Michelle Cirillo. "(Developing) Teacher Discourse Moves: A Framework for Professional Development." *Mathematics Teacher Educator* 1, no. 2 (2013): 181–196.

Hess, Karin K., Ben S. Jones, Dennis Carlock, and John R. Walkup. "Cognitive Rigor: Blending the Strengths of Bloom's Taxonomy and Webb's Depth of Knowledge to Enhance Classroom-level Processes." ERIC ED517804, (March 7, 2009). Retrieved https://eric.ed.gov/?id=ED517804.

Hiebert, James, and Dianna Wearne. "Instructional Tasks, Classroom Discourse, and Students' Learning in Second-Grade Arithmetic." *American Educational Research Journal* 30, no. (1993): 393–425.

Hiebert, James, and Douglas A. Grouws. "The Effects of Classroom Mathematics Teaching on Students' Learning." In *Second Handbook of Research on Mathematics Teaching and Learning,* edited by Frank K. Lester, Jr., pp. 371–404. Charlotte, N.C.: Information Age; Reston, Va.: National Council of Teachers of Mathematics, 2007.

Hiebert, James, and James W. Stigler. "A World of Difference." *Journal of Staff Development* 25, no. 4 (2004): 10–15.

Hiebert, James, Anne K. Morris, Dawn Berk, and Amanda Jansen. "Preparing Teachers to Learn from Teaching." *Journal of Teacher Education* 58, no. 1 (2007): 47–61.

Hiebert, James, Thomas P. Carpenter, Elizabeth Fennema, Karen C. Fuson, Diana Wearne, Hanlie Murray, Alwyn Olivier, and Piet Human. *Making Sense: Teaching and Learning Mathematics with Understanding.* Portsmouth, N.H.: Heinemann, 1997.

Holton, Derek, and David Clarke. "Scaffolding and Metacognition." *International Journal of Mathematical Education in Science and Technology* 37, no. 2 (2006): 127–143.

Hufferd-Ackles, Kimberly, Karen C. Fuson, and Miriam Gamoran Sherin. "Describing Levels and Components of a Math-talk Learning Community." *Journal for Research in Mathematics Education* 35, no. 2 (2004): 81–116.

Hufferd-Ackles, Kimberly, Karen C. Fuson, and Miriam Gamoran Sherin. "Describing Levels and Components of a Math-Talk Learning Community." In *More Lessons Learned from Research: Useful and Usable Research Related to Core Mathematical Practices (Volume 1),* edited by Edward A. Silver and Patricia Ann Kenney, pp. 125–134. Reston, Va.: National Council of Teachers of Mathematics, 2015.

Huinker, DeAnn, and Connie Laughlin. "Talk Your Way into Writing." In *Communication in Mathematics, K–12 and Beyond,* edited by Portia Elliot, pp. 81–88. Reston, Va.: National Council of Teachers of Mathematics, 1996.

Huinker, DeAnn, Janis L. Freckmann, and Meghan B. Steinmeyer. "Subtraction Strategies from Children's Thinking: Moving Toward Fluency with Greater Numbers." *Teaching Children Mathematics* 9, no. 6 (2003): 347.

Huinker, DeAnn. "Dimensions of Fraction Operation Sense." In *Making Sense of Fractions, Ratios, and Proportions,* edited by Bonnie Litwiller, pp. 72–78. Reston, Va.: National Council of Teachers of Mathematics, 2002.

Huinker, DeAnn. "Letting Fraction Algorithms Emerge Through Problem Solving." In *Teaching and Learning of Algorithms in School Mathematics,* edited by Lorna Morrow, pp. 170–182. Reston, Va.: National Council of Teachers of Mathematics, 1998.

Huinker, DeAnn. "Representational Competence: A Renewed Focus for Classroom Practice in Mathematics." *Wisconsin Teacher of Mathematics* 67, no. 2 (2015a): 4–8.

Huinker, DeAnn. "Teaching for representational competence in mathematics." *New England Mathematics Journal* 47, no. 1 (2015b): 18–30.

Inagaki, Kayoko, Giyoo Hatano, and Eiji Morita. "Construction of Mathematical Knowledge through Whole-Class Discussion." *Learning and Instruction* 8, no. 6 (1998): 503–526.

Institute for Learning. *Addition Situations: Solving for the Sum.* Pittsburgh: University of Pittsburgh, 2012a.

Institute for Learning. *Put Together and Compare Situational Tasks: Missing Addend Addition as Subtraction.* Pittsburgh: University of Pittsburgh, 2012b.

Institute for Learning. *Dividing Fractions: Understanding Division With Numbers Less than 1.* Pittsburgh: University of Pittsburgh, 2015a.

Institute for Learning. *Multiplication with Fractions: Comparing Fractions with Common Denominators or Common Numerators.* Pittsburgh: University of Pittsburgh, 2015b.

Institute for Learning. *Multiplication with Fractions: Finding Portions of Numbers.* Pittsburgh: University of Pittsburgh, 2015c.

Investigations Curriculum Center, Education Research Collaborative at TERC. *Measuring and Classifying Shapes.* New York: Pearson Education, 2017.

Jackson, Kara and Paul Cobb. *Refining a Vision of Ambitious Mathematics Instruction to Address Issues of Equity.* Presentation at the Annual Meeting of the American Educational Research Association, Denver, April, 30–May 4, 2010.

Jackson, Kara, Anne Garrison, Jonee Wilson, Lynsey Gibbons, and Emily Shahan. "Exploring Relationships Between Setting Up Complex Tasks and Opportunities to Learn in Concluding Whole-Class Discussions in Middle-Grades Mathematics Instruction." *Journal for Research in Mathematics Education* 44, no. 4 (2013): 646–682.

Jacobs, Victoria R., Lisa LC Lamb, and Randolph A. Philipp. "Professional Noticing of Children's Mathematical Thinking." *Journal for Research in Mathematics Education* 41, no. 2 (2010): 169–202.

Jansen, Amanda, Tonya Bartell, and Dawn Berk. "The Role of Learning Goals in Building a Knowledge Base for Elementary Mathematics Teacher Education." *The Elementary School Journal* 109, no. 5 (2009): 525–536.

Kamii, Constance, Lynn Kirkland, and Barbara A. Lewis. "Representation and Abstraction in Young Children's Numerical Reasoning." In *The Roles of Representation in School Mathematics*, edited by Albert A. Cuoco and Frances R. Curcio, pp. 24–34. Reston, Va.: National Council of Teachers of Mathematics, 2001.

Kapur, Manu. "Productive Failure in Mathematical Problem Solving." *Instructional Science* 38, no. 6 (2010): 523–50.

Kazemi, Elham, and Deborah Stipek. "Promoting Conceptual Thinking in Four Upper-Elementary Mathematics Classrooms." *The Elementary School Journal* 102, no. 1 (2001): 59–80.

Krathwohl, David R. "A Revision of Bloom's Taxonomy: An Overview." *Theory into Practice* 41, no. 4 (2002): 212–218.

Ladson-Billings, Gloria. *The Dreamkeepers: Successful Teachers of African American Children.* 2nd ed. San Francisco: Jossey-Bass, 2009.

Lampert, Magdalene, Heather Beasley, Hala Ghousseini, Elham Kazemi, and Megan Loef Franke. "Using Designed Instructional Activities to Enable Novices to Manage Ambitious Mathematics Teaching." In *Instructional Explanations in the Disciplines*, edited by Mary Kay Stein and Linda Kucan, pp.129–141. New York: Springer, 2010.

Lampert, Magdalene, Timothy A. Boerst, and Filippo Graziani. "Organizational Resources in the Service of School-Wide Ambitious Teaching Practice." *Teachers College Record* 113, no. 7 (2011): 1361–1400.

Leahy, Siobhan, Christine Lyon, Marnie Thompson, and Dylan Wiliam. "Classroom Assessment: Minute by Minute, Day by Day." *Educational Leadership* 63, no. 3 (2005):18–24.

Leonard, Jacqueline, and Smita Guha. "Creating Cultural Relevance in Teaching and Learning Mathematics." *Teaching Children Mathematics* 9, no. 2 (2002): 114–118.

Lesh, Richard, Tom Post, and Merlyn Behr. "Representations and Translations Among Representations in Mathematics Learning and Problem Solving. In *Problems of Representation in the Teaching and Learning of Mathematics*, edited by Claude Janvier, pp. 33–40. Hillsdale, N.J.: Lawrence Erlbaum Associates, 1987.

Lipsey, Mark W., and David B. Wilson. "The Efficacy of Psychological, Educational, and Behavioral Treatment: Confirmation from Meta-Analysis." *American Psychologist* 48, no. 12 (1993): 1181–1209.

Lotan, Rachel. A. "Group-Worthy Tasks." *Educational Leadership* 60, no. 6 (2002): 72–75.

Maloney, Alan P., Jere Confrey, and Kenny H. Nguyen. *Learning Over Time: Learning Trajectories in Mathematics Education.* Charlotte, N.C.: Information Age Publishing, 2014.

Maloney, Erin A., and Sian L. Beilock. "Math Anxiety: Who Has It, Why It Develops, and How to Guard Against It." *Trends in Cognitive Sciences* 16, no. 8 (2012): 404–406.

Marshall, Anne Marie, Alison Castro Superfine, and Reality S. Canty. "Star Students Make Connections." *Teaching Children Mathematics* 17 no. 1 (2010): 39–47.

Martin, Danny Bernard. "Learning Mathematics While Black." *The Journal of Educational Foundations* 26, no. 1/2 (2012): 47–66.

Martin, W. Gary. "The NCTM High School Curriculum Project: Why It Matters to You." *Mathematics Teacher* 103, no. 3 (2009): 164–66.

Martino, Amy M., and Carolyn A. Maher. "Teacher Questioning to Promote Justification and Generalization in Mathematics: What Research Practice Has Taught Us." *The Journal of Mathematical Behavior* 18, no. 1 (1999): 53–78.

Marzano, Robert J. *What Works in Schools: Translating Research into Action.* Alexandria, Va: ASCD, 2003.

Mayer, Richard E., Valerie Sims, and Hidetsugu Tajika. "Comparison of How Textbooks Teach Mathematical Problem Solving in Japan and the United States." *American Educational Research Journal* 32, no. 2 (1995): 443–460.

McClure, Lynne. "Using Low Threshold High Ceiling Tasks in Ordinary Classrooms." Cambridge, Mass.: University of Cambridge, 2011. http://nrich.maths.org/7701

Mehan, Hugh. "'What Time Is It, Denise?': Asking Known Information Questions in Classroom Discourse." *Theory into Practice* 18, no. 4 (1979): 285–294.

Mehan, Hugh. *Learning Lessons: Social Organization in the Classroom.* Cambridge, Mass.: Harvard University Press, 1979.

Meikle, Erin M. "Selecting and Sequencing Students' Solution Strategies: Reflect and Discuss." *Teaching Children Mathematics* 23, no. 4 (2016): 226–234.

Michaels, Sarah, Catherine O'Connor, and Lauren B. Resnick. "Deliberative Discourse Idealized and Realized: Accountable Talk in the Classroom and in Civic Life." *Studies in Philosophy and Education* 27, no. 4 (2008): 283–297.

Michaels, Sarah, Mary Catherine O'Connor, Megan Williams Hall, and Lauren B. Resnick. *Accountable Talk Sourcebook: For Classroom Conversation that Works.* Pittsburgh, Pa.: Institute for Learning, 2010.

Moser, Jason S., Hans S. Schroder, Carrie Heeter, Tim P. Moran, and Yu-Hao Lee. "Mind Your Errors: Evidence for a Neural Mechanism Linking Growth Mind-Set to Adaptive Posterror Adjustments." *Psychological Science* 22, no. 12 (2011): 1484–1489.

Moss, Connie M., Susan M. Brookhart, and Beverly A. Long. "Knowing Your Learning Target." *Educational Leadership* 68, no. 6 (2011): 66–69.

Nathan, Mitchell J., Martha W. Alibali, Kate Masarik, Ana C. Stephens, and Kenneth R. Koedinger. *Enhancing Middle School Students' Representational Fluency: A Classroom-based Study* (WCER Working Paper No. 2010–9). Madison, Wis.: Wisconsin Center for Education Research, 2010. Retrieved from http://www.wcer.wisc.edu/publications/workingpapers.

Nathan, Mitchell J., and Eric J. Knuth. "A Study of Whole Classroom Mathematical Discourse and Teacher Change." *Cognition and Instruction* 21, no. 2 (2003): 175–207.

National Council of Teachers of Mathematics. *Curriculum and Evaluation Standards for School Mathematics.* Reston, Va.: NCTM, 1989.

National Council of Teachers of Mathematics *Principles and Standards for School Mathematics.* Reston, Va.: NCTM, 2000.

National Council of Teachers of Mathematics. *Curriculum Focal Points for Prekindergarten through Grade 8 Mathematics: A Quest for Coherence.* Reston, Va.: NCTM, 2006.

National Council for Teachers of Mathematics. *Principles to Actions: Ensuring Mathematical Success for All.* Reston, Va.: NCTM, 2014.

National Council of Teachers of Mathematics. *Procedural Fluency in Mathematics: Position Statement.* Reston, Va: NCTM, 2014.

National Governors Association Center for Best Practices (NGA Center) and Council of Chief State School Officers (CCSSO). *Common Core State Standards for Mathematics*. Washington, D.C.: NGA Center and CCSSO, 2010. http://www.corestandards.org.

National Research Council. *Adding It Up: Helping Children Learn Mathematics*. Washington, D.C.: National Academy Press, 2001.

Nelson, Melissa N., and Christian D. Schunn. "The Nature of Feedback: How Different Types of Peer Feedback Affect Writing Performance." *Instructional Science* 37 (2009): 375–401.

Organization for Economic Co-operation and Development (OECD). *Ten Questions for Mathematics Teachers… and How PISA Can Help Answer Them*. Paris: OECD Publishing, 2016.

Pape, Stephen J., and Mourat A. Tchoshanov. "The Role of Representation(s) in Developing Mathematical Understanding." *Theory into Practice* 40, no. 2 (2001): 118–127.

Parrish, Sherry D. "Number Talks Build Numerical Reasoning." *Teaching Children's Mathematics* 18, no. 3 (2011): 198–206.

Perry, Michelle, Scott W. VanderStoep, and Shirley L. Yu. "Asking Questions in First-grade Mathematics Classes: Potential Influences on Mathematical Thought." *Journal of Educational Psychology* 85, no. 1 (1993): 31.

Piaget, Jean. *The Psychology of Intelligence*. Totowa, N.J.: Littlefield Adams, 1960.

Ramirez, Gerardo, Elizabeth A. Gunderson, Susan C. Levine, and Sian L. Beilock. "Math Anxiety, Working Memory, and Math Achievement in Early Elementary School." *Journal of Cognition and Development* 14 (May 2013): 187–202.

Redfield, Doris L., and Elaine Waldman Rousseau. "A Meta-analysis of Experimental Research on Teacher Questioning Behavior." *Review of Educational Research* 51 (1981): 237–245.

Reinhart, Steven C. "Never Say Anything a Kid Can Say!" *Mathematics Teaching in the Middle School* 5, no. 8 (2000): 478-473.

Resnick, Lauren. *Education and Learning to Think*. Washington, D.C.: National Academy Press, 1987.

Riordan, Julie E., and Pendred E. Noyce. "The Impact of Two Standards-based Mathematics Curricula on Student Achievement in Massachusetts." *Journal for Research in Mathematics Education* (2001): 368–398.

Rivard, Léonard P. "A Review of Writing to Learn in Science: Implications for Practice and Research." *Journal of Research in Science Teaching* 31, no. 9 (1994): 969–983.

Rivard, Léonard P. "Are Language-based Activities in Science Effective for All Students, Including Low Achievers?" *Science Education* 88, no. 3 (2004): 420–442.

Rivard, Léonard P., and Stanley B. Straw. "The Effect of Talk and Writing on Learning Science: An Exploratory Study." *Science Education* 84, no. 5 (2000): 566–593.

Rowe, Mary Budd. "Wait Time and Rewards as Instructional Variables, Their Influence on Language, Logic, and Fate Control: Part I—Wait Time." *Journal of Research in Science Teaching* 11, no. 2 (1974): 81–94.

Rowe, Mary Budd. "Wait Time: Slowing Down May Be a Way of Speeding Up!" *Journal of Teacher Education* 37, no. 1 (1986): 43–50.

Russell, Susan Jo. "Developing Computational Fluency with Whole Numbers." *Teaching Children Mathematics* 7 (November 2000): 154–158.

Ryan, Allison M., Margaret H. Gheen, and Carol Midgley. "Why Do Some Students Avoid Asking for Help? An Examination of the Interplay Among Students' Academic Efficacy, Teachers' Social–Emotional Role, and the Classroom Goal Structure." *Journal of Educational Psychology* 90 no. 3 (1998): 528–535.

Sadler, Royce. "Formative Assessment and the Design of Instructional Systems." *Instructional Science* 18, no. 2 (1989): 119–144.

Samson, Gordon K., Bernadette Strykowski, Thomas Weinstein, and Herbert J. Walberg. "The Effects of Teacher Questioning Levels on Student Achievement: A Quantitative Synthesis." *Journal of Educational Research* 80, no. 5 (1987): 290–295.

Schoenfeld, A. H. "Making Mathematics and Making Pasta: From Cookbook Procedures to Really Cooking." In *Thinking Practices: A Symposium on Mathematics and Science Learning*, edited by J. G. Greeno and S. Goldman, pp. 299–319. Hillsdale, N.J.: Lawrence Erlbaum Associates, 1998.

Schoenfeld, Alan H. "What Makes for Powerful Classrooms, and How Can We Support Teachers in Creating Them? A Story of Research and Practice, Productively Intertwined." *Educational Researcher* 43, no. 8 (2014): 404–412.

Schoenfeld, Alan H. "Making Mathematics Work for All Children: Issues of Standards, Testing, and Equity." *Educational Researcher* 31, no. 1 (2002): 13–25.

Silver, Edward A. and Mary Kay Stein. "The QUASAR Project: The 'Revolution of the Possible' in Mathematics Instructional Reform in Urban Middle Schools." *Urban Education* 30, no. 4 (1996): 476–521.

Sleep, Laurie, and Timothy A. Boerst. "Preparing Beginning Teachers to Elicit and Interpret Students' Mathematical Thinking." *Teaching and Teacher Education* 28, no. 7 (2012): 1038–1048.

Smith, Margaret S., and Mary Kay Stein. "Selecting and Creating Mathematical Tasks: From Research to Practice." *Mathematics Teaching in the Middle School* 3, no. 5 (1998): 344–49.

Smith, Margaret S., and Mary Kay Stein. *5 Practices for Orchestrating Productive Mathematics Discussions*. Reston, Va.: National Council of Teachers of Mathematics, 2011.

Smith, Margaret S., Elizabeth K. Hughes, Randi A. Engle, and Mary Kay Stein. 2009. "Orchestrating Discussions." *Mathematics Teaching in the Middle School* 14 (May): 548–56.

Smith, Margaret, Victoria Bill, and Elizabeth Hughes. "Thinking Through a Lesson Protocol: A Key for Successfully Implementing High-level Tasks." *Mathematics Teaching in the Middle School* 14 no. 3 (2008): 132–138.

Stahl, Robert J. "Using Think-Time and Wait-Time Skillfully in the Classroom." *ERIC Digest*. Bloomington, Ind.: ERIC Clearinghouse, 1994.

Star, Jon. R. "Reconceptualizing Procedural Knowledge." *Journal for Research in Mathematics Education* 36 (November 2005): 404–411.

Stein, Mary Kay, and Margaret S. Smith. "Mathematical Tasks as a Framework for Reflection: From Research to Practice." *Mathematics Teaching in the Middle School* 3, no. 4 (1998): 268–275.

Stein, Mary Kay, and Suzanne Lane. "Instructional Tasks and the Development of Student Capacity to Think and Reason: An Analysis of the Relationship between Teaching and Learning in a Reform Mathematics Project." *Educational Research and Evaluation* 2, no. 1 (1996): 50–80.

Stein, Mary Kay, Suzanne Lane, and Edward Silver. "Classrooms in Which Students Successfully Acquire Mathematical Proficiency: What Are the Critical Features of Teachers' Instructional Practice?" Paper presented at the annual meeting of the American Educational Research Association, New York, April 1996.

Stein, Mary Kay, Barbara W. Grover, and Marjorie Henningsen. "Building Student Capacity for Mathematical Thinking and Reasoning: An Analysis of Mathematical Tasks Used in Reform Classrooms." *American Educational Research Journal* 33, no. 2 (1996): 455–88.

Stein, Mary Kay, Margaret S. Smith, Marjorie Henningsen, and Edward A. Silver. *Implementing Standards-Based Mathematics Instruction: A Casebook for Professional Development.* 2nd ed. New York: Teachers College Press, 2009.

Stein, Mary Kay, Randi A. Engle, Margaret S. Smith, and Elizabeth K. Hughes. 2008. "Orchestrating Productive Mathematical Discussions: Five Practices for Helping Teachers Move Beyond Show and Tell." *Mathematical Thinking and Learning, An International Journal* 10, no. 4: 313–40.

Steuer, Gabriele, Gisela Rosentritt-Brunn, and Markus Dresel. "Dealing with Errors in Mathematics Classrooms: Structure and Relevance of Perceived Error Climate." *Contemporary Educational Psychology* 38, no. 3 (2013): 196–210.

Stigler, James W., and James Hiebert. "Improving Mathematics Teaching." *Educational Leadership* 61, no. 5 (2004): 12–16.

Stigler, James W., and James Hiebert. *The Teaching Gap: Best Ideas from the World's Teachers for Improving Education in the Classroom.* New York: Simon and Schuster, 2009.

Stigler, James W., and James Hiebert. "Improving Mathematics Teaching." *Educational Leadership* 61, no. 5 (2004): 12–16.

Sztajn, Paola, Jere Confrey, P. Holt Wilson, and Cynthia Edgington. "Learning Trajectory Based Instruction Toward a Theory of Teaching." *Educational Researcher* 41, no. 5 (2012): 147–156.

Thames, Mark Hoover, and Deborah Loewenberg Ball. "What Math Knowledge Does Teaching Require?" *Teaching Children Mathematics* 17, no. 4 (2010): 220–229.

Tobin, Kenneth. "Effects of Teacher Wait Time on Discourse Characteristics in Mathematics and Language Arts Classes." *American Educational Research Journal* 23, no. 2 (1986): 191–200.

Tobin, Kenneth. "The Role of Wait Time in Higher Cognitive Level Learning." *Review of Educational Research* 57, no. 1 (1987): 69–95.

Tripathi, Preety N. "Developing Mathematical Understanding through Multiple Representations." *Mathematics Teaching in the Middle School* 13, no. 8 (2008): 438–45.

Ukpokodu, Omiunota N. "How Do I Teach Mathematics in a Culturally Responsive Way?: Identifying Empowering Teaching Practices." *Multicultural Education* 19, no. 3 (2011): 47–56.

VanLehn, Kurt, Stephanie Siler, Charles Murray, Takashi Yamauchi, and William B. Baggett. "Why Do Only Some Events Cause Learning During Human Tutoring?" *Cognition and Instruction* 21, no. 3 (2003): 209–249.

Wagganer, Erin L. "Creating Math Talk Communities." *Teaching Children Mathematics* 22, no. 4 (2015): 248–254.

Wagner, David, and Beth Herbel-Eisenmann. "Re-mythologizing Mathematics through Attention to Classroom Positioning." *Educational Studies in Mathematics* 72, no. 1 (2009): 1–15.

Warshauer, Hiroko Kawaguchi. "Productive Struggle in Middle School Mathematics Classrooms." *Journal of Mathematics Teacher Education* 17, no. 4 (2015a): 375–399.

Warshauer, Hiroko Kawaguchi. "Strategies to Support Productive Struggle." *Mathematics Teaching in the Middle School*, 20 no. 7 (2015b): 390–393.

Watanabe, Tad. "Ben's Understanding of One-half." *Teaching Children Mathematics* 2, no. 8 (1996): 460–464.

Webb, David C., Nina Boswinkel, and Truus Dekker. "Beneath the Tip of the Iceberg: Using Representations to Support Student Understanding." *Mathematics Teaching in the Middle School* 14, no. 2 (2008): 110–113.

Webel, Corey. "Shifting Mathematical Authority from Teacher to Community." *Mathematics Teacher* 104, no. 4 (2010): 315–318.

Weiss, Iris R. and Joan D. Pasley. "What is High-Quality Instruction?" *Educational Leadership*, 61 no. 5 (2004): 24–28.

Wiggins, Grant P., and Jay McTighe. *Understanding by Design*, 2nd ed. Alexandria, Va.: ASCD, 2005.

Wiliam, Dylan, and Siobhan Leahy. *Embedding Formative Assessment: Practical Techniques for K–12 Classrooms.* West Palm Beach, Fla.: Learning Sciences International, 2015.

Wiliam, Dylan. "Keeping Learning on Track: Classroom Assessment and the Regulation of Learning." In *Second Handbook of Research on Mathematics Teaching and Learning*, edited by Frank K. Lester Jr., pp. 1053–1098. Greenwich, Conn.: Information Age Publishing, 2007.

Wiliam, Dylan. *Embedded Formative Assessment*. Bloomington, Ind.: Solution Tree Press, 2011.

Wlodkowski, Raymond J., and Margery B. Ginsberg. "A Framework for Culturally Responsive Teaching." *Educational Leadership* 53 (September 1995): 17–21.

Wood, Terry, and Tammy Turner-Vorbeck. "Extending the Conception of Mathematics Teaching." In *Beyond Classical Pedagogy: Teaching Elementary School Mathematics*, edited by Terry Wood, Barbara Scott Nelson, and Janet Warfield, pp. 185–208. Mahwah, N.J.: Lawrence Erlbaum Associates, 2001.

Yackel, Erna and Paul Cobb. "Sociomathematical Norms, Argumentation, and Autonomy in Mathematics." *Journal for Research in Mathematics Education* 27, no. 4 (1996): 458–477.

Yamakawa, Yukari, Ellice Forman, and Ellen Ansell. "Role of Positioning: The Role of Positioning in Constructing an Identity in a Third Grade Mathematics Classroom." In *Investigating Classroom Interaction: Methodologies in Action*, edited by Kristiina Kumpulainen, Cindy E. Hmelo-Silver, and Margarida César, pp. 172–202. Netherlands: Sense Publishers, 2009.

Young, Christina B., Sarah S. Wu, and Vinod Menon. "The Neurodevelopmental Basis of Math Anxiety." *Psychological Science OnlineFirst* (March 20, 2012). DOI: 0956797611429134